Unveiling MARY MAGDALENE

LIZ CURTIS HIGGS

Best-Selling Author of *Bad Girls of the Bible*

WATERBROOK
PRESS

UNVEILING MARY MAGDALENE
PUBLISHED BY WATERBROOK PRESS
12265 Oracle Boulevard, Suite 200
Colorado Springs, Colorado 80921
A division of Random House, Inc.

Praise for
UNVEILING MARY MAGDALENE

"I love Liz's work! She entertains while teaching and leaves me with points to ponder long after. Her insights are fresh and exciting and will draw readers back into the Word."
—FRANCINE RIVERS, author of the Lineage of Grace series and
Redeeming Love

"In a style all her own, Liz Curtis Higgs tells the story of Mary Magdalene. And what a distinctive, refreshing style it is. Her books are always placed at the top of my 'must read' list. *Unveiling Mary Magdalene* is just one more reason why."
—ROBIN LEE HATCHER, author of *Ribbon of Years*

"Wow! What more can I say? Liz Higgs has found her groove. This lady knows how to paint a story. The lesson of *Unveiling Mary Magdalene* lingers like good perfume. But most of all what Liz is offering in this masterful rendering of story/allegory and sound biblical teaching is hope and liberation. And it's yours for the reading."
—MICHELLE MCKINNEY HAMMOND, author of
How to Be Blessed and Highly Favored

"I love Liz Curtis Higgs because she extended her love to me first. In this new book, Liz extends that same compassionate love while she challenges our preconceived notions about Mary. Some of her challenges may encourage you, but some may disturb you—this is the way with most things that help us grow. But in the end, you will be drawn back to the good medicine she offers and the irresistible, unconditional love that shines through on each and every page!"
—SHARON EWELL FOSTER, author of *Passing by Samaria*

"Liz has done it again! She captures the heart and circumstances of a woman of Magdala and brings her into the twenty-first century. Then after captivating us with Mary's story and with careful and detailed research, Liz unveils the biblical and historical truths of a demonized woman misunderstood by many but gloriously set free by Jesus Christ. What hope and promise this will bring to many women who cannot comprehend how very precious they are to God."

—KAY ARTHUR, author of *Lord, Give Me a Heart for You*

"This book gives genuine insight into who Mary Magdalene *really* was, and it does it in a very personal and revealing way. I was definitely drawn into the character of Mary, as Liz Curtis Higgs brings her to life from the pages of the Bible. She presents the unforgettable portrait of a courageous woman who will be forever remembered as the first evangelist to proclaim a risen Jesus!"

—REBECCA ST. JAMES, recording artist

Unveiling
MARY
MAGDALENE

OTHER BOOKS BY LIZ CURTIS HIGGS

NONFICTION FOR WOMEN

Really Bad Girls of the Bible

Bad Girls of the Bible

FICTION FOR WOMEN

Fair Is the Rose

Thorn in My Heart

Bookends

Mixed Signals

FICTION FOR YOUNG CHILDREN

Go Away, Dark Night

The Pumpkin Patch Parable

To all who have searched for light in the darkness.

To all who have waited for grace to be spoken.

To all who have longed for his appearing.

CONTENTS

ACKNOWLEDGMENTS

To those who have encouraged my Mary heart through the writing process: Sara Fortenberry, Rebecca Price, Carol Bartley, Lisa Bergren, Erin Healy, Laura Barker, Diane Noble, Lois Luckett, MSW, LCSW, the Summit Sisters—Glenna Salsbury, Elizabeth Jeffries, Gail Wenos, Naomi Rhode—and John F. Kartje of Saint Clement Church in Chicago. Bless you each and every one.

And—above all and through all—to my husband and best friend, Bill Higgs, whom I owe a debt of gratitude so great it can never be paid in this lifetime. I love you with all my heart.

WINGS OF MADNESS

Today I felt pass over me
A breath of wind from the wings of madness.
CHARLES BAUDELAIRE

Jake didn't see her until it was too late.

A woman disguised as a bundle of rags bolted out of the Park View Pet Shop and directly into his path, nearly knocking him to the icy sidewalk. Instead, she was the one who landed there in an awkward heap, her face crimson, her eyes averted.

He bent toward her, shielding her from the bitter January wind. "Ma'am, are you okay? I'm sorry I—"

She looked up at him, and the words froze on his lips.

Lord, help me. He was face to face with a madwoman.

Wide, unfocused eyes lit by an unseen fire stared blankly back at him. Dark smudges down her cheeks—dirt? makeup? dried blood?—seemed days in the making. Her black hair was matted against her head, and her prominent nose ran unchecked.

Jake yanked out a clean handkerchief and knelt by her side, lowering his voice as though speaking to a child. "Let me help you get up."

She shrank back from him, a bony hand tightening around a threadbare striped scarf. The woman might have been his mother's age, in her midforties. He studied the lines around her mouth. *No, older.* The sad wildness in her eyes hinted at decades of pain.

OCt 22, 2008

When she dropped her chin and mumbled an incoherent word or two, he leaned closer. Maybe she would mention her name, where she lived, something.

Except what she said made no sense at all…

———

Maybe you're thinking the same thing: *This makes no sense at all! I thought this was a book about Mary Magdalene, one of the Bad Girls of the Bible.*

Oh, it is, dearie. You've come to the right place. No bait-and-switch here.

I simply asked myself the question, "What if Mary Magdalene walked among us today?" That's the *Story* part. Before doing that, I immersed myself in the biblical accounts of her life. That's the *Study* part. In the process, I discovered a very different woman than I'd expected. Although "her name has come to us laden with infamy,"[1] most of us don't know what she's famous—or infamous—for doing.

Clearly she must have done *something*. Of the seven Marys in the Bible,[2] Mary of Magdala is mentioned *fourteen times,* more than any other woman in the Gospels except Mary, the mother of Jesus.[3]

Hmm.

When I asked my Christian writing sisters what they remembered about Mary, most of 'em were convinced Mary Magdalene was a bona fide Bad Girl.

"Wasn't she a prostitute? Worse than other sinners?" *Sue*

"A good heart for Christ but a bad reputation." *Jan*

"She had a lot of hard knocks and made some bad choices." *Janet*

"She was definitely a bad girl…the proverbial 'tender-hearted whore.'" *Karen*

"I'm confused. Was she the woman who washed Christ's feet? An adulteress? A murderer?" *Debbie*

Yes, there's *something* about Mary. We just can't figure out what it is.

> "I don't know if she would be classified as 'bad' per se, or
> simply afflicted with a terrible case of PMS." *Carolyn*

Hey, that's it! Blame the hormones. Works for me, babe.

Speaking of hormones, if you've heard the rumors about Mary Magdalene and Jesus being lovers, being married, being *parents*—don't get your toga in a knot. Matthew, Mark, Luke, and John, who provided first-century, eyewitness accounts and knew Jesus and Mary Magdalene as well as anyone, never speak of them as a couple, let alone as husband and wife. More on that subject in chapter 11, but I want to put your mind at ease: It's the Mary Magdalene of the Bible we're unveiling here, not the mythical version.

So then. Was the real Mary M. good…or bad?

> "Not necessarily bad, but she must have opened the door to
> those demons…" *Angela*

Uh…*demons?* Nobody ever talks about *that* part of her life. Except the apostles.

> When Jesus rose early on the first day of the week, he
> appeared first to Mary Magdalene, out of whom he had
> driven seven demons. *Mark 16:9*

Wait a minute. The woman was a *demoniac?* Of all the people he might have appeared to first, Jesus chose a former…well, a *madwoman?* Sorta like that person who came tearing out of the pet shop a few minutes ago? Whoa.

Now you can see why this book was first published with the title *Mad Mary.* The bad news is, most folks browsing through a bookstore missed the Mary Magdalene connection altogether. Many apologies. The good news is, we've unveiled Mary's story with a new title and a new cover, yet with the same eye-opening truth inside.

Mary Magdalene was indeed a demoniac—one of the Mad Girls of the Bible—until Jesus appeared and changed her forever. Girlfriend, we gotta find out how she got rid of the demons in her life. And why Jesus trusted a woman with a devilish past to reveal his heavenly future. Contemporary story first, biblical study second, let's explore what it means to be utterly, completely, amazingly transformed.

Darkness to light, death to life.

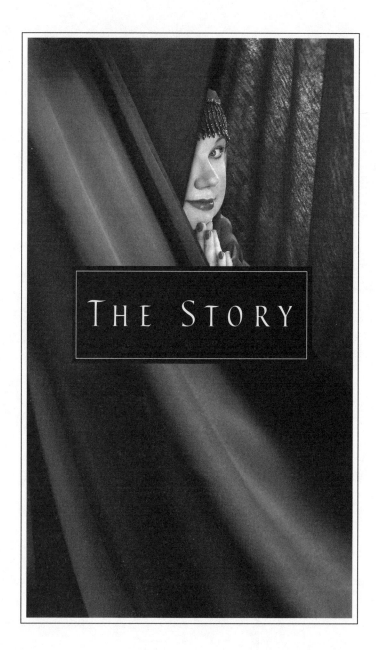

THE STORY

Chapter One

DARKNESS AGAIN AND A SILENCE

Only a look and a voice;
then darkness again and a silence.
HENRY WADSWORTH LONGFELLOW

"Luna," she whispered.

Jake leaned closer and nodded, wanting to encourage this stranger sprawled on the sidewalk before him, hoping his face didn't mirror her confusion nor broadcast his.

Luna?

When she said it again, he heard the muffled tinkle of a tiny bell. She stuffed her other hand into her pocket, but not before he caught a glimpse of something bright and soft, like a child's toy, still in its plastic packaging. His gaze followed hers, trained on the shop door behind them. *Ah. A pet toy maybe.* Was Luna the name of her cat?

Jake turned back toward her and smiled, then slipped his arm underneath hers, gently easing her to her feet. "So, is that a treat for Luna?"

She shoved the object deeper inside her coat, a wary expression crossing her troubled features. Whoever—or whatever—Luna was, Jake felt certain the package in the woman's pocket wasn't paid for. Hadn't she come out of the pet shop in a mad dash?

Ignoring his offered handkerchief, the stranger wiped her nose on her scarf. She backed up as she did so, clearly eager to move on.

Jake eyed the busy flow of traffic on Clark Street. It was past five, nearly dark. Letting her stumble across the intersection on her own would be risky. Her too-big gray coat might camouflage her presence in the fading twilight.

Maybe that's the whole idea, Jake.

Three years of starting churches in urban neighborhoods had taught him something about dealing with street people and others on the edge. This woman was definitely edgy. He inclined his knitted ski cap toward the pavement. "Pretty slippery tonight. Can I help you get somewhere?"

She shook her head, then turned and stumbled forward, her mismatched boots shuffling along the snow-banked sidewalk, heading north toward Tower Records. He caught up with her in two steps, being careful to give her some elbowroom, and shortened his long stride to match her halting one.

"I'm Pastor Jake Stauros from Calvary Fellowship." Did she flinch at that, or was it simply the darkening skies obscuring his vision? Undaunted, he slipped a business card out of his pocket and pressed it into her hand. "Our church is right up the street across from Reebie Storage." Not that Calvary looked anything like a church. The three-story brick eyesore had recently been resurrected, saved from the wrecker's ball after months of lobbying by its Lincoln Park neighbors. "Do you live around here? Sure would love to have you visit us this Sunday."

It was an invitation he extended everywhere he went. Some folks took him up on it. Most didn't. "Church full of misfits," a visitor once grunted on his way out the door. Jake chuckled, a mental picture of his congregation coming into focus. The guy wasn't far off the mark. They *were* a ragtag bunch. Suzy with her two-tone orange hair. Bruce with his armful of tattoos. And four dozen more with their own stories to tell.

This woman and her Goodwill wardrobe would fit right in.

He watched her struggle to keep her footing on the icy walk as a fresh wave of compassion flooded his chest, stinging his eyes. *Father, protect her.* Broken and desperate, she was the kind of person he'd come to Chicago to help.

When they reached the 7-Eleven at Belden Avenue, she darted across the street without a word. Her shapeless gray form never hesitated, oblivious to the angry honks and rude gestures from drivers impatient to get home and gulp down dinner in time to catch the Bulls on TBS.

Jake waved at her, knowing she wouldn't see it. Maybe they'd get another chance to talk, another time. Fishing in his jeans pocket for change, he ducked in the corner store in search of a cold Dad's Root Beer and a bag of chips. It wasn't dinner, but it was close enough.

She hadn't meant to let him get that close.

Mary shivered under her moth-eaten coat, pausing long enough to watch him disappear through the door of the 7-Eleven before aiming her steps toward home.

To her right, a frozen fountain piled high with evergreens and twinkling lights served as a welcome signpost. Half a block more and she'd be hidden behind the thick walls of her brownstone, away from staring eyes and wagging tongues.

And preachers up to nothing but good.

What had he said his name was? *Jake something.* Too eager to help and not much to look at, that one.

Oh, and what are you, Mary Margaret Delaney?

Ugly as Medusa and scared spitless of him—that's what she was.

She kept her head down as she quickened her wobbly steps, squeezing the toy in her pocket to keep her spirits up. *Ha!* A grim smile moved across her chapped lips. The spirits were up, all right, rising with the not-yet-visible moon. Winter nights came too quickly and lasted too long, especially this one.

Mary could already sense the full moon tugging at the tattered strings of her soul, unraveling her mind, undoing her tenuous hold on reality. How many days would she lose this time? How many hours of blackness would swallow her whole?

Her turn-of-the-century townhouse loomed before her. Despite its peeling black trim and decaying mansard roof, it was a welcome sight. *Home.* She stumbled up the concrete steps, then shoved the key in the lock, hands trembling. A minute later, both doors safely latched behind her, she took the first deep breath since her headlong collision with that homely young man, he of the gentle words and the sad brown eyes that saw entirely too much.

He knew she'd shoplifted the toy—that was obvious.

But he hadn't seen her bare arms. And he hadn't followed her home. So he didn't know the whole of it. He didn't know about Luna.

A furry tail flicked around the hem of her coat as a chorus of insistent meows echoed through the empty house. "Max!" she cooed, gathering up the striped feline at her feet, cradling it like a baby. One softly padded paw batted at her nose. "Mama brought something for you, boy-o." She lowered him to the worn hardwood floor, then tore off the plastic wrapping and presented the cat with the stolen treasure.

Within seconds Max was joined by an orange tabby, then a black tom with one white leg, each one pouncing in turn on the jingling toy mouse. "Good kitties," she murmured as more cats appeared from various corners of the house, their cries of hunger plaintive and scolding.

When she straightened, Mary caught a glimpse of herself in the antique hall mirror. The bitter taste of bile rose in the back of her throat. How had it come to this? She peered more closely at the stranger with the unfocused eyes and the filthy face. Had she slept somewhere other than her own bed last night? Were these her clothes or someone else's? Had she eaten today? yesterday?

Not remembering things—that was the worst part.

No, the scars. Those were the very worst.

Shedding her coat, she moved through the dimly lit house, noticing how much furniture there was and how it begged to be dusted. Boxes were crammed in corners, stacked in haphazard piles that threatened to topple with the slightest nudge. The rooms smelled stale and acrid, like too many cats and not enough litter boxes. Such a depressing place to call home. Even the kitchen offered a bleak welcome. Empty metal cupboards, a refrigerator without food, dirty dishes littering the sink.

Mary put a pan of water on the stove to boil, grateful to find a few neglected teabags in a chipped porcelain canister. She washed her face with thawing fingers, then dropped into one of the straight-backed chairs that stood around her kitchen table like soldiers awaiting orders.

She had orders of her own to follow, barked by an unseen master. Orders she dare not ignore, even if she had the strength or the courage. Mary Margaret Delaney knew she had neither.

Taking a deep breath, she pushed up the sleeves of an unfamiliar black sweater, then stretched out her arms on the table's yellow Formica surface.

Yes. These were the worst.

She touched one ragged fingernail to each of the scarlet slashes, which stood out starkly against her pale skin. *Cut, cut, cut.* How evenly they were spaced, marching along her forearms. *Two. Three. Six. Seven.* Not deep enough to kill. Just enough to make her bleed, enough to make her weep, enough to make her long for the sweet release that death promised but never delivered.

Luna had been much braver than she.

Mary turned her arms, exposing her blue-veined wrists.

Luna had cut here.

"Cut me some slack, Pete."

Jake tucked the telephone receiver between his shoulder and ear, managing to scrawl his signature on a letter with one hand and wave his secretary into the room with the other. Friday afternoons at Calvary Fellowship were never dull.

"Look, I'll be ready in half an hour, okay? Yeah, yeah, Ranalli's is fine." Any pizza was fine with Jake, but Ranalli's made the best in Lincoln Park. "You'll call the other guys, right? Tell 'em I'm running late? Good. See ya." He hung up and tossed his pen onto a stack of papers, letting out a noisy sigh.

"Another week in paradise, eh, boss?" His volunteer secretary, Suzy, propped herself in the doorway, one slim hip jutted out at a provocative angle. Habit, nothing more. He'd found her in such a pose—wearing a decidedly less conservative outfit—outside an adults-only store on North Halsted last summer.

Jake had known what she really needed that hot August afternoon.

So he'd shared his Father's forgiveness with her. Given her a whole new definition of love. Brought her to church and watched her blossom into the woman God created her to be.

Pure ministry. It didn't get any better than that.

Not long after she'd arrived, Jake discovered the truth about Suzy: Before she'd been forced to peddle her wares on Halsted, she'd worked as a first-rate secretary at one of the big firms on Van Buren. Her organizational skills were the best thing that had ever happened to Calvary Fellowship. Who cared if her hair was a color not found in nature? The woman was a godsend, plain and simple, working nine to three at a neighborhood bank, then offering her talents to the church for the rest of the afternoon—no charge.

"It's almost six," she informed him, tapping her watch. "Time for all good pastors to call it a day."

He couldn't resist a playful wink. "Don't you know the best ministry happens after the sun goes down?"

"Sez you." Suzy grinned back at him and pushed away from the doorframe. "Have fun with the fellas tonight. See ya Sunday."

Jake flapped one hand in farewell as the phone rang again. Propping his feet on the desk, he grabbed the receiver and leaned back in his chair, untangling the cord, preparing for a long conversation. It was, after all, Friday—a day when too-small paychecks, too-long happy hours, weekend custody visits, and a hundred other stressors pushed people toward the brink. Jake wanted to be there if they fell.

"Calvary Fellowship. Pastor Stauros speaking."

The caller was in tears.

"Take your time, ma'am. I'm not in any hurry." And he wasn't. Pizza could wait. Pain could not.

His gaze wandered to the first-floor window facing the alley, the glass as black as the night sky. The elders had recommended putting bars outside the windows, although Jake loathed such measures. What was the point of keeping people *out* of church when they were all working so hard to bring them *in?*

His caller had finally calmed down enough to share her situation with him. Another marriage in trouble. Few things grieved Jake more. After an impromptu counseling session, he made an appointment to meet with both parties in his office, then stretched forward to drop the receiver in place—and promptly dropped it on the floor.

A face stared at him through the window.

He shrank back in his chair, heart pounding.

Mere feet away, the stranger's nose barely touched the glass, tiny circles of steam heating the icy surface. The eyes were vacant, the mouth slack. A woman, he decided. Long dark hair, wax-white skin, strong brows. His own eyebrows lifted in recognition. Not any woman—*that* woman. The one he had run into outside the pet store Tuesday evening. *Definitely.* She was wearing the same gray coat, the same striped scarf, the same haunted expression.

Jake exhaled, letting his heart rate slow down, then smiled in welcome, waving her in. "C'mon." He raised his voice as he stood, realizing she probably still couldn't hear him. "Hang on. I'll open the back door."

Before he could take a step, her eyes widened—in horror or surprise, he couldn't tell which—and she backed away from the glass, disappearing like a disembodied head floating off into the dark night.

Jake felt his stomach tighten and his hands grow cold.

"Get a grip, Stauros." His laugh had a hollow sound. No question, her unexpected appearance had unnerved him. The piercing beep of an unhooked phone brought him back to reality. "She's just lost and confused," he reminded himself, grabbing the dangling receiver and putting it back where it belonged, then easing into his chair.

He went through the motions of straightening his desk, giving his nervous system a chance to regroup, when a sudden knock at the back door launched him to his feet as if he'd been shot out of a cannon. "Who is it?"

"Who else?" a familiar male voice barked back.

Pete.

Jake's laugh was genuine this time as he unlocked the door outside his office and ushered in a noisy foursome—Nick, Joe, Little John, and Pete—all members of his congregation and the closest thing Jake had to a ministry-support team. When it came time for him to move on, they'd be the ones to carry the ball and run with it.

"What's keepin' you, bro?" Pete slapped him on the back as he stepped inside. "We hung out at Ranalli's for a while, then figured we'd better haul you outta here."

Joe rubbed his ungloved hands together, then plunged them into his pockets. "Bundle up. We nearly froze our parkas off walkin' over here."

"Sorry, fellas. Long story." Jake grabbed his coat off a nearby chair. "I'll tell ya over pizza."

A mountain of a man they called Little John flashed a gap-toothed grin. "Tell us now, Jake, or you're buyin'."

"Always hungry for a story, aren't you, John?" Jake chuckled at his friend's enthusiasm. As he dug around in his coat pockets searching for gloves, he explained about his counseling call and then described the woman who'd appeared at his window.

Nick exchanged nods with the others. "We've seen her around too." Glancing toward the alley, he added, "She's a neighborhood fixture. Mary Margaret somebody."

Jake's eyebrows shot up. *Mary.* His mother's name.

"Folks call her Mad Mary," Pete added, his features reflecting Jake's own discomfort. "Looks the part, doesn't she?"

Jake couldn't argue with that. But could he *do* something for her? The question haunted him all evening, as did the stark memory of her grief-lined face.

Mary Margaret Delaney faced the icy gravestone, touching it with trembling fingers, her knees barely denting the frozen grass. She'd agonized all week, longing to be here in the moonlight, knowing the gates of Graceland Cemetery were locked at sundown.

They were open now. On this melancholy afternoon there was neither moon nor sun that she could see. Only tombs. It felt like her second home.

Eternal Silence.

That was the name the sculptor had given the gruesome creation looming before her, which guarded the remains of Dexter Graves. The hooded statue stood in front of a slab of black granite, its robes reduced to weathered bronze. Mary lifted her gaze, stopping short of the figure's dark countenance. Hidden in the folds of the robe, masked by one perpetually raised arm, was a face black as midnight.

Don't look, Mary. Don't look!

According to local legend, to stare into the face of the "Statue of Death"— the name familiar to Chicagoans—was to risk catching an unwelcome glimpse of one's own death.

She laughed then, a laugh that sounded strange even to her frozen ears. The maniacal sound crackled through the wintry air like glass shattering on a marble floor. *Foolish woman!* Death posed little threat. Let it come, and soon. No, remaining alive when the one she loved most was dead—*that* was the feared thing, the dreaded reality.

"Luna," Mary whispered, rising unsteadily to her feet. She'd chosen the name in happier times when she'd considered a full moon lovely and roman- tic, not frightening and overpowering. Mary passed Graceland Chapel, ignoring its silent invitation. There was no grace there, not for her. Not for Luna.

Tears blurred her vision, stinging her cheeks as the wind off Lake Michi- gan turned them to ice. Step by step Mary drew closer to the one grave that held her heart and would not let go.

Your fault, the voices chided her. *All your fault.*

Mary stared at the pink granite, her tears falling in earnest. Who was to say it wasn't her fault? She'd failed Luna somehow. Just as Mick had failed her as a husband. Just as she had failed him as a wife.

Failure, failure, the voices taunted, and she nodded in weary agreement.

Out of the corner of her eye, Mary saw a young man walking along the row of mausoleums pushing a wheelbarrow full of dead poinsettias, his drab uniform soiled with dirt. When he turned toward her, she ducked her head.

Leave this place! The voices were louder now, more insistent.

Mary scurried toward the gate and away from the whistling young man, wondering how she'd gotten there and how she was going to get home. She'd managed before, of course. Wiping away the last of her tears with the tail of her scarf, she glanced down and realized she'd smeared a fresh layer of dirt on her face.

The last thing Jake expected when he unlocked Calvary's front door Sunday morning was to see her face, still grim and tormented even in the light of day.

Mary—no matter how jumbled her mind was, he couldn't bring himself to call her "Mad"—stood across the street, huddled outside Walgreens as though waiting for permission to go inside. She wore shoes this time, not boots. A fur-trimmed hat that'd seen better days. The same sorry wool coat. The same look of utter desolation.

He called out, waving as he did. "Mary. Ma-ary!" *No use.* His words were swallowed by the stiff morning wind. If he wanted to get her attention, he'd have to cross the street.

After checking his watch, Jake pulled the door shut behind him and sprinted toward her, then waited patiently at the curb while a CTA bus lumbered past, belching exhaust fumes. When the bus was gone, so was Mary. Her spot on the sidewalk was vacant, as though she'd never been there. Had she slipped inside Walgreens? If he followed her there, would she feel hounded? Trapped, even?

Jake perched on the curb, hands shoved into his pockets. As much as he longed to make visitors feel welcome, flagging them down in drugstores might be overdoing it a tad. People came to church when they were ready.

"Taken to preaching on street corners, Pastor Stauros?"

He turned to find sour-faced Charles Farris, one of Calvary's few senior members, standing on the front steps of the church, thumping his cane on the concrete in a staccato rhythm that marked his displeasure. "Ought to be inside the church, greeting those who want to hear you, eh, Pastor?"

Jake bit his tongue, suppressing the snappy comeback he longed to let fly. What purpose would it serve except to ease his ego? *And blow your morning message to bits, Jake.*

He walked toward the older man, hand outstretched. "Welcome, Charles. You're looking well."

"*Harrumph.*" The man turned abruptly and stalked inside.

Jake followed close behind him, smiling. Nothing felt better than doing the right thing, no matter what it cost him.

They entered through a small, windowless foyer that new light fixtures failed to brighten, then stepped into the main space—a former living room and dining area now converted into a sanctuary of sorts. The old house creaked and groaned beneath the feet of its latest tenants, its scarred wooden floors covered with serviceable brown carpeting, its white plaster walls freshly painted. They'd been there only a few months, but it was beginning to feel like home.

Jake checked his watch again, encouraged by the turnout. Fifteen minutes until the opening song, and already the folding chairs were filling up. He took his time moving down the aisle, making eye contact with his flock one by one, shaking hands when he could reach them, feeling his shoulders bend slightly under the weight of their myriad problems.

JoAnn, Calvary Fellowship's bookkeeper—a volunteer, like Suzy—sat by herself near the back, the corners of her mouth turned down with disappointment. Another Sunday without her husband, Cash, by her side. The man was too busy trying to please his boss to bother pleasing God. Too busy making money to make time for his quiet, undemanding wife.

Though JoAnn insisted her pronounced limp was nothing more than arthritis, Jake suspected Cash and his volatile temper might have had something to do with it. A jolt of righteous anger skittered down Jake's spine as he watched her shift in her seat, wincing at the effort. JoAnn was one of Calvary's most faithful supporters. Time, money, talent—the woman was the definition of sacrificial service.

His mother, Mary, sat a few chairs down. A seat carefully chosen so she could keep an eye on JoAnn, he suspected. The woman really was a saint, always looking out for those who were hurting or needy. She winked at him now, her face shining with maternal pride. Streaks of silver shot through her auburn hair and fine wrinkles gathered around her eyes and mouth, but she was still young in spirit.

Mary Stauros had been his biggest supporter from day one. A widow not yet fifty, she'd followed him to the Near West Side, then on to Lincoln Park, leaving behind their hometown of Naperville to make herself useful around the small, urban churches Jake had planted. When she wasn't busy filling communion cups or straightening chairs, she was sneaking into his apartment to take care of his laundry or to slip a casserole into his empty freezer.

Encouraged as always by her faithful presence, he smiled broadly and mouthed, *Thanks, Mom.* Jake had a feeling he'd be saying that until the day he died.

Moving forward, he noticed a young skinhead named Bruce slouched in a nearby chair, feigning indifference to his surroundings. Pierced and tattooed, with a defiant expression to match the angry images on his skin, Bruce was new at Calvary, a silent visitor who'd stumbled in the door a few Sundays back. Jake nodded at him, saying what he could with his eyes. *No pressure, Bruce. We're here for you.*

He squeezed the broad shoulder of Carter Johnson, nodding at the man's wife and two daughters beside him, then shook hands with Mike and Patty, a newlywed couple visiting the fellowship for their third week in a row. *Bind them together, Lord.*

As he neared the front, Jake focused his prayers in the direction of a wheelchair parked in the aisle. Gary's twisted body was propped at an angle inside its metal confines, but his young face was joy itself. Jake couldn't help but smile as he patted Gary's back in passing. "Glad you're here, buddy."

Pete and Little John were working their way around the high-ceilinged room, handing out hymnals and general goodwill, as Jake took his seat behind the music stand that served as a pulpit. All he needed was a place to rest his white leather Bible. The morning message would come straight from his heart.

After a few hymns and contemporary praise choruses led by Marijane— not a trained choral director, just the most musical among them—Jake stepped forward and rested his hands on the black metal stand. "Our story today comes from the tenth chapter of Luke's gospel," he began, flipping open to the text, then training his eyes on the fifty or so souls sitting before him.

Teach us, Father.

"A man once asked Jesus, 'Who is my neighbor?'" Jake let the familiar parable sink in as he shared a dozen verses that told of a man who fell into the hands of some thugs who robbed him, stripped him, beat him, then left him for dead. "According to the story, the pastor did nothing for the poor man, the head of the deacons did nothing, but a stranger took pity on him, bandaged the man's wounds, took him to a hotel, and paid for his care out of his own pocket."

Jake paused before posing the critical question that Jesus asked: "Of these three, which one do you think acted like a real neighbor to the poor guy who got mugged?"

Pete, never one to hold back, forgot himself for a moment and hollered out, "Well, *duh!* The Samaritan, who else?"

Jake chuckled along with everybody else. "You got it, Pete. Jesus called him 'the one who had mercy.' So what are we supposed to learn from this story, brothers and sisters?"

The room grew silent. Fidgeting and page turning ceased. Throats were cleared with muffled coughs. Finally Little John spoke, holding up his Bible as he read aloud, "'Go and do likewise.' Least, that's what it says here."

"Good. So how can we 'go and do' as a church?" Jake stepped away from the makeshift pulpit and moved down the center aisle, noting how many at Calvary Fellowship that morning carefully avoided his penetrating gaze. "Is there a neighbor here in Lincoln Park who needs our help? Someone who might—"

Jake looked up and stopped abruptly, the words stuck in his throat.

Mary.

The madwoman emerged from the dim foyer into the quiet sanctuary, her gaze darting from one corner to the other before it settled on him. No one saw or heard her enter. Except Jake.

He swallowed any apprehension with a single gulp, then offered his warmest smile and stretched his hand toward her. "Folks, I'd like you to—"

As quickly as she'd appeared, Mary was gone. If the door hadn't banged softly behind her, Jake might have decided she was a ghostly apparition. Had she been hiding in the foyer the entire service? Watching through the crack between the door and the jamb? Listening to his sermon?

Several church members turned around to follow his gaze while others merely waited, their attention fixed on their pastor, who was speechless for the first time in many a Sunday.

Jake brushed away his bewilderment with a wave of his hand. "As I was saying, I'd like you to think of somebody this week you might help. Someone who lives nearby, who shops where you do, who takes the same bus, who…" He pressed on, encouraging them to put the words of Jesus into action, even as the still, small voice in his heart spoke so loudly Jake feared the others might hear.

Help Mary.

Stunned, Jake dropped to his seat as Marijane led the group in a closing hymn. How could he help Mary when he didn't know her last name, didn't know where she lived, and didn't know what her problem was? *Make that plural—problems.*

Minutes later he stood at the front door of the church, shaking hands, sending his sheep out to ice-covered pastures. "Good sermon, Pastor." Little John slapped his shoulder blade with a meaty hand. "Think I'll help the older lady who lives upstairs. Buy her groceries or somethin'." He studied Jake, listening with his eyes. "So, d'ya know who you're gonna help this week?"

Jake's words felt like a vow. "Yes, I do." A dark-haired, gray-swathed woman tugged at his conscience. "If she crosses my path again, I'll be ready."

Mary had crossed the threshold of Calvary Fellowship without thinking, drawn there—no, *pushed* there—by a force stronger than any she'd ever known.

She'd trembled at the young man's words, especially when he'd read from that…that *book.* The words frightened her. Disgusted her. Her stomach had threatened to retch them onto the foyer floor like so much tainted food. Restless, she'd swayed back and forth without making a sound, torn between listening and pressing her hands against her ears, between stepping inside the room where she could be seen and running where she could never be found.

One finger had absently picked at the angry red scars on her forearms. Deep inside her mind, dark thoughts had streaked across black, moonless skies and stumbled through fog-shrouded graveyards, where death lurked behind every tomb. *Especially in that room, that room with the people and the man speaking those terrible words.*

After many agonizing minutes, Mary had heard him ask a question about their neighborhood, about Lincoln Park. About helping someone.

Help me!

It was a different voice, *her* voice, close to her heart. It had cried out so loudly she knew, she *knew* he'd heard it.

He was going to speak her name. She'd known that, too.

So she'd stepped into the room. And he'd stopped speaking. Then she'd stopped breathing when she saw mercy shining like sunlight on his face.

Run, run, run!

When the voices gave orders, she was powerless to ignore them. Mary ran, ran, ran all the way to her house, all the way to her third-floor bed, shaking off a blanket covered with cats to burrow beneath its polyester darkness.

"Luna!" she sobbed, rattling the bed with her shivering, the preacher's kind expression already forgotten. When Luna was alive, life had made sense. It made no sense now. If she wanted to be with Luna again, she would have to be brave and do exactly what Luna had done. It'd happened on a Wednesday—of that, Mary Margaret Delaney was utterly certain—at four in the afternoon on the windy, grassy expanse of Lincoln Park, one block north.

She would gather the necessary things and wait then.

Wait for Wednesday.

Chapter Two

THE WOUNDS WITHIN

We cannot heal the throbbing heart
Till we discern the wounds within.
GEORGE CRABBE

Nothing ever happened on Wednesdays.

Jake glanced at the digital clock on his desk, a gift from his mother a couple of years back. It was a frigid day, no sun in sight, with temps hovering in the twenties. Maybe the thing was frozen. In any case the numbers weren't moving. They'd been stuck at 3:55 for at least an hour.

He craned his neck toward Suzy's tiny office next door. "Any messages?"

"Not since you asked me ten minutes ago," floated back her cheeky reply.

Grinning, he tackled a pile of paperwork he'd avoided for days. Jake had all the time in the world for people but no patience with paper and zero interest in fund-raising. The only thing he raised was a prayer toward heaven, leaving the rest to his generous Father, who always provided. *Always.*

When he'd made a sufficient dent in the stack, Jake pushed back from his desk and reached for his coat, suddenly feeling restless. "I'm gonna head home and work on my sermon," he announced, pausing at the doorway into Suzy's converted-pantry workspace. He watched her for a moment, this woman who'd chosen to bring her formidable skills to his small, drab office, brightening the place with her contagious enthusiasm. His voice thickened. "Thanks for everything you do for Calvary, Suze. You're a gem, you know that?"

"Sez you." She tried to hide a smile behind her armful of Manila file folders. "Don't forget your gloves, boss. It's worse than usual out there. And take your cell phone, would you?" Suzy tipped her head toward the slim black phone on her desk, a gift from a generous member. "Never know when I might need to reach you in an emergency. Even if it is Wednesday."

"Yes ma'am." Jake dutifully yanked his gloves out of his pockets, sliding the cell phone down where it would be safe. He seldom used the thing, preferring to speak to people face to face, but he'd humor Suzy and take it. "I'll be home by 4:30. If you need me, feel free to call there."

"Don't forget your shirts." She pointed to the hangers on the back of her door. Four freshly washed, neatly pressed white dress shirts, dropped off earlier by his mother, hung there, waiting for him to take them home.

"Thanks," Jake mumbled, wishing his mother had dropped them off at his apartment instead of here, then feeling guilty about his ingratitude. The fact was, he wore them to bless her. He'd have been perfectly happy in jeans and a sweatshirt on Sabbath mornings. But he couldn't bring himself to disappoint his mother nor dishonor his father's memory. Rev. H. M. Stauros never once stepped into the pulpit without wearing his best suit, a clean white shirt, and his most conservative tie.

Jake didn't own a suit. His standard Sunday wardrobe was a pair of jeans or Dockers and a bright red tie, the only decent one he owned. A white, long-sleeved Arrow was his only concession to tradition. "Nice shirt," his mother often said, patting his shoulder. If this widow, who'd suffered much in her young life, could be made happy by a small effort on his part, it was the least Jake could do.

Hooking two gloved fingers through the hangers, he slung the shirts over his shoulder and headed out to face the elements. He'd make tracks for his two-room apartment, have an early dinner, then work on his Sunday message. It was quieter there. Sometimes a guy had to get off by himself to think.

Jake zipped up his parka all the way, pulling the collar tighter around his neck. It wasn't the worst weather he'd ever seen, just typical for January in Chicago—biting winds, a piercing cold that penetrated to bone and marrow, and no color anywhere. Even the snow turned dingy by the time it landed.

He neared the corner, noticing for the umpteenth time the sign in the window of Gus's Shoe Repair: *Time Wounds All Heels.* He grinned at the clever turnabout, then sobered as he remembered how many funerals he'd attended where people murmured to one another, "Time heals all wounds." *Not all of them.* Time didn't have that kind of power. The fact that plenty of people carried childhood wounds to their graves proved it. Only God's love had the power to heal completely. It took time, but it also took God.

Jake crossed Fullerton at the light, then headed east toward Lincoln Park, still mulling over last week's sermon. He'd encouraged them to "go and do likewise," to care for their neighbors. Already a few reports had come in from Pete, Little John, and some of the others—things they'd done, how they were received. Not always favorably, according to JoAnn, who visited her neighbors with a plate of cookies only to be sent home with them, the paranoid couple fearful they were laced with PCP.

Helping others was risky, no question.

He turned north, the wind stinging his face, blowing full off the lake and across the icy stretches of Lincoln Park. Glancing over, he did a double take when he recognized a woman in a gray coat—as gray as the sky, as gray as the lake, as gray as the frozen ground—stumbling along the slippery park walkway toward North Pond.

Mary.

Her striped wool scarf was blowing behind her like a flag. Jake stopped, craning his neck to watch her. What in the world was she doing out in this weather, let alone without a hat or gloves? *Maybe the same thing you are, Jake. Trying to get somewhere.*

His brow tightening with concern for her safety, if not her sanity, he slowed his steps, his eyes still trained on her. "Watch it!" an older man barked at him, swerving around him. After bumping into two more people, Jake pulled his gaze away from Mary and forged on toward home, fighting his conscience.

He didn't want to make a nuisance of himself, right? A pushy pastor, shoving the gospel down somebody's throat, wasn't his style.

Who is my neighbor?

His own message banged on the door of his heart like a drum.

Two blocks later Jake stopped and glanced over his shoulder. He'd feel better if he could *see* her, talk to her for a minute, make sure she was okay, find out if she had a warm place to sleep tonight, something to eat for dinner. *Something.*

Starting back the way he'd come, Jake found his feet picking up speed, his breath coming in shorter, tighter gasps as he jogged across the park, scanning the bleak scenery.

Then he saw her.

He stopped to catch his breath, gripping his dress shirts with fingers that were steadily growing numb. Mary sat fifty yards ahead of him on a park bench by the pond, hunched over, with her back toward him. A small, motionless form, nearly invisible in the late afternoon light.

Would it frighten her if he approached her, spoke to her? The park was deserted on such an inhospitable day. Could be that's why she'd come. Still…if she needed something, if he could help her…

He moved closer, noticing that she was bending over farther, as if looking at an object on the ground between her feet. What had she dropped? As he closed the gap another few yards, she seemed to sink farther into the bench. Her arms, no longer inside her coat sleeves, flopped down by her sides. What was she doing? With growing apprehension, he walked faster, jogging by the time he reached her, the shirts slapping against his back as he ran.

Jake stopped mere feet behind her. "Mary?" he said softly, not wanting to make her jump. No answer. "Mary?" He said it louder this time, taking one step closer. "It's Jake Stauros from Calvary."

Then he heard her moan so low it sounded like the wind. "Lu-na."

Easing his way around the bench, not wanting to scare the troubled woman, he took a deep breath, preparing himself for what he might find.

But he was not prepared for this.

Mary's chin slumped onto her chest, her eyes half-closed, unfocused. Her mouth hung slack. The sleeves of her blue dress were pushed above her elbows, exposing bare arms covered with fresh blood, flowing down like sap from a wounded tree. Beside her right hand on the frozen grass lay a straight-edge razor.

"Mary!" He threw his shirts on the bench and fell to one knee, yanking off a glove to gently touch her face and feel for a pulse along her neck. It was there but barely. Her eyes didn't respond to his touch or to his voice. "Mary, can you hear me? Mary?"

Jake could barely swallow. *Father God, what now? What now?* He dove in his pocket for the cell phone, thanking Suzy with every punch of every button.

"911. Where are you located?"

Jake slumped forward, weak with relief. "Lincoln Park. I need an ambulance. I'm…" He cleared his throat and started again, raising his voice above the wind. "I'm Reverend Jake Stauros. I've got a…an attempted suicide on my hands here."

"Where is 'here,' sir? Where exactly in Lincoln Park are you?"

"Near Saint James…west side of North Pond…park bench," he said, gulping between each detail. "She's slit both her forearms, lengthwise along the vein." Mary's eyes had grown cloudier still, her breathing more shallow. And the blood, the blood wouldn't stop.

"Wrap clean cloths tightly around her arms. Don't try to move her. Hold a second while I dispatch EMS."

Jake took a deep breath, struggling to keep his wits about him while he listened to her terse instructions. He touched Mary's shoulder and heard her soft, guttural moan. *Oh, Mary.*

The woman came back on the line. "We'll have EMS there as soon as—"

"*How* soon?" The sharpness of his tone made Mary's head twitch slightly. *Good, good. Still conscious.* "Sorry, ma'am. Didn't mean to raise my voice, I'm just…"

"They're on their way, sir."

"Bless you." Jake punched the OFF button and slid the phone into his pocket, his mind reeling. *Clean cloths?* Nothing about Mary's attire was remotely clean. His sweater and jeans weren't much more sanitary, not for open wounds. Then Jake's gaze landed on the forgotten dress shirts, tossed aside earlier without a second thought. *Clean. Cloth.*

He shot to his feet, tearing off the flimsy plastic bag and jerking the shirts free from their hangers, buttons flying. Piling them on the plastic, he knelt on the ground before her, compassion flooding through him from an unseen but most welcome source. "Don't be afraid, Mary." His hands steady for the first time in many minutes, he took one carefully pressed shirt and wrapped it around her right arm, pulling it tight like a tourniquet.

Her wounds wept blood like tears. *Mary. Oh, Mary.* His own tears were hot against his wind-burned face as he touched her wet fingers. Familiar words came unbidden. *For I am already being poured out like a drink offering, and the time has come for my departure.*

"No, Father!" he pleaded aloud, starting on her left arm. Mary stirred, the slightest shift of her shoulders, but it gave him hope. In the distance the whine of an ambulance siren cut through the frosty air. Her blood soaked through the first pair of shirts immediately, the red stains stark against the pristine white cotton. Jake discarded them and reached for the other two, breathing a prayer of thanks that God had provided exactly what was needed.

He took off his knit cap, sliding it over her thick hair, then tucked the loose ends of her scarf back in place around her neck, whispering encouragement. "Hang in there, Mary. They're almost here." An ambulance pulled up, the siren winding down, the rotating globe slicing across the landscape in a blinding arc of light. Jake stood, waving them over.

Stepping around the pile of bloodied shirts, two young men nodded at him and went to work, asking questions as they lifted Mary onto a gurney lowered to the ground and then pulled it waist high with a practiced yank on the handles.

"Is she a relative? A friend?"

Jake stood back, wishing there was more he could do. "She's a...neighbor."

"Uh-huh." They lifted her into the ambulance and followed her in, crouching beside her to check her vitals. With efficient movements they replaced Jake's shirts with sterile bandages and started an IV. Standing a few feet behind the vehicle, Jake could hear them asking her questions but not, it seemed, getting much response. The taller man leaned toward the door, eying Jake with a curious gaze. "Where does she live?"

"I don't know exactly." Jake felt foolish not having more answers. "Could be Belden Avenue, but I'm not sure. Her first name is Mary."

The other crew member slid a hand in her coat pocket and pulled out a business card. "Hey, here's somebody we can call. Her minister." He peered at the card. "A Reverend Staur…uh, Stauros. From—"

"That's me." Jake eyed the card, surprised to see it was already worn around the edges. "I gave her that card a week or so ago when we…when we met on the street near my church."

"I see."

Jake couldn't begin to guess what the guy saw.

All Jake saw was a woman in great pain, inside and out. A lost soul who needed Christ. Who needed help. Who needed him.

The tall fellow jumped out, closing one door. "She's lost quite a bit of blood." He glanced at the pile of shirts littering the ground. "Sorry about your laundry."

Jake shrugged, gathering up the only dress shirts he owned and stuffing them into a nearby trash can. "A good cause, I'd say."

"Mighta saved her life, mister." The two men's gazes met as the wind whipped both their coat collars, nearly drowning their voices. "Do you wanna ride up front with me? Grant Hospital's right around…"

Jake was already moving toward the passenger side.

The young driver shouted over the wind, "Got any idea who we oughta list as the responsible party?"

"Yeah, I do." Jake ducked inside the ambulance, squaring his shoulders as he slammed the door. "Put my name down."

She was sinking down an inch at a time, like a body being lowered into a grave.

Voices were muffled, growing more distant as the darkness closed in, shielding her from the bright, intrusive lights above her. Her wrists throbbed, pumping life from her veins. *Soon…soon…*

Suddenly a male voice, vaguely familiar, cut through the thick cloud around her. "Mary," he said, slicing the air as cleanly as the razor had pierced the fragile skin of her wrists. "I'm right here, Mary. I'm with you."

Her descent stopped as her mind struggled for an answer. *Who? Who was he?* She no longer had a husband. She'd never had a son.

Luna, Luna, Luna.

She hadn't found Luna after all. Oh, she'd sensed her nearby, watching over her in the park, but everything went blank after that. Only the pain shone through, wrapped in a violent laughter. And the cold. The bitter, freezing, wind-driven cold.

Red blood on the silvery white ice along North Pond.

The invisible man was speaking again. "Mary, it's Jake Stauros. From Calvary Fellowship." She sensed the faintest touch on her shoulder. Warm. Gentle. Like his voice.

"We saw each other last Sunday morning. Do you remember?"

Remember? *No, no.* She wanted to forget. Forget living, forget the pain. Her arms ached from shoulder to fingertips, and her mouth tasted as if someone had packed it with rags soaked in cider vinegar.

"I'm going to see about getting you admitted, Mary."

She formed one word and blew it out on a puff of stale air. "Where…?"

"The safest place for you, ma'am. Grant Hospital."

"No!" She struggled to sit up and realized she was strapped to a gurney. *No, no, no, no!* Fighting the canvas straps with strength far beyond her own, she twisted right, then left, straining to get free, to get out. "Not here!" she shrieked, cursing, hating the sound of her voice, hating this horrible place even more. She bucked, feeling the wheels beneath her shimmy. "No-o-o!"

Firm hands pressed her against the gurney. The straps tightened. A needle pricked her arm. Her eyelids fluttered. After that, nothing.

"Nothing in the hospital records then? And nobody here recognizes her?" Jake ran his hand through his hair, yanking on the ends in frustration. "How can she live in our neighborhood without somebody knowing her name?"

The no-nonsense admissions clerk shrugged. *"You* don't know her name, do you?"

A wave of heat rose to his cheeks. *Got me there.*

Above her the fluorescent light flickered in the windowless room, outlining the woman's pinched features. "No ID. No family reporting her as missing." She pursed her lips. "And no 'Mad Mary' listed in the phone book." She tucked a pen behind her ear, then rolled over to a second computer terminal.

Her fingers twitched over the keys. "Chicago's full of Mary Margarets, Reverend. Did she mention any other names?"

"Sure." Jake chuckled in spite of their dilemma. "The name of her cat: Luna."

"Luna, is it?" The woman chewed on the word as though she were a tabby and it was choice catnip. "Luna, Luna, Luna. A cat, you say? Are you sure?"

"No, I'm…guessing." Jake watched her hands fly over the keys until a screen full of data popped into view.

"Aha!" A triumphant smile transformed her severe features. "Luna Delaney. A former patient of ours, seven years ago. Not many Lunas in the world, you know. And look at the address." She swung the monitor in his direction.

He leaned across the counter to squint at the screen. *Belden.* The very street Mary had hurried across when they'd first met a week ago. "I don't understand the connection though. Does this Luna woman know Mary?"

"Know her?" the woman scoffed, jabbing the PRINT button on her keyboard. "Mary Margaret Delaney was her mother."

His jaw dropped before he could stop it. "So Luna Delaney is her daughter! Still living at the same address, do you think? Is there a phone number?"

"You weren't listening, Reverend. I said Mary *was* her mother."

"'Was'?" he repeated, more confused than ever. "What…?"

"Sorry." The word came out in a lengthy sigh. "I should have put this together sooner." The older woman stood, running her finger along the edge of the freshly printed document, eying him across the top of her reading glasses. "You see, Luna Delaney was in and out of our psychiatric care unit for nearly a year." She bent closer, lowering her voice. "Honestly, I'm not breaching patient confidentiality to tell you this. Her death was in all the papers."

All at once he knew what had happened. Knew before she said it.

"Mary Delaney's daughter committed suicide."

Jake's head fell forward as the weight of a mother's grief dropped onto his back. His throat was so tight he could barely get the words out. "In Lincoln Park?"

She consulted the printed form, then nodded grimly. "Along North Pond. At four o'clock."

His shoulders sagged farther as though a crossbeam had settled there, crushing his heart. *Oh, Mary.* Jake understood now, as he never had before, the terrible truth: Madness has its reasons.

"Be reasonable, Pastor Stauros." The white-coated physician folded his arms over his broad chest, encircling Mary's patient chart, guarding his heart like a fortress. "What you're asking for isn't medicine; it's a miracle."

Jake didn't think he was being unreasonable. Just persistent. Without Mary having any insurance, a medical referral, prior hospital admittance, or any family members to sign the dotted line for her, Jake was having a devil of a time getting her the help she deserved.

Mary Margaret Delaney.

Knowing her full name made her fully real to him now. No longer a shadowy figure in a dark window, she was a flesh-and-blood woman who needed God's healing touch. And the best care modern medicine had to offer.

"All right. Three days." Unfolding his arms with more drama than necessary, the doctor jotted a brief notation on her chart. "That's the most we can give her without some form of insurance or guarantee of payment."

"I'll pay." Jake gulped, knowing how foolish it sounded even as he said it. On a pastor's salary?

"Not necessary. We have procedures in place for such situations. Most hospitals do." The doctor tapped his pen on her chart. "Three days will be sufficient time to get her stabilized, connect her with someone in social services, and start her on a prescription drug that should make her life easier."

Jake knew the truth—it would make everyone *else's* life easier. As for Mary, only time would tell. He stood and extended his hand, determined to show his gratitude. "Appreciate it, Doctor."

The physician's handshake was warm, solid. "No, thank *you*, Reverend." He regarded Jake for a moment as though sizing him up. When he spoke again, his voice had lost its brittle, professional edge. "The truth is, son, you have more to offer Mary Delaney than I do. It's not her body that's sick. It's her spirit."

Jake nodded. On that point they were in total agreement.

"Of course, you'll have to drive out her demons first." He moved past

Jake, slapping him on the shoulder as he did so. "Unless I miss my guess, you're the perfect man for the job."

"Hospital visits are my job, Suzy." Jake yanked a sweater over his shirt, avoiding a second glance at his secretary who was busy broadcasting her blatant disapproval—hands on hips, frown in place.

"On Mondays, sure," she fumed. "This is Friday."

"Yeah, well. I went yesterday, too, and I'm going tomorrow morning when Mary is released." He turned toward her, meeting her gaze, wanting her to understand. "Mary Margaret Delaney has no one else to help her. No relatives we can track down, no friends who've stepped forward. No one but us, her church family."

"Her *what?*" Suzy sputtered. "That madwoman has never set foot in this church!"

"Actually she did. Last Sunday." He kept his voice low, his tone free from censure. "She slipped in the back of the room, so no one saw her but me. It was only for a second, but she *was* here. Maybe she'll come back and stay next time." He lowered his chin, wanting to catch her eye again. "I know you'd want that too, Suze."

The young woman's cheeks colored, and her gaze fell to the hem of her ankle-length skirt. "Guess so."

He would never bring up Suzy's own checkered past or humiliate her, not for one second. Nonetheless, she quickly made the connection herself.

"Jake, did people...um...talk about me? When I first came, I mean?" She lifted her head, a hesitant awakening reflected in her eyes. "All I remember is how...kind everybody was." Her voice dropped to a whisper. "Especially you."

He shrugged, embarrassed by her praise. "Grace is a gift meant for everybody. My job is to hand out presents."

"And make hospital calls." She smiled, her blush starting to fade. "Say hello to Mary for me. Tell her...tell her I'm looking forward to...um, meeting her."

"That's the spirit, Suze." Jake touched her elbow briefly as he passed, a tacit affirmation of the growth he saw in her—from a lonely woman focused only on her own needs to a generous soul willing to extend forgiveness to others. No need to hoard it, fearing there wouldn't be enough to go around. The supply was limitless.

"I'll be back in an hour," he called over his shoulder, heading toward the front of the church, his thoughts already reaching toward the sixth floor of Grant Hospital. A swirl of snow traveling on a bitterly cold north wind greeted him as he tugged the hood of his parka in place and turned south toward Webster. Lake-effect snow, Chicagoans called it. It was effective, all right. Turned the sidewalks into a skating rink.

He skidded along, past the Park View Pet Shop, remembering exactly where he'd collided with Mary Margaret Delaney—what, ten days ago? That unexpected meeting had led to another, then another. Clearly the Lord had a plan for Mary, a plan that included Jake's intervention in her life.

"Fine, well, and good," he muttered to no one but himself, tromping around a small mountain of sooty snow. He'd ministered to those broken in two by sins of their own making plenty of times. Women like Suzy, guys like Bruce, people with moral issues. Yeah, he knew what paths to take on those journeys.

But where to begin with a madwoman? She hadn't brought this on herself—not her daughter's suicide, nor her own severe depression. If she didn't start it, how could she *stop* it? More to the point, how could *he* help her stop? What was he supposed to do first?

When the main entrance to Grant Hospital came into view, so did the simple answer to his many questions.

Show up, son. Make an appearance.

And leave the rest to God.

Relieved, Jake lifted his chin and walked through the revolving doors, determined not to be put off by the uninspiring view. Tan walls offered a lackluster welcome, tan furniture provided a dubious resting place, and the tan carpet was stained with melting snow and chalk white circles of ice-melting compound tracked in from the street. He passed the gift shop, brightly lit but deserted, waved at the familiar face behind the reception counter, then punched the button for the elevator.

The doors ground open before he was ready. Jake stepped inside and prayed silently for strength as the car lurched upward. *Sixth floor.* His second visit in as many days to the psychiatric unit, where a dark-haired, wild-eyed woman lay strapped on a bed, her every vital sign carefully monitored—except the one that mattered most.

Nothing mattered anymore.

Mary eyed the plastic bracelet fastened around her wrist. *Delaney.* How could a strip of vinyl know who she was when she didn't have a clue?

She shivered and shifted her weight around, finding a warmer spot on the bed. Outside her window snow fell in thick, fat flakes, turning her surroundings into a white blur—the sheets, the curtains, the lab coats, the filmy privacy curtain with the noisy silver rings. White, white, white.

Not Mary though. She was black inside and red all over, covered with angry scars and a head-to-toe tint of shame.

Every inch of her body felt like a battleground. On one side of the bloodied field stood a tenacious young preacher who'd visited her room entirely too often these three days—or was it four? He never stopped talking about God. His weapons were soft words, but they bruised her heart like blows from a blunt mallet.

On the other side were all the terrifying memories she'd hoped never to face. "Demons" the pastor called them. Their wicked weaponry, anything but soft, cut with the precision of surgical knives. Wherever they touched her, she bled, pierced by unholy memories of nocturnal jaunts beneath the glow of a full moon and suicidal nightmares that sent her stumbling along the banks of North Pond looking for Luna.

Luna, Luna, Luna.

Her only daughter, Luna had been the bright and shining product of Mary's marriage at age twenty to Mick Delaney, a transplanted Irishman who had landed in their tree-lined Chicago neighborhood and stolen her heart. For nearly two decades, life had been up and down with the Delaneys. Mostly up. They'd bought a fine house, had they not? Mortgage paid in full. And had the prettiest daughter at Saint Clement Church—none could deny it.

But when Luna had left this world by her own hand at seventeen, darkness had settled over Mary's days like a March fog rolling off Lake Michigan, relentless and unstoppable. *Seven years of darkness.* Her charmed life had slowly dismantled itself. Released by her employer, abandoned by her husband, neglected by her neighbors, discarded by society, Mary had become all too familiar with suffering and well acquainted with sorrow.

Mad Mary.

Oh, she knew what they called her. In her lucid moments, she hated them for it. In her murky moments, she agreed with them completely.

The metal bars of the hospital bed offered a cold and stark reminder that she was imprisoned in a madness not of her own making. "Let Christ set you free," this Jake person had said. This do-gooder with his nice words and his Bible verses and his honest smile.

When he'd touched her shoulder yesterday, it had burned her skin.

Danger, danger, danger.

The voices inside her had given up whispering altogether and were shouting at her now.

DANGER, DANGER, DANGER!

The pastor *did* seem to know too much about her. Her full name. Where she lived. That she'd once had a daughter.

He would come again this morning, he'd said. Come to walk her home.

Mary blinked at the clock mounted on the wall, certain the hands were visibly moving. "Time flies," she croaked, attempting a smile, feeling her chapped lips crack with the effort. The medicine that had dripped through her veins all day yesterday had made her woozy. Today they'd given her pills instead. It was better, but she still felt odd. Not like her old self.

Which old self, Mary?

There were too many old selves, too many voices, too much noise.

Minutes later she didn't hear the door open and was startled when she turned her head and found Jake, the dangerous one, standing at her bedside, smiling down at her pillowed head.

"What have you to say for yourself, Mary Margaret Delaney?"

She squinted at him, momentarily blinded by his radiant face. For a plain man, he certainly could work up a shine. "You know what the Irish say, don't you?" She grimaced in a palsied sort of way. "'May you be in heaven half an hour before the devil knows you're dead.'"

"You're not dead, Mary. And trust me, the devil knows it."

She'd never seen a man smile yet be so serious at the same time. "Nor am I alive." She swung her chin in the direction of the monitors standing guard over her bed. "I hate all this garbage."

"Which means you're ready to go home." Jake gently squeezed the fingers of her right hand, sending an unseen spark skipping up her bare, razor-scarred arm. Before she could comment, he turned toward the door. "Isn't that right, Doc?"

"She's ready as she'll ever be." Her physician strolled into the sterile room, adding little warmth with his presence. "The paperwork is waiting for you to sign, Mrs. Delaney."

Mrs. Delaney. She hadn't heard that in years.

He consulted his chart rather than meet her bleary gaze. "Within the hour you'll be a free woman."

Free? She'd forgotten the meaning of the word.

The physician checked her monitors with a practiced eye, jotted down a few notes, then slipped her chart into a filing tray mounted by the door. The sight of his lab coat disappearing through the wide doorway was the last of him, though it was soon obvious he'd issued an order at the nurse's station. A matronly woman appeared moments later with a bulky plastic bag.

"Your clothes, Ms. Delaney."

Ms. Mary liked that better. *Not Mrs.* Not since the day Mick Delaney had divorced her without a second thought. "My loony wife," he'd called her right before making her his loony *ex*-wife.

The nurse pulled the curtains closed. "I'll be waiting for you with some forms that need signing. Don't be afraid to ring the CALL button if you need help getting dressed." The older woman's gaze shifted toward Jake, and her eyes softened. "In the meantime you're in good hands." The door closed with a muffled thump. Then silence.

They were left regarding one another—a compassionate young preacher who, Mary was certain, knew nothing about life's travesties, and an exhausted woman old enough to be his mother, whose ravaged soul could not account for seven years lost with nothing gained.

"Are they?" She stared at his fingers resting on the bedrail. "Are they good hands?"

He paused, swallowing. "No one is good except God."

"Then how can you help me?" She heard a hint of desperation creeping into her voice, pinching the words, transposing them up a note.

"Ah, Mary." Much as she resented it, his tender sigh reminded her of a fresh spring morning. "All I can do is see that you get home safely. But God can do more than you might ask or imagine."

"My imagination is pretty vivid, boy-o." She forced her slack features into a half smile, sure the results were less than satisfactory.

"Ask him then." He rested his hand on hers and bowed his head.

No! She swallowed hard, her throat tightening. *Not prayer!* Beneath his warm touch, her hand began to tremble. Somewhere inside her, warning bells began to clang and a chorus of voices screamed at her. *Stop! Stop it!* Prayer—talking to God—no, no, she couldn't do that. Hadn't done so since her daughter went to Lincoln Park seven years ago and never came home.

She slipped her hand out from under his, then quickly grasped the lowest rung of her bedrail, determined to hang on. "You and your God can wait in the hall," she growled, a wave of nausea rushing through her. "I'll be ready to leave soon enough. No need to wait if you don't want to."

Long pause. "I'll wait."

Infuriated, she stared at the rumpled sheets, refusing to acknowledge him. He stepped into the hallway outside her door without another word, and she felt the air suddenly cool at his departure. *Pain-in-the-neck preacher!* She slid to the end of the bed, past the rail, then waited while the room spun around a few times. She'd need his help to walk the four blocks home, but after that, he could point his sad brown eyes some other direction.

She yanked an ugly blue dress out of the bag, depressed at the sight of it, knowing it was the same dress she'd worn on Wednesday to Lincoln Park, hoping to be dead by now, to have the pain over for good. When she stood to her feet, shaking uncontrollably, and slipped it over her head, the feel of it against her skin repulsed her. Blood-stained and torn, two sizes too small, it clung to her bony frame, buttons straining, its long sleeves not long enough, exposing her bruised, purple wrists. Where had she found such a rag anyway?

It was the smell of it that disturbed her most. She leaned toward one shoulder, sniffing tentatively at the fabric. Beneath the acrid scent of dried sweat and faint traces of antiseptic slathered on her arms in the emergency room, there lingered a familiar fragrance. Sweet and floral. Yet unpleasant. Unsettling. Familiar but not welcome.

She leaned closer and sniffed again. Bile rose in her throat, nearly choking her.

Luna. It was Luna's perfume. Luna's dress.

What was she doing in Luna's dress?

Mary swallowed repeatedly, desperate to remember. Had she resurrected the dress from some drawer in Luna's empty room one forgotten night? What was she thinking, saving such a thing? Wearing such a thing?

The voices taunted her without mercy, whispering her deepest fears, her secret longings. *You hoped Luna would recognize you in the park, Mary.*

"But she didn't!" It came out on a sob. "Luna didn't see me, didn't know her own mother."

Luna wasn't there, Mary. Luna is dead.

The room was spinning again, now on a sickening tilt. Mary pulled a name out of thin air as her body pitched forward. "Jake! Ja-a-a-ake!"

The green tile floor rose to meet her when two strong hands suddenly appeared and caught her beneath the arms. She sagged into them, too weak to resist as the younger man lifted her to her feet in one graceful move.

How had she ever remembered his name? She tried to look away but could not. His face was kindness incarnate.

"I'm here, Mary." He said her name as though he knew her. Knew her well and overlooked all that he knew to be true.

"Why are you here?" she whispered, dreading his answer.

"My Father sent me." The corners of his mouth turned upward, as though he'd had a revelation. "Are you ready, Mary Margaret Delaney?"

"R-ready?" She clutched the vinyl hospital bag and held it tightly against her chest. "Ready for wh-what?"

"No need to be afraid, Mary." The young pastor named Jake inclined his head toward the door. "I've come to take you home."

Chapter Three

POWER OF THE VISIBLE

*The power of the visible
is the invisible.*
MARIANNE MOORE

Mary's home was nothing like Jake expected.

He was prepared for a rundown, third-floor apartment in a building crawling with DePaul students in the fall and roaches in the spring. Instead he found himself steering Mary up the steps of a classic Victorian brownstone. Squeezed between two twentieth-century buildings and only half a block from upscale Lincoln Park West, it was a valuable piece of real estate.

Of all the things he imagined Mary to be, affluent wasn't one of them.

On closer inspection, though, the house's age was showing. The bay windows on the first and second floors needed washing. Badly. So did the lace curtains in the windows. The wrought-iron rail wobbled beneath Mary's grip, and the stark black trim, long overdue for a fresh coat of paint, made the house look gloomy and foreboding.

Head bent, Mary fumbled with the key as Jake stood behind her, waiting for some cue. "Do you need me to come in with you?"

She slowly pivoted around. Her pupils were dilated—pharmaceutically, he guessed—and her features expressionless. "Why would I need your help inside my own home?"

Heat stung his cheeks. "Sorry, Mrs. Delaney." The woman had a point.

He'd walked her the few blocks between the hospital and her house, mostly to make certain she didn't slip on the ice. Her steps had been surprisingly sure, her gait steady. No more than ten words had passed between them—eight of them his—and she'd made it abundantly clear with her distant demeanor that his company was neither necessary nor welcome.

The woman's glazed eyes narrowed, and her chin jutted out. "What happened to Mary?"

She really is mad. Swallowing his dismay, Jake found himself at a loss for words.

She spoke instead, her tone peevish. "You called me *Mary* in the hospital." One eyebrow lifted, forming a question mark on her face. "Why not now?"

"Oh, I see." *Not so crazy after all.* "I didn't know your last name at first. Now that I do, *Mrs. Delaney* seems…I dunno." He shrugged, searching for the right phrase. "More respectful."

She smiled at that. Nothing more than a slight twitch of her lips, but it altered her features dramatically. "Your mother raised you right, boy-o. Good for her."

Unwittingly, Mary had handed him the perfect opening.

"Speaking of my mother," he began, leaning cautiously on the rail. "She would love to meet you. I'm guessing you're about the same age—"

Her harrumph cut him short. "*Old,* you mean."

"Did I say that?" He held up both palms in mock resistance. "Quite young actually. She lives by herself, not far from here. A finer woman you'll never meet, Mrs.—"

"Mary," she corrected him firmly.

Good. "*Mary* then. As it turns out, that's my mother's name as well. Why not join us at Calvary Fellowship on Sunday? You can sit with—"

"What *is* it with you and that church?" The hint of a smile disappeared as a bitter scowl hurried to take its place. "Do you think the whole world needs your…religion?" She spat the word out like sour milk, stepping back toward the half-open door. "I've had a bellyful of your verses and your prayers. It was good of you to see me home, but now if you don't mind…"

She jerked around and shoved the door open farther. Jake caught a brief glimpse of a cluttered interior and the distinct aroma of cat litter before he finally remembered the package in his coat pocket.

"Mary, I…I have something for you." Jake watched her pause and turn only partially toward him. The timing was wrong, all wrong; he knew that. He'd meant to give it to her earlier, *should* have given it to her at the hospital. Still, if he never saw her again…well, it had to be now. Fishing the slim Bible out of his pocket, he held it out gingerly, wondering if she might slap it out of his hand.

Instead, she stared at it, her brow drawn into a knot. "What am I supposed to do with that?"

"Um…read it?" He couldn't keep the playful words from slipping out. Wasn't it obvious what one did with a Bible?

Not to Mary apparently. Speechless, she took it from him with exaggerated care, as though it were a sleeping cobra. Holding it by her fingertips, she stepped inside the house and with a nervous flick tossed the red volume onto a nearby table.

He swallowed his disappointment whole and pressed on. "Would you…?"

When she ignored him and started closing the door, Jake slapped his hand against it. "Mary Margaret Delaney, would you please listen to me?"

She looked up, startled, gripping the doorknob for balance, and truly met his gaze for the first time that morning. The sorrow in her eyes was deeper than a well and every bit as dark.

Poor Mary.

Jake softened his voice and infused it with prayer. "Will you read a page or two? Please? I've marked a good place to begin." When she didn't argue, he stepped closer and touched her arm. "And will you let me know if you need anything? Anything at all?"

Mary didn't speak, didn't move. She simply stood there in the doorway, her eyes on him. "I will," she said at last, surprising them both.

The last thing Jake needed was a forty-degree sanctuary and no working furnace.

He rubbed his hands together, warming them with steamy breaths, as he surveyed the empty room, imagining his members shivering in their seats come eleven o'clock. The meager morning light in the front windows high-lighted the still air, cold as a tomb. January couldn't end soon enough to suit him. Not that February in Chicago was any improvement.

Jake checked the watch hidden under the sleeve of his heaviest sweater. *Nearly nine.* Little John was handy with plumbing and electrical stuff, but this furnace fiasco might tax even his considerable talents. Nonetheless, he'd call him, and Pete, too. Get them working on things downstairs while he located some space heaters or, at the very least, ski caps. No good delivering a heartwarming sermon to a crowd with frozen ears.

Jake settled into his office, his membership roster spread out on the desk, and started punching numbers. Little John sounded confident on the phone, promising he'd arrive in ten minutes, toolbox in hand. When he did, Jake followed him down the stairs, armed with flashlights and a battery of prayers. Pete showed up soon after, giving orders as usual while John struggled to bring the decades-old furnace to life again. The thing looked like an oversize octopus, dependent on gas, electricity, *and* gravity to work its magic. If it could be repaired, the big man with the big heart could handle it.

Trusting their expertise, Jake finally left the dank basement behind and climbed the rickety steps that led to his office—the kitchen of the old house—where he found JoAnn filling communion cups by the sink. Her blond head was bent as she carefully poured a swallow of purple liquid into the tiny plastic cups.

"Why not stick a toothpick in each one?" he suggested, watching her tip the jar again and again. "Then we can serve 'em like little Popsicles."

She laughed, almost spilling the grape juice. "It *is* an icebox in here."

"Which is why I'm headed out to see what I can find at Walgreens." Jake grabbed the Calvary checkbook off his desk. "You're in charge while I'm gone."

"Better hurry back then," she called after him, still laughing.

He zipped his parka as he strode through the building toward the front door, his thoughts centered on the people who made Calvary a going concern. Could they manage without him? Someday they'd have to. Maybe sooner than later, although he couldn't pin down a date yet. He'd know when it was time to move on.

Jake understood his calling—starting new congregations, not maintaining established ones. "Church planting" they'd called it at seminary. Once the seedlings had strong roots, his work was done.

Striding across the street, he made a beeline for the pharmacy, smiling at the names and faces that crowded his mind. JoAnn could certainly handle the finances without his help. Little John knew every nook and cranny of that old building. Pete knew his way around the Bible and was born to preach—*if* he got his impulsiveness in check. Joe and Nick had generous hearts with a bent to serve. And Suzy would keep the whole lot of them in line. *Charles Farris included.*

Jake smiled, yanking open the glass door. His job at the moment was keeping them all warm.

Wide aisles and bright fluorescent lights greeted him as he hurried through the store, waving at the clerks he passed en route to the hardware section. Unfortunately, the pickings were slim. One small space heater sat on an empty bottom shelf, the only unit left after a bitterly cold month. He tucked the box under his arm, then cleaned out a wire bin of knitted caps in assorted colors. Even if Little John succeeded in fixing the furnace, the church wouldn't be comfortably heated until long after the service was over.

The clerk, a tiny woman with pale olive skin and long black hair, regarded him with amusement as she rang up the unruly pile of caps spilling over her counter. "You takin' your congregation skating this morning, Jake?"

"Not unless my sermon is on thin ice," he quipped, counting caps. *Three dozen. Might be enough.* In brutal weather most people bundled up before they braved the elements, but he'd have something to offer the ones who arrived bareheaded.

Minutes later he found Little John up to his elbows in grease and soot, the furnace still uncooperative. "I called in a pro," John admitted, wiping his brow with a handkerchief, clearly defeated. "He's coming by at three. Sorry, Jake."

Jake brushed off his friend's concern with a wave of his hand. "No problem. God will provide, you know that. Meanwhile, I have the perfect thing to keep us toasty warm, at least from the ears up." He held up one of the caps, then inclined his head toward the stairs. "Come help me hand them out, brother."

Ever-resourceful Suzy, digging around various storage cabinets, had already unearthed stacks of Girl Scout sit-upons—hand-stitched vinyl cushions stuffed with old *Tribunes*—courtesy of the Junior troop that used Calvary's facilities on Tuesday nights.

"Nothing colder than a metal folding chair," she explained, placing the cushions on the seats and pulling them closer together. "A little shared body heat won't hurt either." His mother, swathed in wool from head to toe, showed up moments later and went to work making hot coffee in a gallon-size silver urn while Pete fired up the space heater.

Jake helped where he could and praised their efforts, pleased to see them pulling together, working as one.

Little John, his arms scrubbed clean, yanked a knitted cap over each bare head that stumbled through the door. "No wind chill in here," he announced cheerfully. "And a full twenty degrees warmer than it is outside."

"Don't we even get to pick the color?" whined one teenager.

Jake stifled a laugh as he watched bear-sized John silence the boy with a fierce glare. "You don't even get to *keep* it," John informed him, pointing to a box near the door. "Deposit it there on the way out so we can take 'em to a homeless shelter this afternoon."

Jake nodded, secretly delighted with their good stewardship. *They'll do fine without me, Father. Tell me when it's time.*

As the minutes ticked by, he offered his customary greetings to each member. He barely had to move to do so—everyone had squeezed into the first three rows without a vacant chair left among them. When Marijane stood to lead the first chorus, Jake glanced over his shoulder and spied a familiar face in the foyer entrance.

Mary Delaney. He hadn't seen her all week, not since their walk home from the hospital.

Little John held out a cap to her. Even from a distance it was obvious to Jake that he did so reluctantly. *C'mon, John. Nothing to be afraid of.* As she pushed the cap away, Mary's gaze flitted around the room, then landed on Jake, like a moth drawn to a light bulb. He nodded, wanting her to know he was glad to see her, then turned toward the front. Better not to focus too much attention on her, make her feel self-conscious.

She was *there;* that was the main thing.

Twenty minutes later, when he rose to share his sermon, she was still there. Alone, in the last row, no hat to warm her head, no sit-upon to warm her seat, but she was *there.* In her left hand, clutched tightly against her shabby coat, was a thin red book with gilt-edged pages.

Try as he might, Jake couldn't keep a smile from spreading across his face. *Welcome, Mary.*

Mary threw the book on her kitchen table, a knot of angry tears tightening her throat. *Some welcome!*

Oh, he'd *looked* at her. He'd *smiled.* But then he'd spoken to those other people who'd hung on his words like hungry birds. *Fools.* She'd left before he finished speaking, confused by what he'd said. More than confused. It scared her. Made beads of sweat dot her forehead, even in that freezing cold room.

She vowed she would never go there again.

But she did.

The first Sunday in February found her tiptoeing in while they were singing, still arguing with herself as she scanned the few empty seats. *What are you doing here, Mary Delaney?* She had no answer, no clue to what drew her to this man and his message.

At least the place was warm that week. Too warm perhaps. Thirty seconds after she crossed the threshold, a fine sheen of perspiration already ran across her brow. She sat in the second row from the back, trying to blend in, to disappear in her nondescript coat.

It didn't work. When the song finished, the young preacher stood and turned to face his congregation. And promptly met her gaze with a broad smile. All at once she felt sick. *Run! Run!* She stood, knocking her chair to the floor with a loud *thump.*

"Mary." His calm voice stopped her. His compassionate gaze wouldn't let her go. "I'm glad you came back." He waved his hand across the rows of chairs. "I'm sorry that chair isn't comfortable for you. Why not choose another one? Perhaps a little closer to the front?"

She felt trapped like a butterfly in a net. Moving forward, her knees shaking, she dropped into an empty chair, aware that every eye in the place was

trained on her. *Assessing, judging, condemning.* She refused to look at them—
or at him—and focused instead on the red book in her lap.

She'd thrown it away twice, disgusted by what she'd read, then retrieved it
from the trash, ashamed of herself. It was, after all, a gift. A gift with something astonishing on the cover: her name. *Mary Margaret Delaney* printed
with gold letters in a fanciful script on dark red leather, the color of wine.

The color of blood, Mary. Your own blood, shed for no one but yourself.

The voices in her head, held at bay since her dismal failure in Lincoln
Park, screamed for attention this morning. She could barely hear the words
the pastor was saying. After several agonizing minutes, the onslaught was
finally over, and she sagged forward in relief.

Why were they bothering her now? She'd had such a good week. The
medicine was helping her think more clearly. Almost like a sane person.
Almost. Her gaze took in the attentive congregation, their Bibles in hand,
their heads nodding. *Of course.* It was this place, this sacred room. Her
demons didn't like it, not one bit.

She found herself fidgeting in her chair until Jake's sermon ended and he
moved to the front door. All around her, people stood and greeted one
another with handshakes and hugs. No one stretched out a hand seeking
hers in return. A few aimed tentative glances in her direction, but they eventually wandered out into the blustery day without coming any closer than
necessary.

Not a soul spoke to her. The only thing they offered was a cold shoulder
or a cursory glance. More than one person wore a candid look of fear as they
gave her a wide berth. And some well-dressed older man pointed his cane at
her, complaining to Jake as he stood at the door.

Hot tears stung her eyes. *Foolish, Mary, to get your hopes up!* Why would
anyone want to speak to a woman with a trace of madness still lingering in
her gaze and arms streaked with scars, the calling cards of self-mutilation?

She rose to go, shaking with frustration.

"Mary." Jake's voice echoed across the empty sanctuary. "Glad you're still
here." A few lengthy strides and he was beside her, his eyes filled with concern. He motioned her back into a chair and sat down beside her. "My

mother is home ill this morning but sends her best." He paused for a long time, studying her. "How are *you* feeling?"

"Neglected," she confessed with a rueful sigh. "Disposable." Her voice dropped another notch. "I get the feeling people around here would be happier if I went away and didn't come back."

"At Calvary Fellowship?" His brow wrinkled, and a slight frown creased his face. "I'm very sorry to hear you say that."

He *looked* sorry—she had to admit that much. This young man who made the whole world feel welcome probably couldn't imagine what it was like to be despised and rejected. Maybe she would show him, let him see how it felt to be treated like last week's garbage.

"Busy this afternoon, preacher?" *That* got his attention. "I've got some grocery shopping to do. Thought you might keep me company." She stood, buttoning her coat. "Ought to be a real education for you."

"If you say so, ma'am. Lemme grab my parka." He was gone only a moment, then led her out the front door, locking it behind him. "I assume we're headed to Big Apple."

She nodded, then bent her head into the wind. Across the street and half a block north stood the neighborhood grocery store. BIG APPLE was spelled in tall white letters across the brown shingle facing, though the B had disappeared one Windy City day. The red-and-white signs plastered across every inch of the windows shouted the bargains that waited inside: EDY'S ICE CREAM $2.99. IDAHO POTATOES, 29¢ A POUND, BAGS ONLY.

"That's the problem," Jake murmured, pointing at the sign as they pushed open the door. "What single guy can get through a whole bag of potatoes before they sprout legs?"

A blaring radio and a mingling of smells greeted them. The bananas were overripe, and the meat case needed a good scrubbing. Mary waited while Jake found her a chrome cart with a bright green handle and wheels that worked. "Don't walk with me," she insisted. "Keep a little distance so people won't know we're together."

"Why?" He grabbed a cart for himself, then caught up with her, clearly perplexed. "What's this all about?"

Turning her back toward him, Mary smeared her lipstick across her face with a quick swipe, then opened her coat and wiped her hand clean on her white blouse. She redid the first few buttons so they were mismatched and yanked the shirttails out of her skirt, then pulled her hair loose until it stuck out in clumps.

Her transformation complete, Mary swung back and met his gaze with an intentionally half-lidded one. "I want you to see how the world treats a madwoman."

She stumbled past the rows of bread, ignoring him as she filled her basket with fresh vegetables, mumbling to herself. Right on cue, a woman started to turn her direction, then beat a hasty retreat. A trio of children taunted her with cruel words and raised voices. The man behind the meat counter took one look, then shook his head in derision. So it went aisle after aisle. Unkind comments, rude stares, pointing fingers.

On her worst days, Mary guessed, she hadn't even seen how people had responded to her. On more lucid days, she'd pretended not to notice. With her newfound toehold on reality, the dire truth was all too apparent. No wonder her cupboards had stayed bare. Going out in public was more painful than living with an empty stomach.

Not far behind her, she heard Jake tossing grocery items into his basket. Was he paying attention? Could he possibly comprehend what it was like to endure scorn and ridicule?

He followed her to the checkout line, neither making eye contact, both going about their business. When they met on the street, she turned to find his brown eyes clouded with tears.

"Mary, Mary." He gently took her bag of groceries, adding it to his own. "I'm so sorry."

His pity—that *was* pity in his eyes, wasn't it?—angered her. "Why should you be sorry?" she snapped, jerking her chin as she wiped away the lipstick on her face with a tissue. "What have you done wrong?"

"What have I ever done to *stop* it? That's the real question."

"You don't have that kind of power." She tried to take her groceries back, but he pulled them tighter to his chest.

"Let me help you, Mary." His voice was kind but firm. "It's too cold to stand outside when your warm house is waiting right around the corner. C'mon, I'll walk you home."

He matched his stride to hers as they headed down Clark, shifting into single file when the piles of snow along the curb turned the wide sidewalk into little more than a footpath. They were soon standing at her doorstep, Jake holding two heavy grocery sacks as if they were full of feathers, Mary digging in her purse for a house key. Once the door swung open, she turned and plucked the brown paper bags out of his arms, then stepped inside, blocking the entrance.

"Look, Jake." She stared down at his earnest face, determined to make him go away and take his best intentions with him. "You can't change my...my condition. And you can't change how people treated me."

He backed down the steps, his steady gaze never faltering. "Nor can I change what I'm called to do."

Stubborn lad! "Which is what, exactly?"

"Convince the world that God can do both those things." He started down the sidewalk, calling over his shoulder, "See you next Sunday."

"Not if I can help it," she grumbled and slammed the door.

Thursday night, standing in the open doorway staring out at the rain, Mary couldn't help herself.

She'd watched the calendar, counted the days, hoping the medicine would be potent enough to stop her. But it was nearing midnight, and she could fight the urge no longer. The pull of the moon was too powerful, too demanding.

Like a magnet, it drew her out the front door and toward the park. Though the temperature was unseasonably mild, a wind had kicked up, blowing pellets of rain against her cheeks. She pulled her hood over her face until all she could see were her boots scurrying through the dark, wet night. That was enough. Her feet knew the way to Lincoln Park. Hadn't they taken her there against her will on many a moonlit outing?

Imposing high-rise apartments loomed on both sides of her, their rows upon rows of menacing black windows staring down at her. *Better not to see them.* She quickened her steps, dashing across the parkway, only slowing when she recognized the curving park sidewalks and felt her heart ease its frantic beating. The meandering shores of North Pond were not far ahead.

She hadn't brought anything dangerous with her. The medicine had helped her past *that* sinister temptation. Nor would she throw herself in the pond's icy waters seeking some final release from life's burdens.

When she reached the shoreline and realized it was frozen solid, Mary chuckled. *A good sign, old girl.* Not that the pond was still frozen, preventing her from drowning, but that she'd chuckled.

She risked a faceful of rain to look up at the cloud-covered sky. No moon in sight. Oh, it was up there somewhere, full as could be, make no mistake. The calendar said so, and her emotional state confirmed it. But not seeing the single, luminous eye staring down at her provided a small measure of comfort.

Nor was there any sense of Luna's presence hovering in the midnight air. "Thank you," she whispered, not knowing or caring who might be listening. She needed to be alone—away from the voices, away from Luna's ghostly specter, away from the moon—to sort through her jumbled thoughts and feelings. Mary began the half-mile walk around the pond, talking louder to herself with each step.

If someone wandered by and heard her, what of it? Let him think she was crazy. That's what Mick Delaney thought, and it drove him away. Maybe it would do the same for any ne'er-do-wells who might wander through the park at such an ungodly hour.

"Leave me alone," she announced to the night.

Leave me alone, Luna.

Her daughter's suicide was in all ways unexpected, tragic, needless. There was no warning in the weeks before, no note left for the stunned survivors. Yes, Luna had struggled emotionally. There had been personality changes and periods of severe withdrawal. Hospital stays and psychiatric evaluations. But nothing insurmountable, nothing beyond the reach of modern medicine and a mother's loving care.

Or so Mary had thought. She had been wrong.

None of the details of those days remained in her memory banks. The desperate trip to Grant Hospital, the endless decisions, the funeral, the burial at Graceland Cemetery, the choosing of a headstone—all a meaningless blur. Nothing remained but the guilt, an enormous, smothering mass that crushed Mary's spirit as surely as Luna's velvet-lined casket pressed into the ground beneath it.

Mary swore she would never attend another funeral, not even the death of her marriage in a judge's chambers. The divorce not only went uncontested, it went unnoticed, so lost was she in a maze of depression. As the years passed, the leafy walls of that maze climbed higher around her, blocking the sunlight. The only thing Luna had bequeathed to her mother, it seemed, was a map that led to a solitary and hopeless destination.

Now a young man whose very countenance was hope itself held out a different set of directions entirely, squeezed between the covers of a book. "Choose life," he'd said last Sunday. Had he looked at her intentionally, or was it nothing more than her overactive imagination?

It was a life with God he was talking about, and that's what scared her most. She'd known who God was since childhood—what good Irish Catholic girl didn't? The priests at Saint Clement had done their best to fill her with images of a loving Savior who cared enough to die for her, sin-laden though she certainly was. And she, good mother that she'd tried to be, had reared Luna in the same cozy parish on Deming Place, not six blocks from home.

Had the church failed her? Indeed not. She had failed the church.

Had the Christ failed her?

She stopped with a lurch and sank onto a nearby park bench in a soggy heap.

"Oh, Jesus." She hadn't spoken his name in seven years. The words came slowly, like drops of blood from an old wound. "Where were you?" she whispered. "When Luna was alone in this park, *where were you?*"

Ugly voices inside her head answered instead. *Where were* you, *Mary? You were her mother. Where were you?*

The words came out in sob. "I was making...her...supper."

She collapsed then, bending in two, tears mingled with rain streaming down her coat. If getting well meant feeling all this pain, reliving all this sorrow, then she was not ready. She would never be ready.

Jake hoped they were ready, prayed they'd have ears to hear.

He might not be able to convince the entire world that the Mad Marys among them deserved compassion and respect. But persuading the growing number of souls sitting before him—nearly sixty now—seemed a good place to begin.

"It was the Sabbath, Luke tells us, and Jesus was busy teaching in the synagogue. A woman was sitting among them who'd been crippled by an evil spirit for eighteen years." *Evil spirit. Yeah, that got their attention.* Jake saw their eyebrows lift, their mouths open in surprise.

"Eighteen years is a long time. No way could she have faked it. Besides, it was obvious something was the matter. She was bent over and couldn't straighten up." He leaned forward until his back paralleled the floor. "Be kinda hard to miss somebody who walked into church like this, wouldn't it?" He hobbled forward, penguinlike, and the congregation laughed. "Bet everybody in town knew this lady. Probably called her some clever name— 'Bent Brenda'—to remind her she was different. That she wasn't one of them."

The laughter died down as Jake straightened. *They know where I'm going with this.* They would not find a hint of judgment in his eyes because there was none. Only love. And the truth.

He walked back toward the pulpit, scanning their faces. "Jesus saw her and called her to the front." He didn't dare look at Mary Delaney, sitting wide-eyed in the last row, his mother by her side. "Think how quiet that room got, and fast!" Jake moved slowly down the center aisle, wanting to connect with every gaze, touch every heart. "Can't you see it? People stepping aside, making way for this woman bent in two, shuffling silently forward."

When he reached Mary, Jake paused, waiting one beat, then two, letting her see his face and understand his purpose in telling this story. Her story. *To set them free to love you, Mary. To set you free to love them back.*

He began backing up, as slowly as he'd come forward, drawing their eyes with him. "All he asked her to do was walk forward. Not say some special words or bathe in a pool of magical water or kiss the hem of his garment." Jake had reached the first row again and stopped, resting his hand briefly on young Gary's shoulder. "Just come to him. That's all he asked the woman to do. Know what he said next?"

Pete called out impatiently, "No! What?" and the congregation laughed good-naturedly.

"Hang on, brother. I'm gettin' to it." Jake picked up his Bible and read, " 'Woman, you are set free from your infirmity.' In fact, I like the old King James way of putting it: 'Woman, thou art loosed!' "

Out of the corner of his eye he caught a glimpse of Mary Delaney straightening in her chair, more lucid than he'd ever seen her.

Jake continued, encouraged by her attentiveness. "He put his hands on her, and right away she straightened up and praised God."

"Well, I guess so!" Pete looked highly satisfied with the happy ending. "Bet the whole place praised God right along with her."

Jake carefully placed his Bible on the stand and stepped closer. "No, they didn't, Pete. The guys in charge were too worried about Jesus' delivering and healing on the Sabbath—in other words, breaking the rules—to care about this woman and her evil spirit and her bent body."

Now came the hardest part of all: resisting the temptation to look Charles Farris right in the eye. He'd been the first to come to Jake complaining about *that woman* and demanding to know what she was doing in their church.

Jake looked instead toward the front door and the wooden cross that hung above it, his constant source of inspiration. "The Lord called them hypocrites. Frauds. But he called the woman a daughter of Abraham. You won't find that phrase anywhere else in Scripture, folks. Rocked their world, I can tell you. But it needed rocking."

He closed his Bible, feeling the weight of God's mercy. "So does our own, brothers and sisters. So does our own."

"You may own this house, Mrs. Delaney." The woman from the social services agency looked down at her through sharp-edged glasses. "But that does not give you the right to jeopardize the public's health. You have one week to find homes for these cats or have them destroyed."

Mary looked down at her precious Max, curling around her ankles, and felt faint. "*All* of them?"

The tall, sixtyish woman—*Kathleen Jensen,* her crisp business card said—gazed about the messy room, her lips pinched. "You may keep one, provided it's properly cared for. And what about all"—she swept her hand through the air—"all *this?* What plans do you have for making your living conditions more…sanitary?"

Plans? Mary bit her lip. She barely planned from one hour to the next. Had it truly become as disgraceful as this woman seemed to think? Glancing about the room, Mary realized the furniture might indeed need a good dusting. The look on the woman's face assured her it was worse than that, probably far worse than Mary understood. *Help. Somebody.*

"I'll see to things," was all Mary could bring herself to say, sliding toward the front door, anxious to have the house to herself again. Ever since her visit to Grant Hospital, she'd known a visit from some agency type or another would be inevitable. Now there would be more it seemed.

"I'll be back next Tuesday. Say two o'clock?" Ms. Jensen marched down the front steps, brushing her coat as though to shake off any remnants of their visit. "Call me if I may be of further assistance," she said, although the woman's tone suggested quite the opposite.

Mary stared at the overcast sky, colorless like her future. Overcome, she closed the door and clung to the knob, pressing her forehead into the wood. The dreaded day had come. Whatever pain the process might entail, it was time to begin living again.

She would have to make decisions. That was the worst of it. Endless decisions about what to wear, what to eat, whether to read or watch television, stay home or go out. The concept exhausted her. She would need some sort of regular routine, Ms. Jensen had insisted. "Buy a daily calendar and a watch, if you don't have them."

Mary had neither.

Calendars and watches could be bought. What Mary's life needed most was more priceless and rare. She needed a friend. Someone who could walk her through dark, overgrown paths and back into the bright world of the living.

She pushed away from the door and sighed heavily, moving toward the kitchen. "And who do you think would willingly take on *that* thankless job, Mary Delaney? Anyone you know?" Pausing to stare at her reflection in the hall mirror, it was clear what such a friend would be up against. A weary woman in her midforties with a house full of junk and a heart full of pain and a life full of confusion.

"And eleven cats," she announced to the mirror with a nod of finality. She'd counted them after breakfast, fearing the social services woman might ask about them. Which she did, with the saddest possible outcome.

Mary's throat constricted at the thought of them. *Dear kitties.* They were her only true friends. They kept her company, kept her warm at night, kept her from losing all touch with reality. She never came home to an empty house, never ate a meal by herself because of her beloved cats.

"Oh, Max!" Her heart breaking, she scooped up the purring bundle, burying her face in his thick winter fur. Tears fell among his stripes as she stroked under his chin and down his chest, just the way he liked, and felt him *thrumming* under her fingers. "They can't have you, old friend," she whispered, touching her nose to his. "They simply can't. You're all I have."

Was that true? Was there no one else in her life that mattered to her? No one who cared if she lived or died? No one who wanted to see her get well?

Jake.

At the thought of his name, she smiled for the first time that day.

Yes, Jake. He was her friend. Not a close friend, she quickly reminded herself, yet he cared about her. Not like a husband, yet he watched over her. Hadn't he told his congregation—not in so many words, naturally, but woven all through his sermon—hadn't he told them that she, Mary Margaret Delaney, was worthy of respect and compassion, like the woman bent in two?

He was young enough to be her son, yet he had the wisdom of a man twice his age. Older than that. Jake could help her a little, couldn't he? Sort things out, put things in motion? He'd saved her life, hadn't he?

But asking Jake for help meant hearing more about Jesus.

Mary felt a churning inside. The voices were grumbling, as though arguing among themselves, while another voice—a calmer one—rose above the ungodly noise.

Fear not.

She swallowed the lump that threatened to choke her, letting Max slip to the floor in a furry heap. No question, Jake's faith would be part and parcel of their friendship. Last Thursday she'd been so sure she wasn't prepared to change, wasn't ready to be whole again, to be well again. To seek God again.

Unbidden, her sainted mother's words came to her. An Irish proverb from her mother's great storehouse. "Mary Margaret, remember this: 'However long the road, there comes a turning.'"

"Yes, Mama," Mary whispered to the fetid air around her, imagining for a moment it was fresh and clean again. *The turning is coming.*

Chapter Four

PILGRIM SOUL

But one man loved the pilgrim soul in you,
And loved the sorrows of your changing face.
WILLIAM BUTLER YEATS

Jake saw the change in her face the minute she opened the door.

The grief was still there, lingering faintly behind her eyes, and pain had etched a cluster of vertical creases between her eyebrows. Yet, smiling as she was now, the lines vanished without a trace.

"Come in, Jake."

"You mean I can actually step *inside?*" he teased her. Whatever lay beyond the threshold, whatever prompted her unexpected invitation that chilly Saturday morning, he was grateful for her trust. *Lord, let me be worthy of it.*

A strange mix of aromas assaulted him as she closed the door and waved him forward. The delicious scent of bread baking—he never got that one wrong—competed with less pleasant, musty smells. Like all townhouses, this one had windows only front and back, so the interior rooms remained gloomy even on the brightest days.

This was hardly that kind of day. Snow showers were in the forecast, and it felt like ten degrees outside. Mary's house was warm enough, but he blinked trying to adjust to the dim lighting. Not certain where she intended for him to land, he continued slowly through the rooms, trying not to stare at what appeared to be an indoor flea market without the price tags.

"I have a treat for you," she said behind him, her tone more buoyant than he'd ever heard it. "That's it, right in there where the table is set."

Jake knew he was looking at a kitchen. It had a stove, a fridge, cabinets, a table, and chairs. But it also had two sofas from different decades, a lawn-mower, several Casio keyboards, and boxes upon boxes crowding every bit of floor space in stacks so tall they covered the windows. The only light was from a flimsy ceiling fixture that dangled over the table, showing the yellow Formica's age.

He sat down at one of the place settings, too dumbfounded to speak.

Mary busied herself stirring a battered copper pot on the stove, her back toward him. "I know what you're thinking." She tapped the wooden spoon clean on the edge of the pot, laid it gingerly on the stove, then turned around. "You're wondering if I play music."

Of all the things he was wondering, that was tenth on the list.

He swallowed his surprise. "Well, *do* you?"

"No. But I got a good price on those keyboards." Mary nodded at the hodgepodge of black instruments perched on X-shaped stands, as though everyone kept a few handy in their kitchen. Without another word she bent to peer into the stove, releasing a wave of fragrant heat into the room.

Despite his uneasiness Jake smiled. *Fresh bread.* Mary might need some serious help with interior decorating, but her baking talents were promising. He watched her pour piping hot tea into two cups. She smiled as she did so, but her trembling hands gave her away.

"Mary, are you okay?" He had to start somewhere, had to get her talking. The woman hadn't invited him over simply to eat lunch, and they both knew it.

She put the teapot down with an awkward *clink,* then met his gaze, her forced smile replaced by an earnest, open expression. "Lunch first. Then I'll work up the nerve to ask you some hard questions."

"Deal," he agreed with a nod, undone by her candor. He'd never seen her more stable—nor seen her surrounded by more visible evidence of her long affliction. However much they'd witnessed, these silent walls could never tell her story. He hoped that Mary could.

An unkind comment Charles Farris made last Sunday popped into Jake's mind as he spooned sugar into his tea. "Pastor Stauros, why doesn't that woman snap out of it?" Charles had fumed. "Lots of people have problems. No need to bring them to *our* doorstep."

"I can't think of a better place," Jake had responded as gently—and firmly—as possible. "It's not the healthy among us who need a doctor, Mr. Farris. It's the sick."

"Then let her go to a *hospital!*" Charles had shot back, stomping out the door, never realizing Jake was referring to him.

A tricky business, showing people their weaknesses in order to help them grow in grace. An overwhelming task, in fact. During his morning prayers Jake often asked the Lord, *Whose idea* was *this?* then laughed when the answer quickly followed: *Mine.*

Jake sipped his tea, nearly burning his tongue, then eased the cup down and waited patiently while she ladled thick soup into two bowls. Looked like good bone china, though he was hardly an authority on such things. With her expensive plates and her well-worn Formica, Mary Margaret Delaney was becoming more of an enigma by the minute. She placed the steaming bowl before him and an oversize silver spoon with it. *Genuine silver.* Even he knew that much.

"Let me get the bread," she murmured, making short work of breaking the round loaf into quarters. She seemed at home with herself and her work, efficiently handling the final details of their meal. Whatever Mary was nervous about, it wasn't her cooking. Finally seated with bread, butter, and soup in place, she inclined her head toward him hesitantly.

"Would you like me to pray, Mary?"

She nodded, then bowed her head, eyes shut tight.

Smiling, he lowered his chin. "Lord Jesus, may this wonderful meal strengthen our bodies. And may the words we speak strengthen our friendship. In the name of the Christ. Amen."

When they lifted their heads in unison, he discovered a look of astonishment on her face. "What is it?" He grinned, certain he knew. "Too short a prayer for a preacher, right? Ha! You don't know how good this food smells."

"No...not the length." She averted her gaze, her lips moving silently as though she were reciting the words to herself. "You said...you said *our friendship*. Is that...true?"

He held his spoon poised over the creamy soup. "Of course. I'm your pastor, Mary. Your shepherd, if you will." The relief on her face when she met his eyes warmed his soul. "You definitely are my friend, and I hope I'm yours."

"You are." She nodded rapidly. "Yes. Yes." Mary began stirring her soup, then abruptly dropped her spoon in place and grasped the plate of bread, nearly poking him in the chest with it. "Have some," she prompted.

"You don't have to ask twice," he assured her, sliding one of the wedges onto his plate. "So will you tell me what's on the menu here?" He winked at her. "Always helpful to know what you're eating before you swallow it."

She straightened in her seat, as though grateful to return to a safer topic. "The soup was my father's favorite. Potato and leek."

"That's funny." He made a big show of looking around the bowl, hoping his foolishness would put her at ease. "I don't see any leaks." Watching Mary roll her eyes, he knew he'd succeeded.

"Leeks are an herb," she informed him, pretending to be offended. "From the lily family, if you must know."

"I must, absolutely." He stared down at his bowl. "What else is in there besides potatoes and green lilies?"

"The usual." She ticked them off on her fingers. "Onion, celery, parsley, bay leaf, rosemary, light cream, butter—"

"Enough," he groaned, diving in. "I'll have to run an extra half-hour tomorrow morning as it is." He pointed to the mound-shaped loaf. "What kind of home-baked delicacy is this?"

The corners of her mouth turned up, and a faraway look fell over her features. "Irish soda bread. My grandmother's recipe from County Kerry."

"Mmm," he managed between bites, sinking his teeth into the fresh-from-the-oven bread. They ate in a comfortable silence for several minutes, enjoying one another's company. Despite the encroaching boxes, no mention was made of their unusual surroundings.

Unusual to you, Jake. Home to Mary.

When he finally sat back, filled to the brim with her Irish repast, he studied her head bent over a last bite of soda bread. It was time to move on to the purpose of his visit. "How can I help you, Mary?"

She jumped, caught off guard, knocking her butter knife onto the worn linoleum floor.

He'd spoken too soon. "I didn't mean to rush—"

"I need a friend," she blurted out, then clamped her lips shut.

He could see she was fighting tears, and he reached out to touch her arm in assurance. "I *am* your friend, Mary. And I think there are several women at Calvary who would be honored to step into that role as well. My mother, Mary Stauros, for one. Suzy and JoAnn in the office—"

"T-today," she said, her voice quivering. "I need a friend today. Right now. To help me d-do…help me t-take…" Her tears were flowing in earnest now. She tried to keep speaking between gasps. All he could make out was that it had something to do with cats.

He smiled, hoping to calm her. "I thought you might have a cat or two." No need to mention the telltale aroma that gave away their presence. As tenderly as he could, he asked her again: "How can I help you, Mary?"

She took a deep breath and managed to get it all out at once. "Eleven. I have eleven cats, and I have to…to…give them away."

He was shocked. "*All* of them?"

Mary nodded forlornly. "All except Max. You'll meet him in a minute." She paused, searching his face. "That is, if you're willing to help me."

"You bet." How could he not? He'd never known a person who needed his help more. "What do you have in mind?"

"PAWS." The word came out on a long sigh as she stood. "You've seen it on Clark Street. 'Pets Are Worth Saving.'"

He nodded slowly, trying to place it. "Right next to the Big Apple?" He'd never been inside but had passed it plenty of times. "Sure they're interested?"

"They usually rescue animals from the pound," she said, still sniffing. "But they said they'd make a special exception for me." With that, she disappeared into the hallway. He heard her climb the steps, then open a door somewhere above him.

"Here we come," she called out.

Jake was soon up to his knees in felines of every size and color, rubbing against his jeans, imploring him with piteous meows. They were woefully underfed, their coats dull and in poor condition. But they were obviously beautiful to Mary, who insisted on brushing each cat, head to toe, saying her teary good-byes as she did, crooning their names and telling them how much they meant to her.

The social services people were right—the cats needed a more sanitary environment and so did Mary—but Jake could hardly stand to watch the sad procession of animals being showered with affection by a woman who last Sunday morning could barely make eye contact with the members of Calvary Fellowship.

No wonder she was desperate to count him as a friend. She was bidding ten others farewell in one afternoon.

"This is Max, my oldest buddy," she struggled to say, lifting his paw out in greeting.

Jake dropped to his haunches and shook the cat's paw solemnly. "Good to meet you, Max. Glad you'll be staying." He eyed Mary carefully, trying to gauge her mercurial mood. "Is this the kitty you bought the toy for? On the day we met?"

Mary wrinkled her brow for a moment, then a mottled blush moved across her cheeks, and she lowered her gaze. "I didn't...buy it." She exhaled, as though relieved to make a full confession. "I stole it."

"Appreciate your honesty," Jake said softly. "You didn't have to tell me."

"Yes, I did," she said, lifting her chin. "You're my friend."

"So I am." He smiled, then straightened up, stretching his arm muscles for the job ahead. "Time I earned my lunch, don't you think? I'll need some empty cardboard boxes."

Finding them was the easy part. Filling them was not.

Jake finally managed to coax the cats into boxes while Mary watched, crying softly, tying her wet handkerchief in knots as she hung on to Max like a security blanket. Jake made quick work of it, not wanting to drag things out a minute longer than necessary.

By no coincidence whatsoever, he'd brought his mother's car. Normally he never bothered with wheels. Didn't own a car—not when parking on the street was impossible and the self-park garage wanted $9.75 per hour. *Nah.* The El got him anywhere he needed to go. That morning he'd had a strong sense he might need a car for this visit, never dreaming who—or what—his passengers might be. Now he knew.

With Mary in the front of the Toyota and five boxes of cats jammed into the backseat, it was a tight fit but a blessedly short drive. "Thank you, Jake," Mary said, her voice breaking. "I could never have done this without you."

The women at PAWS were more than accommodating, immediately punching the door buzzer that allowed the two of them to come inside and not asking many questions as they helped them with their boxes. Clearly they lived in the neighborhood, had seen Mad Mary around, and had put two and two together.

"Good homes, please," Mary whimpered, lingering near the office, still teary as she and Jake waited for the door to be buzzed open once again. "Please?"

The manager's eyes were filled with empathy. "That's the only kind we look for, ma'am. Good homes. Not to worry."

Jake helped her in the car, not content to let her walk home, no matter how close it was. He wasn't worried about the cats. He was worried about Mary Delaney. Her medications had made a marked difference in her, but they couldn't do the work of living for her.

Only Christ could make that kind of difference in her chaotic life. It was up to him—her pastor, her friend—to make certain Mary understood. Jesus was the friend she was looking for, not him. Jake would do what he could to help her, but he knew his stay at Calvary Fellowship was short and his list of skills and abilities shorter still.

He caught a glimpse of himself in the rearview mirror and shook his head with a wry grin. Carrying boxes full of cats? Now *that* was right up his alley. But delivering Mary from her past, making her whole for the future? That was a miracle only Jesus could handle.

Suzy raised an almost-orange eyebrow, dyed to match her vivid hair. "Can you handle a word processor?"

Mary gulped, squeezing her clammy hands around her church bulletin. "Is it...like a typewriter?"

Suzy's lips pressed together, as though she were weighing something in her mind or holding back her frustration. Mary wasn't sure which.

Finally the younger woman answered, "Kinda like a typewriter. Anyway, there won't be a lot for you to worry with there. Couple of letters for Jake now and then, although he handwrites most of his notes." Suzy shook her head, laughing. "The guy is definitely from another century. The fewer machines involved, the happier Jake is." Her bright voice softened a bit. "I know he appreciates your offer to help in the office, Mrs. Delaney."

"Mary," she corrected gently.

"Right." Suzy laughed again. "*Mary*. That'll take some getting used to."

Instead of Mad *Mary, does she mean?*

Mary stepped aside, letting Jake's mother ease past her en route to the church foyer, following the flow of departing worshipers. Mary Stauros was quiet and elegant, yet her passing smile warmed Mary's soul. It was easy to see why Jake had turned out to be such a good son.

She turned back to Suzy, grateful for the young woman's willingness to let her invade her domain as a fellow volunteer. "You're sure you don't mind if I use your desk in the mornings then?"

"What, are you kidding?" Suzy flapped her hands in the air like a graceful, tangerine-colored bird. "Everything in that tiny room belongs to the church. Besides, Jake needs all the help he can get with paperwork." She winked dramatically. "You'll see soon enough."

"I just want to be...useful." Mary explained, knowing deep down there was more to it than that. Jake had not only taken care of her kitties yesterday. He'd come back to the house and helped her haul half a dozen boxes to the car so he could drop them off at a thrift store, never once complaining.

Much more than that, Mary. He probably saved your life.

The truth was, she owed this man a debt of thanks she could never adequately repay. But she could try. A few hours each morning in his office seemed a small gift to give, but give it she would, and gladly.

Answering phones, a little filing, stuffing envelopes, running errands— even those things would be a big stretch after years of barely functioning at home. Her heart pounded at the mere thought of it. If she didn't have to turn on the word processor, she'd be fine.

"Thanks, Suzy," Mary added as the young woman turned to go. "You've been very...kind." Whatever judgment Mary had felt those first weeks had evaporated. Maybe Suzy had a story to tell as well, something she wasn't proud of. Mary watched the younger woman bounce out the front door, purse swinging behind her, then stared down at her wrists protruding from her long-sleeved dress. She yanked the fabric over them with furtive tugs, wondering if Suzy had seen them. Wondering if Jake noticed anymore.

On cue he strolled up, his mother beside him, both of them smiling as if they'd heard good news. Jake spoke first. "Mary, you know my mother, don't you?"

"Of course."

The women exchanged handshakes and nods. Mary felt no hesitation on his mother's part, just a caring sense of curiosity about her. They were about the same age, but what different lives they'd led! She hoped they'd find a point of common ground, and soon. Something told her Mary Stauros could teach her a great deal about how best to serve Jake and his church.

Jake folded his arms over his chest and exhaled noisily. "Two Marys around here, and a Marijane as well. Won't *that* make life interesting?" He mimicked Suzy answering the phone, aiming his voice at her soprano pitch. "Calvary Fellowship. You want to speak to Mary? *Which* Mary?"

All three of them laughed, then Mary stepped back, suddenly uncomfortable. Her many years hiding at home had siphoned away her social skills. Small talk seemed beyond her grasp, making her feel foolish and out of touch.

Jake, who had an uncanny ability to sense her changes in mood, stretched out a hand. "Don't leave yet, Mary. We can easily solve that problem. Mind if we tag on your middle name—*Margaret?* It's a beauty."

She nodded, wetting her lips. "That's...that's what my mother always called me."

"Perfect. Mary Margaret it is then." Jake eyed his mother. "Uh...Mom and I were talking this morning about your house, and how...well, how she, JoAnn, Sallie Mae, and Marijane might..."

Mary Stauros interrupted by graciously clearing her throat. "What Jake is trying to say is that the girls and I would be delighted to come over and help you do some...well, some spring cleaning. That's always such a thankless task. We'd love to help you tackle it, if you're willing."

Spring cleaning? Mary couldn't think of the last season—the last *year*—her three-story house was truly cleaned from top to bottom. "Is that what Jake said it needed?" Mary asked, her voice echoing the uneasiness she felt. She looked at Jake, then at his mother, feeling her insides turning into one huge knot. "A simple afternoon of spring cleaning, is that what you're expecting?"

"No, not at all." Mrs. Stauros clasped her hands behind her back, her expression growing more serious. "Jake gave me a pretty clear picture of what you're up against." She glanced at her son. "I hope you don't mind, Mary Margaret. He meant no harm by telling me, I can assure you. Sometimes we have to get rid of the old things in our lives to make room for the new. Is that how you see it?"

"What I see," Mary began, her voice shaking in earnest now. "What I see is a house full of heaven-only-knows-what. Honestly, I don't even remember buying most of it or know where it came from." She looked at the toes of her shoes, dropping her voice to a shame-filled whisper. "Or how I paid for it. *If* I paid for it. Or what I thought I was going to do with it all."

She looked up again, certain she would find pity in their eyes. Or loathing. Or disgust.

It was none of those things. It was mercy.

"We'll sort it all out, room by room," Jake's mother assured her confidently. "Inch by inch, if necessary. Nothing I like better than a project that's beyond my grasp."

"Wh-what?" Mary stared at her, confused by her enthusiasm.

"Absolutely," the woman said with a nod, pulling a small notebook out of her purse. "When it's too big for me, it's the perfect size for God." Mary Stauros glanced down at a calendar full of notations. "Jake tells me you'll be working in the office each morning. The whole church is thrilled to hear it, believe me."

Mary Margaret wasn't the least bit convinced. Jake had announced it this morning during his sermon on stewardship. She'd only mentioned it to him before the service, never dreaming he would take to the idea so quickly. The others seemed amazed—no, *shocked*—when Jake said blithely, "As a good example of giving your time and your talents, Mary Margaret Delaney will be donating three hours a day to help in our church office, Monday through Friday, nine to noon."

A few heads nodded, and Pete beamed at her. The rest simply stared, wide-eyed, trying to imagine Mad Mary doing word processing. Now that she'd chatted with Suzy, Mary Margaret had a hard time picturing that one herself.

"Why don't we start Friday at noon?" Mary Stauros was saying, tapping a pen on her notebook. "Get a running start on the weekend. Jake can spare Suzy in the office later that afternoon. We'll meet you here with some lunch, then walk over to your place together. Will that suit?"

Mary was stunned at the generous offer. "I…I don't know what to say."

Jake grinned. "Say yes, Mary."

There was no getting around it, not when she needed their help so desperately. She nodded first, then made herself say the word: "Y-yes."

"N-no. I'm not sure what happened to it."

Jake watched Mary Margaret fidget with a button on her sleeve, near tears. She'd lost yet another important letter addressed to him. Add that to the coffee stains on the annual financial report, the misfiled correspondence from his seminary, and a stack of jumbled phone messages, and it was obvious Mary Margaret considered her first week at Calvary Fellowship a full-blown disaster.

Jake couldn't argue with that. It *was* a disastrous beginning. What she needed to know was that it was a *beginning,* not an end, and that things would get easier. "Let's look together in my office, okay?" He inclined his head toward his door. "Ten to one that letter is hiding on my desk."

He followed Mary into the converted kitchen, watching her gaze dart around the room as though the letter might jump out unexpectedly from a shadowy corner.

"Have a seat, Mary. We'll each take a stack and see what we can find."

They both settled down with several inches of papers, going through them piece by piece, keeping an eye out for the telltale letterhead with the royal blue edging.

When Mary found it minutes later, her eyes and mouth flew open in delight. "Here it is!" she announced, proudly holding it up between two fingers. "Am I forgiven?"

"Of course," Jake assured her. "Around here, forgiveness is as close as your next breath." He pointed to the framed prayer on the wall next to his desk. "Have you ever taken time to read that, Mary?"

"Read it?" she said with a huff, lifting her chin proudly. "I can say it by memory." She proceeded to do so with her eyes closed and her heart, it seemed, wide open.

> Christ be with me, Christ within me,
> Christ behind me, Christ before me,
> Christ beside me, Christ to win me,
> Christ to comfort and restore me,
> Christ beneath me, Christ above me,
> Christ in quiet, Christ in danger,
> Christ in hearts of all that love me,
> Christ in mouth of friend and stranger.

Jake applauded warmly when she finished. The woman certainly was full of surprises. "Mary Margaret Delaney, you astound me."

She pointed her nose in the air. "D'ya think the granddaughter of a County Kerry woman would be likely to forget the words of Saint Patrick?" Mary ladled out an Irish brogue thick as her potato soup. "Me sainted mother had the same prayer hangin' on her kitchen wall, so she did." Her voice softened and returned to a flat Midwestern pitch. "It gave me great comfort as a child. To know that the Christ was behind, before, beneath, and above."

Jake chose his words with care. "If that assurance comforted you then, why not now?"

"I'm not sure." Her slight shoulders lifted and fell. "Not sure about anything anymore." She met his gaze, then looked away, staring instead at the windows that faced the alley. "Those windows look familiar."

"They should, Mary Margaret." He'd watched her memory come back in bits and pieces, surfacing at odd moments. He was hoping this scene might stay forgotten, but there was no getting around it now. "You once peered in at me. On a Friday night about seven. Do you remember it?"

"I…I peered in at…?" She looked as if she might be ill. "I was a *peeping Tom?*"

"No, you were a peeping Mary," he teased her, wanting to lessen her embarrassment any way he could. "Besides, it was only for a second. I scared you away."

"You scared *me?*"

"I invited you in, but you bolted."

She shot to her feet, her cheeks stained a dark pink. "Bolting sounds like a good idea about now."

"Nonsense, Mary. It was nothing. No need ever to think about it again." He pointed to his desk clock, eager to change the subject. "Mom should be here any minute with the troops. Gonna be quite a cleaning crew descending on your house this weekend."

Mary seemed nervous about that, too, judging by the way she was fidgeting with her new watch. "Y-yes, I guess so."

"Mary Margaret, if this is too much, too soon, it can wait—"

"No, it can't," she interrupted, her words firm. "Ms. Jensen has been very patient with me about…things. But she has insisted the first floor be made more…uh, sanitary. Immediately. Or she'll call the Board of Public Health."

"Then our timing is perfect," a woman's voice sang out from the doorway.

Mom. He smiled at the sight of her in one of his father's old shirts and a pair of decrepit jeans. "Don't you look ready for action?"

"Right now I'm ready for lunch." She held up a small cardboard box. "The girls will be right along. Meanwhile, anybody hungry for a corned beef on rye?"

If Mary never saw the inside of another cardboard box, she would die a happy woman. That seemed unlikely with only two rooms down and too many to go.

She wiped her damp forehead with the back of one hand and smiled wearily at her colaborers. Suzy, Marijane, and JoAnn were dragging boxes toward the hall while Mary Stauros, covered with dust from shoulder to shin, stuffed plastic lawn ornaments in a carton destined for Goodwill. "Really, Mary Margaret, what were you thinking?" the woman said, her tone lightly teasing but not unkind. "Buying lawn ornaments when you have no lawn?"

"I wasn't thinking at all," Mary confessed, chagrined they'd discovered yet another odd purchase, price tags still attached. "*That* was the whole problem."

They'd worked nonstop for nearly a day and a half, going through box after box, salvaging a few valuables, packing the rest for trash or giveaway. Sallie Mae—like Mary, a newcomer to Calvary—poured her heart into her work, undaunted by long-legged spiders or layers of dirt. "Girl, you shoulda seen my Aunt Louisa's house," she sang out in a voice sweet as peaches from Georgia. "After she died, my sister June and I spent months gettin' to the bottom of it all." She surveyed the living room, her pixie features decorated with dust and grime. "Shucks, this is nothin'. Another weekend, and we'll be done. Don'tcha think, Mrs. Mary?"

Jake's mother merely raised her eyebrows, saying nothing, while Suzy shook her head, her vibrant hair visible even in the gloomy hallway. "Don't get your hopes up, honey. We have two more floors like this one."

Oh! Mary Margaret's heart sank to her knees. She'd hoped they hadn't been upstairs, hadn't seen how much more work awaited them. What if they gave up and left, disgusted? What if they never came back but the Board of Public Health *did?* She dropped onto a couch, sending a flurry of dust motes into the air. "I'm so sorry," she moaned. "Can't we leave stuff where it is and let Goodwill send their customers here?"

"Wait...that's *it!*" Sallie Mae squealed. "We'll have a yard sale *right here in the house!*"

"Brilliant." Suzy clasped her hands together and brought them to her chest, a look of wonder crossing her features. "It's the perfect solution. We'll close one room on each floor to store the things Mary wants to keep and let 'em stroll through the rest of it and buy, buy, buy."

"Hang on." Marijane dug through her purse, pulling out a tablet and pen. "Let's make it easy. All the stuff in each room will be the same price. This will be the twenty-dollar room—"

"Ten dollars," Mary Margaret interrupted, surprised to find herself laughing when she said it. "Not a thing worth twenty dollars in any of these boxes."

"Right," Suzy agreed. "Priced to sell. Even so you should get a nice little nest egg for all your…um, treasures, Mary Margaret."

"A nest egg?" Mary shook her head, brushing the dust off her jeans as she stood. "Whatever money we make won't be for me. We'll give it to the church."

"Really?" Jake's mother nearly dropped the box she was holding. "That would be wonderful, but can you…afford to do that? I mean…" A rosy tint covered her cheeks. "I'm sorry," she murmured. "That's really none of my business."

Mary Margaret stepped toward her, determined to put her at ease. "After all your hard work, I'm not ashamed for you to know anything about me. Yes, I think I can manage just fine. I'd like nothing better than to have a yard sale—"

"Estate sale," Suzy corrected, winking. "Sounds better. Anyway, you don't have a yard, remember?"

"Let's pick a Saturday." Quiet, practical JoAnn had her calendar in hand. "Sometime next month. We still have plenty of cleaning and organizing to do. What about March 17?"

"Perfect." Mary Margaret smiled all the way to her soul. "Saint Patrick himself will be most welcome."

Mary Delaney was snug in her third-story bedroom when the storm hit, unwelcome and unexpected.

It'd rained all day while the six of them cleaned and boxed, but the winds picked up considerably after the women left at dinnertime. Mary, who'd braved many a Chicago winter, seldom gave in to the weather hysteria that filled her television screen. A wind advisory crawled across the bottom of her screen throughout the evening. Forecasters on all the local channels, includ-ing WGN, warned of a strong low-pressure system moving up from the south, dragging warmer temperatures and high winds along with it.

Mary had crawled into bed at ten, unconcerned, only to be awakened by Max's jumping skittishly around her bed in the middle of the night. "What is it, boy-o?" She threw off the covers and slipped on her robe, shivering all the while. Warmer temperatures, did they say? Max was pacing in front of the window, tail twitching, a low keening in his throat.

"Easy now." She reached out a hand to pet his arched back. Max's ner-vous state quickly escalated her own. Outside, the winds were fierce, bending the lone maple tree in front of her house until she feared it might snap in two. Its spindly branches scratched against her window like the tingle of fear now scratching along her spine.

Second by second a growing sense of despair and foreboding crept over her. Things had been going so well. So very well. Working each morning at church gave her a sense of usefulness. New friends had come into her life. Her medicine, carefully monitored by her doctor, kept her emotions in bal-ance and held the darkness at bay.

Darkness.

She peered out the window, suddenly seeing what was upsetting Max. It was pitch black outside. No street lamps. No lights in any of the houses. Trembling, she reached for the nearest lamp and turned the switch.

Darkness.

Her electricity was out, lost to the windstorm. It was no comfort whatso-ever knowing her neighbors had been plunged into the same dreary predica-ment. *She* was the one who was alone—all alone—in her too-big, too-old, too-dark house.

Not alone.

"No!" She screamed, throwing herself against the wall. Terror, like the spiders in her living room, crawled along her arms, across her scarred and ugly arms.

Not alone, Mary.

"No!" She dove for the bed, clawing at the covers, desperate to pull them over her head. *Quickly, Mary, quickly!* Sobs tore at her throat, and the bed shook even as she did, uncontrollably. Why now, now that she wanted to live? Why had the voices come back?

"Leave me alone!" she shrieked, hoping there was no one there to hear, yet knowing the truth. *They are here.* In her house, in her room, in her. The wind blew harder still, rattling the windows until she was certain the glass panes would break. Break into a thousand tiny shards, fly across her bedroom, cut her skin. Cut, cut, cut.

Where were her razors? Could she find them alone, alone in the darkness?

Not alone.

"No! Please, God. Help me!" she screamed with the last of her strength and fell to the floor in a motionless heap.

Chapter Five

WE LOOK FOR GOD

We look for God as though he were not already here.
MERRITT MALLOY

Jake found Mary Margaret Delaney curled up in a tight ball on the front steps of the church Sunday morning.

"Mary! Mary, what's wrong?" He tugged at her arms, coaxing her stiff limbs to unfold, forcing her eyes to open. "How long have you been here? Are you ill? Do you need me to take you to Grant Hosp—?"

"No!" She sat up all at once, her back stiff, her eyes rolling back in her head. "Not there. Not there."

"Okay, okay. Relax now." Jake pressed his hands down on her shoulders, holding her still, letting her feel his warmth. She was soaked and frozen through and through. Why had she come to church at this hour, and why in such terrible weather?

Heavy rains had pounded the lakeshore relentlessly until dawn, when winds had reached fifty miles per hour, toppling trees and power lines. ConEd, the utility company, had its hands full. Some seventy-four thousand people in the city, including him, had awakened to discover they had no electricity.

Jake had come to church earlier than usual, hoping to find they'd been spared. Instead, tree branches were scattered all over the church's small front yard, and the storefronts were unlit.

Ah, well. Last month they'd had church in the cold.

Now they'd try church in the dark.

Had Mary Margaret lost her electricity? Had the darkness frightened her, was that it? Grateful that she was breathing more evenly, Jake helped her stand. "Come, Mary, let's go inside and find something dry for you to wear."

She followed close behind him, silent and shivering, as he unlocked the door and led her through the foyer. It was dry inside, if not terribly warm. With no guilt whatsoever, he raided the church's collection box for two old towels, women's slacks, a sweater, some socks. All were worn, nothing matched, but they would do for the moment. He sent Mary into her tiny office to change, handing her a flashlight, then closed the door behind her.

Minutes later he heard her weeping.

Lord Jesus, show me what to do.

Jake knocked, speaking to her as he might a child. Slowly, gently, calmly. "Have you changed yet, Mary? You haven't? You're still in your wet clothes?" *Oh, Mary.* "I'm sorry. Wait and let me get someone to help you."

One small blessing—the phones still worked. "Mom, I know it's early, but I need you at church right away. It's Mary Margaret. Yes, something's wrong. I'll watch for you." He made a second call to Joe, asking him to pick up a fresh supply of candles and matches on the way in, then stepped into the hall and faced Mary's office door again.

"Mary Margaret?" He tapped on the wooden panel. The weeping had stopped, replaced by an eerie silence. The only sound echoing through the church was the rain pelting the windows. "Mary, it's Jake. Are you all right?"

Uneasy about invading her privacy, yet unwilling to stand there doing nothing, he took a deep breath and turned the knob. The door creaked open a few inches. "Mary Margaret, are you dressed? May I come in?"

Behind him, a male voice growled, "What's going on here?"

His heart in his throat, Jake whirled around to find Charles Farris standing in the hall, his raincoat drenched, his face hard as flint. "Charles! I didn't expect you here. Not this early anyway. What is it, eight o'clock?"

"I was headed out to breakfast and thought I'd stop by, see if the building had any power." The older man's eyes narrowed. "Looks to me as if I got here just in time. Care to explain what an undressed woman is doing in this church alone with you?"

His face warming, Jake stepped back from Mary's door, pulling it shut again with quick yank. "I found Mary Delaney on the steps this morning, soaking wet, and sent her in to change into some dry clothes. That's all, Charles. No need to jump to conclusions."

"Not much of a jump, son," he grumbled. His bushy eyebrows knit into a fierce scowl. "Got nearly sixty folks here looking to you for leadership. Better stick to preaching and forget trying to rescue all these wet, straggly sheep. The neighborhood's full of them."

Mary opened the door with a jerky swing, her hair every bit as wet and straggly as Charles described. Her temporary wardrobe was dry and clean and modestly covered her from head to toe. She clutched the flashlight in one hand, the doorknob with the other. "Mr. Farris," she croaked, her voice weak, her eyes red rimmed. "This is all my fault. Don't blame Jake." Then she turned his direction, her chin trembling. "Jake, I'm sorry."

"Not a thing to apologize for," he insisted, his gaze locked on Charles Farris. "Your church *should* be the first place you turn for help."

Charles cleared his throat, a low, gurgling sound like an ancient motor. "I don't recall Mrs. Delaney stepping forward to be part of this church family. Officially."

Jake shifted his gaze to Mary, gauging her response. He couldn't deny it. She hadn't made any sort of public profession of faith. Was she ready for such a thing?

"Sounds like a good topic for discussion this morning, eh, Mary Margaret?" Jake cupped her elbow, steering her toward his office. "Charles, I'm expecting Joe to show up any second with more candles. Suppose you help place them around the sanctuary, would you? We need all the light we can get this morning."

Charles shuffled toward the front of the building, still grumbling, while Jake got Mary Margaret settled in his office, tracking down another dry towel for her hair. She wound it around her head, turban style, and stared out the back window. Whatever had spooked her last night, it was clear she wasn't free of its clutches yet.

Within minutes his mother appeared, plastic foam cups of hot coffee from the 7-Eleven in hand. "They had a generator going," she explained, prying off the plastic lids. "Just the thing for a blustery morning." She joined them around his desk for coffee, comparing notes about storm damage. Mary Margaret sipped her coffee, nodding but not adding a word to their conversation.

He heard Joe's voice in the sanctuary at the same time Pete and Little John came stomping through the back entrance, shaking their wet heads like terriers. John held up his toolbox, grinning. "Gonna play a little trick on our heating system. Make it think it's got a functioning thermostat. Even with the power outage, the gas heat should still work, and we haven't run out of gravity, have we?"

Soon the place was a beehive of activity. The choir was singing that morning—all six members—so the piano in the sanctuary was getting a workout. Mary Margaret sat in the midst of it all, quiet but attentive, her hands wrapped around her empty foam cup as though waiting for someone to fill it.

Jake stood, feeling a tug in his chest. "Mary Margaret, suppose we duck into your office for a minute? I gotta review my text for this morning's message, and I could use your help." What he didn't mention were the prayers that would be encircling that little room while they talked. A slight nod to his mother, a brief exchange of glances with JoAnn and Pete, and he knew they got the message.

Pray for Mary Margaret.

Two chairs, one small desk, and a tall filing cabinet were all that fit inside the workspace that Mary Margaret and Suzy shared each day. "We could use some light in here, please," Jake called out.

Within seconds, Joe appeared with two fat candles in saucers meant for planters. "It's the best we could dig up, boss."

"They're perfect," Jake assured him, arranging them on the desk so he could read his Bible and Mary's face, the two things that mattered most that morning. "Thanks, Joe. Go ahead and pull the door only halfway shut, if you will." No sense giving Charles Farris more ammunition.

Mary took down her towel turban, rubbing her hair dry in the flickering candlelight, not meeting his gaze.

"Mary Margaret, may I read this morning's verses to you, see what you think of them?" Jake kept his voice even, without inflection. Not pleading, not demanding.

She paused, giving it some thought, then nodded and went back to drying her hair, never once looking up.

He breathed a silent prayer, then began to read. "This is from the book of Psalms: 'Out of the depths I cry to you, O LORD.'" Jake hesitated, wanting to let the words sink in. "Ever cried out to God from a deep, dark place?"

Her head shot up, and heat flooded her cheeks.

He knows.

Jake was not there in her house last night. But he knew, somehow he knew, that the darkness had returned, leaving her more lost and confused than ever. And scared to the very marrow of her bones.

"Yes," she stammered. "I have cried out to God...like that. Like you said, from 'the depths.'"

"Did he answer you?"

Her lower lip began to quiver, and she dropped her chin. "I don't think so. I hear...other, louder voices though."

"Scary voices?"

She nodded, not daring to meet his gaze.

"Listen for the voice of God, Mary Margaret."

She glanced up to see Jake looking down at his Bible, not at her. The circle of light from the candle fell on the page, illuminating both the paper and his features. He was not a handsome young man. He was not. Yet reflected in his face was something more than good looks. It was goodness itself, a radiance, an unearthly sort of splendor.

Righteousness. Yes, that was the crux of it.

It calmed her heart to watch him. The urge to cry receded, and a sense of peace quietly took its place. "How will I recognize that voice? What makes it...different?"

He looked up then, smiling. "It sounds like grace, not condemnation." He held up the Bible. "It agrees with his written word, which tells us how deep and wide his love is for us. Listen for the tone of grace, Mary."

"Grace, you say?" But what did *that* sound like? Maybe he'd describe it shortly. "Go on, do the next verse."

"'O Lord,'" he read tenderly, "'hear my voice. Let your ears be attentive to my cry for mercy.'" He met her gaze again, apparently pleased with what he saw there. "And have you ever cried out for mercy, Mary Margaret Delaney?"

"Of course I have," she admitted, smiling for the first time that morning. "Who doesn't need mercy, Jake?"

"Ah, exactly right." He nodded, his expression thoughtful. "Is that something we deserve, do you think?"

"I'm not sure." She chewed on her lip, not wanting to disappoint him with the wrong answer. "Are grace and mercy the same thing?"

He liked her question. She could tell by the twinkle in his brown eyes, though it might have been the candlelight playing tricks on her. When he finally answered her, it came on the last note of the choir's rehearsal wafting through the office door.

"Mary, think of it like this: Mercy is the motive. Grace is the gift."

The candles seemed to glow more brightly as she struggled to grasp the difference. "Can you have one without the other?"

"Not if God is the one being merciful. Grace—forgiveness—is an expression of God's mercy."

"I see." And she almost *did* see, as if looking through a kaleidoscope and watching the tiny pieces fall into place. "Jake, how many times does God give a gift like that?"

"No limit," he responded firmly, pointing to the page. "He doesn't count how many times he forgives us. That's what it says here: 'If you, O LORD, kept a record of sins, O Lord, who could stand?'"

"Not me," she murmured, remembering how she'd collapsed into bed last night, shaking and weeping. Was it her demons that had driven her there? Or the fear of God they instilled in her, a God whom Jake insisted was even more powerful than they were?

"I'd be flat on my face myself if God had no mercy on sinners," Jake agreed. "The psalmist has good news for both of us. 'But with you there is forgiveness; therefore you are feared.'"

Mary fell back in her chair, bewildered. "So even though he forgives us, we're supposed to be afraid of God?"

"Not that kind of fear, Mary." Jake leaned across the table, his face aglow as though he were a taper lit by an invisible fire. "Reverence. Awe. Respect. Never taking God for granted, putting him first above all things. It's a healthy fear, not a scary one."

She rubbed her temples, the long, stormy night suddenly catching up with her. "I don't know, Jake. My demons are plenty scary."

He eyed her across the desk, the candlelight throwing dancing shadows around the room. "Is that why you ended up on the church's doorstep?"

Her shrug was answer enough.

"Do you understand that God can rid you of those demons permanently?"

"If you say so." A nauseous feeling had crept into her stomach. "Look, the God I met as a child was to be feared, not befriended. How do I know he won't make things worse?"

Jake's smile was warm, not smug. "Have things been worse since you started coming to Calvary?"

He knew the answer as well as she did.

"So they've been somewhat better, I take it? With more good things to come." Jake stood, stretching the kinks out of his shoulders, and opened the door, letting daylight filter in. "The last verse in my message this morning says it all: 'I wait for the LORD, my soul waits, and in his word I put my hope.'" He scooped up his Bible, gripping it tight. "Wait, Mary. Help is on the way."

Mary closed her eyes, letting the possibility sink in.

She would wait.

Mary Margaret waited, growing more anxious by the hour.

In the morning she loved the warm confines of her little office, the orderliness of her day. In the afternoon she tackled a dusty box or two, slowly getting things ready for their March "estate sale," as Suzy insisted they call it. But at night, the street noise died down, the phone stopped ringing, and no matter how many lights she turned on, darkness still filled the corners of her house and the corners of her heart.

It was clear that, whatever she was waiting for, it was also waiting for *her*. To do something, to ask some question, to make some decision.

On Wednesday, the third day of her waiting, an unusual visitor arrived in Lincoln Park: the sun. Tilted at its low wintry angle, it did little to warm the air, but it was there nonetheless, shining down between the clouds. A good omen for the last day of February, with spring only three weeks away.

Was the first day of spring March 20 or 21? Her breakfast tea in hand, Mary flipped over the page of her new wall calendar, fussing at herself for not being able to keep the date straight after forty-six springs.

Tuesday, March 20. Spring begins. She nodded, pleased to know the truth of it, then let the page fall back into place. Her mother had cautioned her it was bad luck to turn a calendar over to the next month before it actually arrived. "Tempting God," her mother had warned. Eyes like saucers, young Mary Margaret had not required any further explanation. One did not tempt God, whatever that meant.

Her gaze fell on the current date, and her heart ground to a stop. *Ash Wednesday.* How had she forgotten the beginning of Lent, a season firmly etched in her mind since the cradle? All through this hallowed day, in churches all over the world, people who loved God would feel a thumb pressed against their foreheads as the ancient words were recited: "Remember that you are dust, and to dust you will return."

Ashes to ashes, dust to dust.

Mary set her teacup down so hard the fragile cup danced in its saucer.

Her old life was nothing but ashes. Her old house was nothing but dust. She'd sunk to that place of nothingness, closer to death than any sane person would ever want to be. And yet here she stood, alive. More alive than she'd ever remembered.

Because of Pastor Jake. He had saved her. In so many ways he had saved her.

Or had God saved her? That's what Jake kept insisting. But hadn't she disappointed God? Why should God care about her when she'd so blatantly cared nothing about him for too many years to count?

Seven years and counting. Seven.

Mary touched the white square on the calendar, drawing a cross with her thumb. *Ash Wednesday.* Ashes made from the burned palms used last year for Palm Sunday. Purified in the burning. Signifying repentance. A chance to begin again.

She should go tonight. Go to Saint Clement, to her parish church, for evening Mass. If her instincts were right, if there was a decision to be made, it needed to be made there, in the church of her childhood, in the sanctuary where she'd first met God so long ago.

She held her breath all day, wondering how it would feel to walk through the century-old doors and confront a God who looked nothing like Jake Stauros. Mere weeks ago she'd wanted to die. Would it happen tonight? Would God strike her dead?

It was the longest Wednesday she could ever remember.

At seven o'clock she finally stepped across the threshold of Saint Clement, still a bit numb at the thought of actually *being* there. Lent at Saint Clement meant there was not a flower to be found. The sanctuary was unadorned except for a large wooden cross—empty, waiting—draped with a purple cloth.

Every wooden pew overflowed with parishioners. Heart racing, she commandeered a folding chair, then immediately offered it to an elderly woman who hobbled in, looking lost. Mary would stand along the outer edges with the others. It was only an hour. An hour to reconcile the God she'd once known with the God who confronted her now.

Leaning against the wall, Mary let her head drop back, drinking in the glory and majesty of Saint Clement. A sense of rightness flowed over her, in harmony with the chords of the opening hymn: "Lift High the Cross." The light marble walls, covered with gold and green vines, surrounded her, embraced her. The organ reverberated against the stone floor, sending the notes up through her shoes. Exquisite stained-glass windows filled with angels hung above her like bright pieces of the night sky. Colorful mosaic pillars stood in silent homage to women saints—Catherine of Sienna, Teresa of Avila, Mary Magdalene.

Everywhere she looked Mary was struck by the beauty of the familiar.

How had she stayed away for so long?

At the start of the reading of the Scriptures, Mary's ears perked up. Jake never failed to emphasize the power of God's Word, the importance of God's Word. Wasn't that what he'd taught her on Sunday? "'And in his word I put my hope,'" she recited so softly that no one heard her.

The first passage read that evening was from Joel: "Rend your heart, and not your garments, and turn unto the LORD your God: for he is gracious and merciful."

Mary smiled, remembering their Sunday discussion by candlelight. *Mercy is the motive. Grace is the gift.* Suddenly verses she'd heard many times before came alive. They made sense, they had meaning, they *mattered* in her life.

Next came one of the psalms. There were so many she didn't recall them by number. A man's voice soared across the assembly. "Out of the depths have I cried unto thee, O LORD."

Mary's mouth dried so swiftly she could barely pry her tongue free. It was the same passage, the very same that Jake had taught her. The same words. The same God. *The same God.*

A teary sob escaped her lips as she read the last verse out loud, partaking of God's Word for herself: "'I wait for the LORD, my soul doth wait, and in his word do I hope.'"

Mary.

Her heart stopped.

Of course. She knew whose voice it was the instant she heard it.

Yes, Lord.

Mary held her breath, waiting for the other voices to protest. She closed her eyes, shutting out her lovely surroundings, allowing the darkness behind her eyelids to reveal the darkness that surely dwelled inside her.

Where are they, Lord?

Amid the blessed silence that reigned inside her came her answer.

They are gone.

Her eyes flew open, and her heart as well. *Oh, thank you, Father!* One voice, the voice of mercy and grace, was the only voice she could hear.

She had not waited in vain.

She had not hoped without reason.

Tears streamed down her cheeks. Not tears of sorrow, tears of *joy.*

Minutes later when she partook of the bread, the body of Christ, her own body was made whole. And when she drank of the vine, the blood of Christ, the blood shed from her wrists was washed clean by his. And when the priest gently rubbed the black ashes into Mary Margaret Delaney's forehead and she repeated the sacred words, she knew the truth.

Yes, to dust she would return. But until then, she would return to Calvary Fellowship and tell a young pastor that he had not waited in vain. He had not hoped without reason. He had not labored and sacrificed and rescued without purpose. Jake Stauros had shown her what Christ's forgiveness looks like and feels like, and in the bargain he had taught her how to forgive herself.

Teacher. That was the best word for Jake's role in her life, she decided as she floated out the door an hour later, content to be alone, to reflect. Jake was her friend, but even more than that, Jake was her teacher.

My great teacher. She smiled as she hurried home, at peace with God and the night.

"This is *not* the way my grandmother taught me to make it," Mary Delaney confessed, unwrapping a fresh loaf of soda bread and holding it out for their inspection. "But it's the way I like it: with raisins."

Five hands reached out at once, each grabbing a piece of the steaming loaf. Moments earlier JoAnn, Mary, Suzy, Marijane, and Sallie Mae—the Sisters, they called themselves—had knocked on Mary Margaret's door, prepared to tackle yet another two days of packing and unpacking.

Mary Margaret was determined to feed them something first.

"Mmm," Sallie Mae groaned, an angelic smile stretched across her face. She propped her elbows on the kitchen table and pulled off hunks of bread, popping them into her mouth with obvious relish and little ceremony.

"My, aren't we casual," Mary Stauros observed, rolling her eyes in mock horror as the others laughed, Sallie Mae included.

Three weekends together and they'd already grown comfortable with one another. Mary had watched them banter back and forth for hours that first weekend before she felt comfortable tossing in a comment here and there. Now they were simply the Sisters, and she was one of them, working toward a common goal: emptying her house and filling up Calvary Fellowship's bank account.

Between boxes, a small miracle had occurred: Mary had learned to trust again, to care about people and call them her friends. When she'd told the Sisters about her experience at Saint Clement's, they'd cried even more than she did, rejoicing over her newfound freedom. In big and small ways, she was learning what it meant to be fully present, moment by moment.

She no longer needed to ask who wanted coffee or how they drank it. JoAnn filled half her mug with milk, Suzy and Marijane drank theirs black, Jake's mother preferred tea, and Sallie Mae wanted two heaping spoonfuls of sugar, minimum. Mary served them accordingly, watching with amusement as the loaf of soda bread quickly dwindled to crumbs.

Suzy downed her coffee, then banged her mug on the table with a sigh of satisfaction. "Whaddaya say we move to the third floor this afternoon?"

Mary's stomach fluttered as though a dozen butterflies had started batting around looking for a way to escape. "The third floor? Uh...not a whole lot up there. A small bath and two bedrooms, including mine." *And Luna's.* She'd never cleaned out her daughter's room, never given away a blessed thing, never *touched* it.

Except for the blue dress. Yes, she'd found that, hadn't she? Hanging in the closet. Hanging on her body. Covered with her own blood. She closed her eyes for a moment, intent on blocking out the dark image. Even when all was going well, the faintest memory could trigger others that were far less sanguine.

"Mary, are you still with us?" JoAnn's voice.

A warm hand brushed hers.

"Give her a second." Suzy that time.

Mary slowly opened her eyes and found five concerned faces focused on hers. "Sorry." Her cheeks warmed. "Sometimes the memories..."

Suzy held up a cautionary hand. "No need to say a thing, Mary. We under—"

"I know you do," Mary jumped in, suddenly compelled to put her fears into words. "But I want you to know all of it, the whole ugly truth." She straightened in her chair, leaning toward them, searching their faces. "There's no easy way to put this: My daughter, Luna, committed suicide when she was seventeen." She swallowed hard, then plunged back in, determined to keep going before she lost her nerve. "I couldn't help thinking somehow it was my fault. That I'd failed her as a mother, that I should have seen the signs, that I wasn't *listening* carefully enough."

She sank back in her chair, overcome by a fresh wave of guilt. "I thought the only way I could…could *pay* for that terrible mistake was to take my own life the same way Luna did. I'd convinced myself that, in God's economy, it would somehow balance things out if I were dead too."

There. She'd said it out loud, given voice to her guilt. There were, thankfully, no ugly internal voices shouting out their agreement. They'd been blessedly silent for two whole days.

But what of the Sisters? Would they condemn her with their words, with their shocked expressions?

Mary Margaret held her breath, watching them. They didn't look shocked. In fact, they just sat there. *Sat there!* Nodding intently—not judging, not pulling away from her in silent disapproval.

Suzy moved first, sliding her chair closer to Mary's. Unbuttoning her left sleeve, the younger woman rolled the fabric up over her elbow with sharp, economical movements, then thrust her arm out for Mary's inspection.

Needle marks. Long faded to a dull red, but still there, still visible against Suzy's fair skin.

Mary shifted her wide-eyed gaze to Suzy's serene face. "H-heroin?"

Suzy chuckled, rolling her sleeve back down. "You don't think I was selling my body for grocery money, do you? I was in serious trouble when Jake found me." Suzy's eyes misted briefly before she grinned and shook her carrot-topped head. "Thank God he found me, huh?"

"I *do* thank God," Mary echoed, grappling with the nonchalant way Suzy bared her skin—and her heart—with such abandon. A quick glance at the others confirmed what she'd already begun to suspect: They knew about Suzy's past. Probably knew all about her struggles as well. *Knew, yet didn't condemn.*

Mary Stauros carried her teacup to the sink, humming a lilting melody that Mary recognized immediately as an Irish tune.

"Do you know it, Mary Margaret?" Jake's mother asked with a sideways glance.

"Don't I though? 'As Sally Sits Weeping,' isn't it?" Mary cleared the table, singing a few bars of the traditional folk song that mourned the deceitfulness of poor Sally's true love. When she turned and found the color draining from Sallie Mae's face, Mary Margaret stopped in midnote, appalled. "What is it? What have I…?"

"You've helped her." Jake's mother nodded at the younger woman, her eyes brimming with empathy. "Go on, Sallie," she murmured. "It will do you good; you know that."

Sallie Mae exhaled heavily, then propped her chin on her folded hands. "That's why I left Atlanta. My husband was…is…well, he cheated on me. So many times I stopped counting."

"I'm sorry," Mary murmured, at a loss. The others nodded sympathetically. It seemed they'd already heard Sallie Mae's sad tale.

"It gets worse," the youngest of the Sisters confessed. "He had a vasectomy without telling me. Don't ask me how I didn't figure that out for myself." Sallie blushed furiously. "All I wanted was a family, and all he wanted was…" She groaned again. "Then he had the nerve to leave me and ask for a divorce. Said I didn't make him happy." Her voice rose. "Well, guess what?" She sat up, throwing her napkin down with a vehement slap. "He didn't make me happy either!"

Mary Stauros rested a hand on Sallie's shoulder. "But you stuck by your vows, Sallie, even when he didn't. You honored God through it all."

"Yeah," Sallie agreed, slumping down in her chair. "I sure tried."

Marijane took a deep breath before plunging into the conversation. "I'm blessed with a great husband, but my two teenage sons are a handful. I'm…" She glanced at the others, who nodded their unspoken encouragement. "I'm seeing a counselor right now, trying to get my anger under control." Her voice dropped another note. "Jimmy and Josiah deserve a mom who doesn't yell all the time."

JoAnn finally spoke up, her tone more playful than usual. "I have a story too, but I'll save it for another day, or this housecleaning will never get done."

"Good point." Mary Stauros chuckled, and they all exchanged grins. "As you can see, Mary Margaret, every one of us has a past we're working through, learning to put behind us."

"Except you, of course," Mary hastened to add, certain the saintly woman had walked the straight and narrow every day of her life.

"Me?" Mary Stauros winked at Suzy. "I got pregnant out of wedlock."

Mary Margaret couldn't keep her jaw from dropping. "You're kidding!"

"Hardly." Jake's mother laughed, her face the very picture of joy. "Ask my son."

The sun had long set by the time the Sisters blew out the door the same way they'd come in, roaring like March lions. Their energy and willingness to work hour after hour left Mary exhausted but grateful.

She surveyed her kitchen, scrubbed clean from corner to corner and no longer cluttered with cardboard boxes and Casio keyboards. Instead, the Sisters had collectively decorated the room with the few pretty and practical items she'd dragged home on her shopping jaunts. Mary was beginning to piece the lost years together—the auctions, the yard sales, the department store closeout bargains—that had added up to a house brimming with wasteful, worthless trash.

"Not trash, *treasures*," Suzy constantly reminded her. All of Calvary Fellowship was on board for their estate sale on the seventeenth. Jake's mother had lined up volunteers to make change and hand out shopping bags, warning Jake that under no circumstances was he to miss his turn at the cashbox.

The Sisters were convinced Mary's many rooms would be junk-free by dinnertime on Saint Patrick's Day. Mary laughed, stepping back to glance at the artfully arranged display of sheer rubbish in her dining room. Hard to believe anyone would really want any of it, though many of the items were brand-new. Mary had the receipts to prove it.

Last week she'd found boxes stuffed with nothing but sales receipts dating back seven years. And canceled checks. And cash. *Cash*. Thousands of dollars crammed into a corner of her third-floor closet. Mary had stared at it for a full ten minutes before she started counting it, putting it into neat piles with shaking hands. It was all hers; the bank statements said so. She'd never paid attention to Mick's wise investments during the early years of their marriage. But they'd resulted in large dividends, which he'd split with her, right down the middle.

WE LOOK FOR GOD   89

With judicious spending it was enough money to live on for a year or two, maybe longer. Sufficient time to put her burdensome past behind her completely and decide what she was going to do with the rest of her life. Last Thursday she'd invested in some nice, basic clothes that would last for more than a season and had put the rest in the bank where it belonged, reminding herself that her security rested not on having money in the bank but on having God in her life.

Mary wiped the counters clean once more, secretly elated that she *could*, that she cared now, that it mattered to her. On the wall above her ticked a shiny new clock, as round and yellow as a full moon. The irony of it hadn't struck her until she took it out of the box and mounted it over the fridge, at which point she'd laughed until she cried.

Near the phone hung her new calendar—scenes of Ireland, naturally—with all the important dates noted in red ink. Saint Pat's, the first day of spring, Palm Sunday, Good Friday, Easter—all loomed on the horizon. But sooner, much sooner than all those, was the notation for tonight, March 9. *Full moon.*

She'd been skittish all morning working at church, then forced herself to forget it the rest of the day while they labored on the house. The Sisters would return first thing in the morning. Would they find her stretched out across her front steps, incoherent and babbling about the moon?

"They will not," Mary announced to her one and only cat as he sauntered into the room, purring for attention. She gathered the fluffy animal into her arms and squeezed him tight. "Good thing I still have you, Max."

At Jake's suggestion she'd visited PAWS last Sunday, inquiring sheepishly about her donated cats. "Go on, show those women that you're 'dressed and in your right mind,'" Jake had insisted.

"That I'm *what?*"

"Gospel of Mark, chapter five," he'd responded with a silly grin.

Just as Jake had predicted, the women were blatantly shocked to see her—not that she'd come, but that she'd changed so dramatically.

"Don't you look…nice?" one of the women had blurted out before assuring Mary that her kitties had all found good homes in the neighborhood. "You've made several new pet owners, and your cats, very happy indeed."

Tonight, however, would be the litmus test. A full moon staring down at her through the clouds. Beckoning her. Bewitching her. She strolled through the house, flicking on more lights than usual, bolting the front and back doors in passing, praying as she went. *I wait for the LORD, my soul waits, and in his word I put my hope.* At eleven, feeling restless, she snapped off the television and checked the locks once more before climbing the two flights of stairs to her bedroom.

Here, too, the cleaning skills of the Sisters had turned her jumbled room into a cozy, restful retreat in blues and lavenders, an altogether feminine palette without a drop of red anywhere. "Nothing red" had been Mary's watchword all through the house as they chose what to keep and what to sell.

"No red!" Suzy hollered any time a scarlet item came up for consideration, gleefully adding it to her own purchases. Suzy loved red.

Draping Max over her shoulder to bolster her courage, Mary left the brightly lit bedroom behind and ventured down the hall to Luna's old room. At her request, the Sisters had steered clear of this one. Mary's simple explanation—"I'm not ready"—was all they needed.

"Maybe tomorrow," JoAnn had said, her tone casual. No pressure.

When will you be ready, Mary Margaret? What are you waiting for?

She paused at the doorway, gripping Max so tightly he nipped at her hand. "Sorry, boy-o," she whispered, easing him to the floor. The room was filled with shadows, illumined only by the traitorous moonlight pouring in the window.

"Turn the light on, Mary." She said it out loud. Not because she was a madwoman, but because it made her feel bolder, more in charge. Her hand reached out and flipped the wall switch, bathing the room in the sickly glow of one sixty-watt bulb, the only one left in the Victorian ceiling fixture that still worked. Four other bulbs, all burned out, hung there, useless.

"I can fix that," she announced, practically marching into the bathroom next door to find a box of fresh light bulbs, one of dozens she'd purchased on an unhinged sort of day. Light bulbs, at least, were a necessary household item, especially at the moment. Fully armed, she returned to the bedroom and pulled over a solid oak desk chair that would easily hold her weight and bring the spent bulbs within arm's reach.

Only one problem remained: She would have to turn off the antique fixture or risk electrical shock. Since it was the only light in the room, that
meant changing bulbs in the dark. *No, worse. By the light of the full moon.*

Mary took a deep breath, filling her lungs with the presence of God.
"Hear my voice, Lord!" she cried out, surprised at how strong it sounded.
Not a quiver. "Let your ears be attentive to my cry for mercy, Lord. I need
your help to do this."

She hit the light switch, plunging the room into darkness. But not her.

Mary Margaret glowed. Light seemed to radiate from her skin. Her eyes
already adjusted, she moved to the center of the room, in awe of how bright
the place had become. Stepping onto the chair, she was amazed to find her
legs were steady. Above her, the brass fixture shone in the moonlight, making
it easy to remove the bulbs and replace them, one after another.

It was only when she stepped down that she began to shake. Not from
fear. From anticipation. She ran to the light switch and flicked it upward with
a shout of victory. Instantly the room was bathed in a light so bright that not
a single nook or cranny remained in darkness. *Not in the room. Not in her.*

The frightening voices were truly gone.

Only one voice remained. And it was good.

As though the light itself were an energy force, Mary found herself working well into the wee hours, emptying drawers and bookshelves, making
stacks of things to sell and things to keep, awash with memories of Luna, all
of them positive. Luna at her first dance recital. Luna making a snowman in
Lincoln Park. Luna smiling up from the pages of her first chapter book.

Long after the moon sank low in the sky and the first tendrils of dawn
touched the eastern horizon, Mary pulled the last of Luna's colorful clothes
out of the wardrobe and folded them neatly into boxes for another teenage
girl who might need them. Her beloved daughter would live in her heart
always. But her earthly possessions could at last be put to better use.

Luna hadn't needed them for seven years.

Mary Margaret would never need them again.

Chapter Six

HINGES OF OUR FRIENDSHIP

May the hinges of our friendship never grow rusty.
IRISH BLESSING

"No rest for the weary," Jake sighed dramatically, grinning as he lugged yet another carton of Mary's treasures out the door on the heels of a satisfied customer.

The weather for their Saint Patrick's Day estate sale could not have been worse. Rain mixed with snow mixed with sleet and temperatures hovering around an icy thirty degrees. Inside Mary Margaret Delaney's house, however, the rooms were a cozy seventy degrees, laughter was in abundance, and the predominant theme was shamrocks.

If Calvary's volunteers weren't wearing green when they arrived, Mary remedied that situation in short order. Plastic bowlers, cheap bow ties, and too-short vests were dispensed with such liberality that soon the customers were bedecked in green as well.

Something was working, Jake knew that much. Bric-a-brac he wouldn't have given ten cents for walked out the door for ten dollars. Smiling people left with armloads of stuff, leaving behind dollars that would go a long way toward furnace repair, insulation, and a dozen other needs the church elders had brought to him last Tuesday.

Thank you, Father.

Holding court near the front door, Mary Margaret Delaney was in her element. Jake delighted in watching her welcome strangers like guests and greet neighbors like old friends. "Everybody's Irish on Saint Patrick's Day," she announced to all who would listen, her face beaming. All morning she'd held sway over a table laden with her Irish soda bread wrapped in cellophane bags with bright green bows and her grandmother's recipe attached. Whatever she was charging, it wasn't enough. The round loaves were gone before noon.

Jake stopped hauling boxes long enough to help her fold up her empty card table, pouting as he did. "You didn't even save a loaf for me?"

She arched an eyebrow. "And who says I didn't, lad?"

"God bless you, Mary Margaret," he sighed with a grateful bow.

She curtsied in return, sweeping her skirts like a dairymaid from County Kerry. "Blessings to you as well, Pastor Jake."

He continued to watch her out of the corner of his eye, marveling at the miracle of Mad Mary. She was simply *gone,* and a brand-new Mary had taken her place, full of joy and light and boundless generosity. *Glad Mary.* Jake smiled. The name suited her to a T.

One neighborhood couple, eyes wide, mouths agape, stared at Mary in utter disbelief. Jake suspected they'd seen her on a moonlit foray or bumped into her at the Park View Pet Shop crying over cat toys. If they'd dropped by this afternoon hoping to get a glimpse of a madwoman and her creepy old house, they'd gotten an eyeful of grace at work instead.

And the house! Not only was it clean, it would soon be *empty.* Even some of Mary's good furniture, the pieces he thought she'd intended to keep, walked out the door with her blessing. Was she fully aware of what she was doing, or had her medicine made her too happy to be rational? Concerned, Jake sidled over to her during a lull in the action.

"Mary Margaret, did you…?" Suddenly he felt foolish. She was his mother's age, a woman more than capable of making wise decisions. But he had to be sure.

Mary looked up at him, her face the picture of contentment. "Did I what?"

"Did you mean to sell that sofa?"

"Of course!" Her laugh was genuine, not the manic cackling of old. "And what a nice contribution that couple made to our church. *Your* church."

"No, *our* church." The sooner the fellowship understood that, the better. Jake looked around at the dwindling merchandise. "But what are you going to sit on, Mary?"

Her eyes twinkled, and he got the distinct feeling she was harboring a secret. "You worry too much, Jake."

Later that afternoon he caught a glimpse of her seated at the kitchen table deep in conversation with a well-dressed gentleman, and Jake felt a strange tug in his chest. Change was in the air, and not only for him. Perhaps for Mary Margaret, too, though he couldn't imagine what she might be planning.

He longed to tell her, to tell all those closest to him, what was going to happen next month. Not today though. No way would he dampen their enthusiasm with his sobering announcement. It could wait another week. Little John, his mother, and the other women who labored so diligently at Calvary would surely celebrate his new mission. But the rest of the church might see it as *bad* news, not good news.

And how would Mary Delaney see it?

Jake watched her as she walked toward him, a loaf of bread in hand and a smile from ear to ear, and knew the answer: She would see his new work for what it was, a calling from God.

He gazed at the fresh loaf, trying not to drool. "Whatcha got there, Mary Margaret?"

"The smallest of thank-you gifts." She held out the bread, tugging on the recipe card. "Whenever you're hungry for more, you can make it yourself, see? I scribbled some extra notes on the back for you."

"Because I'm baking impaired?"

She laughed and nodded. "Something like that."

He flipped over the card and read the handwritten lines aloud. "'No substitutes for the buttermilk.'" He wrinkled his nose. "I hate buttermilk."

"That bread you're about to wolf down has two full cups of it," she said, rolling her eyes. "Stop whining and keep reading."

"'Add a heaping handful of raisins if you like.' Ah, now that I *do* like.

'Don't knead the dough more than a dozen times or your bread will be tougher than Charles Farris.'" Jake chuckled, then glanced over his shoulder to see who was standing nearby before he lowered his voice and asked, "Did Charles even show up today?"

Mary shook her head. "He's the only member of the church who didn't, Jake. Sometimes I wonder if he really supports what you—what all of us—are trying to do."

"Don't give up on him, Mary Margaret. God hasn't."

"If you say so." She stood on tiptoe to look at his recipe card. "Any more notes there?"

"Yup. 'Since you'll probably burn the roof of your mouth trying to eat the bread while it's still hot, slather it with butter first.' Oh, yes ma'am, you can count on it." He pulled the recipe off and stuffed it in his jacket pocket, then reached in the bag and pinched off a piece of bread and chewed it with relish. "Mmm. You sure you can't keep baking this for me?"

"Maybe." She waved her hand with a flourish. "As you can see, my oven is about all that's left in the house. That and a few basic pieces to make the place...uh, livable."

For the time being. Was that what she meant? What was she about to say before she caught herself? Jake gave her a brief hug and headed for the door, her soda bread tucked under his arm.

Whatever her news and whatever her reasons, it was clear that Mary Margaret Delaney was a new person, inside and out. When her faith was tested in the weeks to come, Jake knew she would remain steadfast, her trust in the Lord unwavering. No one could be transformed, madwoman to glad woman, without first seeing the living God face to face.

Jake slowly walked down the center aisle, greeting Calvary's members and guests as usual, though his thoughts and emotions were bittersweet. He would miss this old building with its temperamental furnace and its mud-brown carpeting and its pastor's office that still looked like a kitchen.

But mostly he would miss the people he'd come to love, Charles Farris included. It was easy to see past the old coot's prickly exterior to the wounded heart inside. Jake watched the scowling man sitting by himself at the end of the first row. Who knew? Charles might be the one person there that morning who would applaud when Jake announced his plans for the future.

Jake would know soon enough.

Marijane's music was especially spirited, and the choir sang not only in the same key but also with gusto. Jake was impressed, though it tugged harder still on his conscience. *Give me strength, Father.*

His message was chosen with care. "Let's begin reading in Matthew, chapter 25: 'For I was hungry and you gave me something to eat, I was thirsty and you gave me something to drink, I was a stranger and you invited me in.'" He looked up from his Bible, letting the words sink into his own heart and theirs. "When the Lord brought me to this work, to Calvary, could any of us have imagined what he would build?" Jake gazed at the ceiling that hung above them, swallowing hard as he remembered the weeks of plastering and painting that smooth surface represented, then looked back at the true building: God's people.

"You made me welcome from the first, when I knocked on your doors…" He nodded at JoAnn, who blushed and smiled back. "Or invited you to church…" It was Mary Margaret he looked at then, who met his steady gaze with her own. "Or accosted you on a street corner."

Suzy laughed before he could even look her direction. "Please, no details, Pastor Jake," she called out, making everyone chuckle.

"I don't need to tell your story, Suze," he assured her. "You do a much better job yourself."

He continued, speaking more passionately than ever, longing to lay the groundwork for a conclusion he feared no one would expect. At last he came to the unavoidable end. Taking a deep breath, Jake moved in front of the pulpit, needing to be closer to them, to be sure they saw his face and heard his heart.

"The time has come for me to leave our fellowship," he began, pausing while they gasped, then spoke in agitated whispers, caught off guard as he knew they would be. He'd dropped plenty of hints, but they apparently hadn't sunk in. "It has been an amazing time of ministry. Look at us, seventy strong now and still growing."

He stretched out his arms, wanting to gather them to his side like children needing comfort, like sheep needing a shepherd. "We knew this day would come, when I would move on to another part of the city and begin a new congregation."

Jake glanced at Mary Margaret, then looked away, overwhelmed. Tears were streaming down her cheeks, though it was hard to tell if they flowed out of sorrow or joy. The latter, no doubt.

She was simply not the same woman he'd met in January. That woman had been entombed, obsessed with death. This woman was empowered, infused with life. Her office skills had grown exponentially, right along with her confidence. Her free time was spent immersed in the Scriptures, bathing her in wisdom. Her service to the church had shifted from quiet service to quiet leadership, hosting a weekly women's Bible study in her home and offering encouragement to other hurting women.

Of the many good people before him, he would miss Mary Margaret Delaney and her abundance of tears most of all.

"There will be only one Calvary in my life," he assured them, wanting them to know how much he loved them. "But I believe God has prepared a place for me, and I must be obedient and go there, much as it tears at my heart to do so."

Relieved to have made it that far, Jake shared the specific details of the new church he would be planting with the Lord's help.

"Pretty rough part of town," Pete grumbled.

Jake knew the man's countenance would change as soon as he made the next announcement. "You can jump on the El and visit me anytime, Pete. Just follow the Red Line." He couldn't hold back the smile that was stretching across his face. "Though I'm not sure how much time you'll have for sightseeing since you'll be busy preparing your sermons as Calvary's interim preacher."

"*What?*" A startled Charles Farris dropped his cane on the floor. "Preparing his what?"

"My sermons," Pete repeated, his matching grin the size of Wrigley Stadium.

"Yup," Jake nodded. "Pete's the man for the job. The elders and I discussed it last night. My last Sunday here will be Easter, and Pete will be in the pulpit the following week. We've also arranged for my full-time replacement, set to arrive late this spring."

This was the best part, the good news Jake hoped they would embrace with their whole hearts. "You won't be disappointed, folks. Sit tight for a few weeks, and don't go wandering off in search of greener pastures, okay? This will be the place to be come summer. I promise you."

Mary had promised the Lord that if he made it very clear it was his will, she would move forward with her plans.

Jake's announcement last Sunday had made it abundantly clear. The kind gentleman who'd approached her at the estate sale with a generous offer had given her until the first of April to make her decision. All was decided. Now it was her turn to surprise the congregation.

She rose near the end of Jake's closing prayer, turning around in her front-row seat, hoping she'd have everyone's attention when they lifted their bowed heads. Charles Farris, she noticed, hadn't closed his eyes or bowed his head at all.

"Brothers and sisters," she said in her loudest voice, not nearly as loud as Jake's, but it got their attention. "As a show of support for Pastor Jake's ministry, I've sold my house and will be giving all the proceeds to his new work."

"Mary Margaret!" Jake's eyes widened. "Do you…I mean, are you…?"

"Am I sure? Positively."

"I get it." Pete jumped to his feet, his face a wreath of smiles. "April Fool's, right?"

Mary laughed, grateful for any levity that might lessen the tension in the room, not to mention in her queasy stomach. "No, Pete. It may be the first of the month, but I'm not fooling, not for one minute. I've had a sizable offer on the house, one that I couldn't refuse."

"*Fool* is exactly the word for you!" Charles Farris barked, standing to shake his cane at her. "Throwing your money away like that. You're still a madwoman, Mary Delaney."

She shook her head, surprised that she felt no anger whatsoever. Only pity for his blindness. And an utter sense of peace about her decision.

"Where you gonna live?" Charles demanded, his tone bitter. "Don't expect the rest of us to feed and clothe you. Seems to me we've done enough of that around here."

"I won't need your help," Mary assured him, folding her hands in front of her to keep them from shaking. "Not only do I intend to support Pastor Jake financially, I'll be following him to his new neighborhood and helping any way that I can to reach out to others like…" Her throat tightened, but she kept going, not caring if they heard the tears in her voice. "Like Jake reached out to me. And so did Suzy. And JoAnn. And Marijane. And Sallie Mae. And…and like Mary Stauros, who showed me what the love of God looks like, up close."

The Sisters stood as one, their faces radiant, their eyes shining with unshed tears.

Jake's mother spoke first. "I'm going as well, Mary Margaret. Wherever my son goes, that's where I intend to be."

"Me, too," was all Suzy could manage before she broke down, sinking into her seat to blow her nose, still smiling through it all.

The other three Sisters exchanged glances, then shrugged and said in unison, "Me, too!"

Little John stood, his big shoulders squared but his wobbly chin giving him away. "Guess I better go along too, boss. If all these women are willing to make that kind of sacrifice, well…count me in."

Jake, slack-jawed through it all, finally cleared his throat and stepped forward to speak. "I…I never dreamed my support staff would be so…supportive. Sisters, I cannot begin to tell you what that means to me, how it blesses me. And John, since I have no idea what kind of building we'll be meeting in, better bring your toolbox and a lot of nails."

A few nervous laughs rippled through the crowd that filled the small sanctuary. Mary Margaret saw Jake's brow draw together, as though he'd thought of some stumbling block.

"My only concern," he said with some effort, "is the work we've started here. Are there others who will step forward and fill their shoes at Calvary?"

A middle-aged woman near the back rose to her feet. "I'd be delighted to serve as secretary." She winked at Suzy. "My hair is all one color, but the brain underneath it still works pretty well."

"It works *very* well," Jake amended. "Bless you, Beverly."

Mary Margaret was elated to watch more hands go up as others volunteered to see that things would run smoothly when Jake and his support team moved on. A tight knot in her chest began to unravel, and a sense of freedom quietly took its place, filling her to overflowing. *Where the Spirit of the Lord is, there is freedom.* If she'd had any qualms that selling her house and supporting Jake's ministry were the foolish plans of a crazy woman, such doubts were gone forever.

Mad Mary was no more.

Mary Margaret and the Sisters kept the details of their Palm Sunday celebration under wraps, telling Calvary's members no more than necessary.

Suzy spent her mornings on the phone, JoAnn her afternoons, each spreading the news: "Mary Margaret's house, Sunday at one, bring food." Settlement on Mary's property wouldn't come until after Easter, so it was the perfect send-off for both her old house and their young pastor.

Now that he knew the Sisters were going with him, Jake couldn't stop talking about their new location. "Think big," he told them. "The neighborhood is twice the size of Lincoln Park. Maybe three times. Wait until you see it. Trust me."

It was a phrase he used often that week: *Trust me.*

Mary *did* trust Jake's faith in his godly calling, but she'd heard some rumblings as well. About the sort of reception Jake might encounter there. About the dangers and the uncertainties of that part of Chicago. She would be strong for him and keep her fears to herself. But they were undeniably there.

Keep him safe, Lord. Her prayers increased as the spring temperatures climbed each day. Into the fifties, then the sixties, then the low seventies by Friday morning. Praying for Jake came easily enough. As an afterthought she prayed for her own safety, for John's, for all the Sisters'.

"I feel as if our future is one big question mark," she confessed to Mary Stauros as they readied her house for their Palm Sunday gathering the next day.

Jake's mother smoothed her hand across a white lace tablecloth, then looked up, her eyes clear, her smile confident. "Not at all, Mary Margaret. Our future is one big exclamation point!"

Mary Margaret sighed pensively. "How can you be so certain?"

"I watched Jake grow up. God's hand was on him from the beginning." Her smile was wistful. "Even before the beginning, I think." Mary straightened, the lace tablecloth forgotten, and met Mary Margaret's gaze head-on. "If my son says he is called, you can rest in that. He won't go anywhere God doesn't want him to go."

"Where is it we're going again?" Jake eyed the two Marys standing on the front steps of the church, umbrellas in their hands and grins on their faces.

"Really, Jake!" His mother shot up one eyebrow with a practiced flair. "Aren't you the one who is always saying, 'Trust me'?"

He scowled at them playfully. "It's hard to trust people when your congregation flies out the door like buckshot on my final 'amen.' Where was everybody off to in such a hurry?"

"Home," Mary said, knowing she spoke the truth. They weren't going to *stay* home, just change and pick up their covered dishes, but it was perfectly honest to say they *went* home. For a minute.

"Well, that's where I'm headed. Home." Jake took one step off the porch before they each hooked a hand through his elbows, flanking him.

"I'm going home too," Mary Margaret agreed, then burst out in laughter. Mary Stauros gave her a stern look, though her smile gave her away.

"What Mary's saying, Son, is that we're all going to *her* home today."

"Including me?"

"Especially you." His mother guided them down the walk while thunder rumbled above them. "You are, in fact, the guest of honor. Lead the way."

Within seconds the clouds began to disperse their contents in huge drops. Huddled under two umbrellas, Jake and the two Marys scurried down the street, eager to get inside before the drops turned into a downpour. Suzy and Marijane were already on her doorstep, waving their umbrellas precisely as they'd waved their palm branches in church that morning. "C'mon, Pastor Jake, it's your big day!"

"It is?"

A crack of thunder punctuated the bang of the door, though it would open and close many times that afternoon as seventy members of Calvary

Fellowship strolled over its threshold, casseroles and salads in hand. The house was soon filled with laughter, music, spirited conversation, and mountains of food piled on flimsy paper plates.

Jake finally settled on a corner of the living room rug with his own dinner. "We should have done this a long time ago, Mom."

"No," Mary Stauros countered, shaking her head. "This was the perfect time and the perfect place. And the perfect reason." She lifted her glass of ice water in tribute. "It's the start of Holy Week, Jake. And your last week at Calvary."

Jake nodded, his brown eyes filled with a thousand emotions, which Mary Margaret knew she could never sort through. His voice was low, but his intensity was not. "I know how I'm going to spend Good Friday."

Mary Margaret continued to watch his expressions, aware that Jake would tell her more if she simply waited.

"I'm visiting our new neighborhood. Taking the Red Line down Friday morning."

For no logical reason, Mary Margaret's chest tightened. "A-alone?"

"Sure. No use dragging anyone else along so early in the day. I'll be back before you know it." He studied her face, obviously troubled by what he saw there. "Mary, are you okay? You're not worried about me, are you? This is where I'm supposed to go, remember?" He squeezed her hand and his mother's as well. "Have I told you two lately how much your support means?"

His mother stood, balancing her empty plate in her hand. "There's nowhere else I'd rather be, Jake. I know Mary Margaret feels the same way." She moved toward the kitchen, stepping gingerly around people of all ages and sizes strewn over the carpet like so many house pets.

Mary realized that he was still holding her hand and looked up, surprised to find him gazing at her, an expression of awe on his young face.

"You're a miracle, you know that, Mary Delaney?"

"If I am, I know who to thank," she said, squeezing his fingers affectionately.

"The Lord?"

"Of course," she agreed quickly. "But you're a close second, Jake."

He shook his head. "Not even in the running." He gently let go of her hand and sat back, surveying the room. "I wonder…" Jake ran his fingers through his hair, silent for a moment. "Could we…?" More ruminating. "Do we have enough glasses for everyone?"

"Sure, if we use those plastic ones." She collected their discarded plates, mentally counting their supplies. "JoAnn brought something like ten dozen."

He glanced at her sideways, a solemn and purposeful look starting to envelop his features. "And you still have plenty of your soda bread left, yes? And grape juice?"

"Plenty," she assured him. *What was the man up to?*

"Good. Suppose you pour out cups of juice for everybody. And tuck the bread in some baskets, if you have any."

"I do. And I will." She regarded him thoughtfully. "Is this our last communion together, Jake?"

He nodded, more serious than she had ever seen him. "I'm going to miss this body of believers very much. I want them to know that. And I want them to know that I'll always be part of them, and they will always be an important part of me." He paused then, a look of uncertainty flitting across his features. "Do you think that would be meaningful for them, Mary?"

Oh, this dear man. She could barely get the words out. "Y-yes. I do."

She quickly did as Jake had requested, enlisting the help of the Sisters to pour the juice and prepare the baskets of bread. As word of their plans spread, a hush fell over the group until the entire household waited expectantly, wrapped in a sacred silence. Outside, the rain fell in earnest, more noticeable now that they'd come to such a place of quiet inside.

Mary stood before Jake, her arms loaded with baskets. "Where shall we do this?"

He looked up. "Is there more room on the second floor?"

"Absolutely." Mary nodded, seeing the wisdom of his choice. "Not a stick of furniture up there, and all adjoining rooms. I'll have Little John and Pete steer folks upstairs."

As though in tacit agreement, everyone remained silent as they filed up the steps. Even the younger members of Calvary were attentive, sticking close to their parents as they reconvened on the second floor. The three big rooms were connected by pocket doors, which Mary pushed open, allowing them to gather as one.

Jake stood amid them and held his cup and bread aloft. "Our brothers will be passing these among you. Please take a cup and a bit of bread, then simply hold them until all are served." The men made short work of their duties, and soon all held their juice and their bread, their eyes trained on the young pastor, whose gaze was lifted up to heaven.

"Lord Jesus," Jake prayed. "You once told your followers that whenever they gathered around a table in your name, you would be among them." He swallowed hard, holding his elements up high. "We are here, Lord. And we are grateful beyond words that you are here with us. You who are the bread of life, who come to us that we might never be hungry, feed your flock this hour."

Jake lifted the small piece of bread to his lips and ate, and everyone followed.

"And you, Lord Jesus, who promised to be our living water that we might never be thirsty, quench our thirst this hour."

Jake drank his juice in a single gulp, and the others did likewise.

He slowly lowered his gaze to meet theirs, his face lit with a glow that only Christ could bestow. "When the new church gathered after Christ's resurrection, the Bible tells us they devoted themselves to teaching and fellowship, to the breaking of bread, and to prayer. We've been taught today, we've fellowshipped, and we've broken bread together. Now, let's pray. Pete, will you lead us?"

The rain fell, a soft symphony beneath their words, as prayers were offered aloud by various members, old and new. Entreaties for all those who were hurting and those whose hurting had ceased. For those who were celebrating a new season of life and others who grieved that a season had ended. Through it all, prayers for Jake and his ministry ascended like the smell of fresh bread baking, permeating the second floor with a fragrant aroma.

Time stretched and bent around the believers. No one fidgeted, no one coughed. Even the children behaved themselves. Not a sound broke the mantle of peace that fell over them. Not a thunderclap, not an impatient car horn, not the insistent ringing of a cell phone.

Silence reigned.

Finally when all was said and all was done to the glory of the Savior, Mary Margaret opened her eyes and found Jake smiling in the center of the room. "Have a blessed week, my brothers and sisters," he said, waving a benediction over them. Then he turned and walked toward her, God's love shining in his eyes. "We'll miss this fine house, Mary Margaret Delaney. But I promise you something even grander someday. Wait and see."

"Wait, Jake!" Mary hurried after him, the slim red Bible in her hands.

Jake paused in the foyer while she crossed the empty sanctuary. "Something I'm forgetting, Mary?" he called out, checking his watch.

She'd come to work much earlier than usual that Friday, knowing he was trying to catch the train heading south, compelled to send him on his way with one more item. "This," she said, thrusting out the book he'd given her months ago. "I bought myself one of those big study Bibles, you know. So I thought this one...well, someone might need it...where you're going."

She touched her engraved name, already wearing off from use. "I hope you don't mind, Jake. It was, after all, a gift."

"What's inside it is now inside you," he reminded her. He slipped the red volume in his pocket and patted it, a smile easing away the tension in his features. "Very generous, as always, Mary Margaret."

He zipped up his jacket, his eyes scanning the changeable skies, a mix of clouds and sun. "Pray for me, will you? Heaven only knows what I'll find when I get there." He touched her hand briefly, then took off running, calling over his shoulder. "I'll be back soon enough. The Cubbies have their opening game this afternoon, remember? No way I'm gonna miss that."

Mary watched him until his back disappeared around the corner, knowing the route he would take on foot: west on Fullerton Parkway for several blocks to DePaul University, where he would board the Red Line sandwiched between Sheffield and Bissell. "People do it every day," she reminded herself. It was safe, clean, well lit. *Safe. Clean. Well lit.*

She repeated the words like a litany as she made fresh coffee, expecting Jake's mother to show up at any minute so they could decorate the sanctuary for Easter morning. Both of them were eager to brighten the simple worship center with gorgeous Easter lilies, the fragrant white blooms and purple foil pots beautiful enough to fill anyone's senses.

She glanced at the calendar hanging behind Jake's desk, and her heart skipped a beat. On Palm Sunday night a full moon had come and gone and she'd never even noticed. *Thank you, Lord.*

"Mary Margaret?" Jake's mother walked through the front door with a lily in each hand. "Come help me unload them, sis. My poor Toyota smells like a funeral home."

It took several trips to bring in the plants, which had filled her car and trunk to overflowing. Even after Mary's careful arrangement on white wooden pedestals, though, the twenty-four pots were lost in the high-ceilinged room.

"It looked like so many in the car," Jake's mother mused, shaking her head. "Do you want me to go back for another dozen? Or two?"

"Maybe…" Mary wondered what Jake's preference would be for his last Sunday at Calvary. More flowers meant less money for the poor, less money for Bibles. If only he were back in his office where she could ask him. *So much to learn, Mary!* Once they were settled in their new neighborhood, she intended to sit at the feet of her teacher and soak up his wisdom on such things.

"Yes or no, Mary Margaret?" Mary Stauros stood at the doorway, car keys in hand.

They both jumped when Jake's office phone rang, echoing through the empty rooms. Jake's mother got to it first. "Hello, Calvary Fellowship. Yes, this is Jake Stauros's church."

Mary watched the woman's lighthearted expression fade. Her features grew pinched, and her brow creased until Mary Margaret feared it might crack under the pressure. "He…what?" Jake's mother whispered into the phone. "And this is which hospital?"

"Hospital?" Mary Margaret's heart leaped into her throat, beating faster and heavier. Her head suddenly ached, and her lips dried to dust. "Who is it? Who are they calling about?"

In a daze Mary Stauros motioned for her to pick up the other phone, the one in her office. Mary hurried there, breathless after only a few steps, and lifted the phone off the hook, dreading what news she might hear. Was it the Mullins baby? *Please, Lord, not Gary.* Not anyone. Not at Easter.

She held the phone to her ear, praying as she did.

"He's asking for Mary," a young woman's voice was saying.

Mary Margaret couldn't see Jake's mother, but she could hear her muffled sobs.

Desperate for details, she jumped in. "*Who?* Who's asking for Mary?"

"Jake Stauros, ma'am."

"*Jake?* What are you...? Where *is* he?" Her mind froze, refusing to register what the woman was saying. "Wait, never mind. I know where Jake is. He's on the Red Line—"

"Ma'am, this is the ER at Grant Hospital." The woman's authoritative tone pulled Mary back to the present, made her pay attention.

"Y-yes, yes, I'm listening. Grant Hospital." Her throat thickened with apprehension and the threat of tears.

"Look, ma'am, this Mary person he's asking for needs to get here quickly. Are you Mary?"

"We...we both are. She's Mary Stauros, his mother. And I'm Mary Margaret Delaney. His...his friend." She dropped to her knees beside her desk. Every word was an effort. "Tell...me...what's...wrong."

"Jake Stauros has been shot. Accidentally or intentionally, we're not sure. It happened while he exited the train at Thirty-Fifth Street. The gunman has yet to be apprehended. Ma'am, this man is in grave condition. You'd better hurry."

Mary Margaret dropped the phone as though it had burned her skin, then struggled to her feet, her legs like lead. Before she could call Mary's name, her friend was there, a look of horror on her pale face. "Jake..."

"I know." They embraced but only for a moment, anxious to get there, to see him. "Let's walk. It'll be faster." Mary Delaney put her arm around the woman's shoulder and guided her out the back door. "Do you mind if I...come with you?"

"Mind?" Mary Stauros stared blankly at her. "No...*no!* Of course not."

They hurried down the alley in tandem, both too stunned to cry. Only one question troubled Mary Margaret and then only a little: *Which Mary?*

Jake's mother knew her well. When they paused at the curb to check for traffic, Mary Stauros turned toward her, catching her eye. "Mary Margaret, it doesn't matter which Mary he's asking for." She squeezed her hand as they ran across Grant Place. "The truth is, he needs us both."

Chapter Seven

DARKNESS BENDS DOWN

Lo! darkness bends down like a mother of grief
On the limitless plain, and the fall of her hair
It has mantled a world.
JOAQUIN MILLER

I can't watch him die. I can't.

Mary Margaret's steps slowed the closer she got to the hospital. By the time they reached the ER entrance, Jake's mother was practically dragging her.

"Hurry, Mary! He needs us."

And I need you, Lord. Help me! Help me be strong.

They stumbled through the door together, leaning on one another for support as they identified themselves and were led through a maze of gurneys and IV carts to a familiar figure covered with a bloodied sheet.

"Jake!" Mary Stauros lurched forward, stopped from falling by an orderly who put out a steadying hand.

"Easy does it. He's in shock right now, ma'am. Could you have a seat to the side there? You, too, ma'am."

Jake. We're here.

His skin was the color of death.

His clothes lay discarded on the floor, cut away around his waist where the bullet had done its damage, penetrating his side like a sword.

An IV needle pierced his wrist.

"What is all this?" Mary Stauros asked faintly.

A harried nurse took time to explain between issuing orders to her peers. "Fluids. Blood transfusion. Antibiotics. Blood-clotting agents." She paused long enough to look his mother in the eye, lowering her voice as she did. "Are you Mrs. Stauros? Jake's in grave condition, I'm afraid."

"Yes, yes. They told me. Is that...?"

"The worst, ma'am. Unless he improves dramatically, your son is going to die."

Mary Stauros opened her mouth, but no sound came out.

"We'll do everything we can, but..." The nurse lifted her shoulders in a weary shrug, her face reflecting her genuine sorrow. "I'm sorry."

Mary Margaret caught her before she collapsed on the floor. "Mary, Mary, let me help you." She snatched a tissue from a nearby table, whispering comforting words as she wiped the woman's nose and brushed back her hair. *Help her, Lord. Help Mary.* It seems they'd switched roles—she as the comfort giver now, Mary Stauros as the needy one. *So be it, Lord.*

As the minutes ticked by, reality began to set in. Mary Margaret could taste the bitterness of it in her mouth, feel the coldness in her veins. Seven years ago she'd sat in this room, this very room, and watched her daughter bleed to death.

Your daughter is going to die.

She could not stop death's cruel hand then. And she feared she could not stop it now.

Your friend is going to die.

Mary Margaret bent in two. A searing pain, so acute it left her gasping for breath, sliced through her chest like a scalpel. *No, no, no!* Losing Jake would be like losing Luna all over again. She could not bear it alone. *Lord, please!*

Darkness pressed down on her like a shroud, smothering her, blocking every particle of light.

Then Mary Stauros squeezed her hand.

Not alone. She had Mary. She had the Sisters. She had all of Calvary Fellowship. She was not alone, not this time.

Mary Margaret rose to her feet, weaving a bit yet still standing, her purse dangling from her shoulder. "We need to tell the others what's going on. I'll be right back."

Patting Mary's hunched shoulder, Mary Margaret made her way back into the ER reception area where she vaguely remembered seeing a pay phone. A whole bank of them waited for her, all empty.

Marijane burst into tears when she told her and had to be consoled before Mary could give her sufficient information to pass on to others. "Make some phone calls, honey. Then come. Quickly."

Her duty done, Mary Margaret hurried back to her station, relieved to find a doctor hovering over Jake as he shone a tiny flashlight into his patient's eyes.

"Please tell us something," she pleaded, peering over his shoulder from a safe distance. "Do you know what happened?"

"Police could tell you more than we could," he grunted, putting away his penlight, then pressing gently around Jake's wound. "If it's any consolation, the other two are in worse shape."

Mary Stauros blinked, suddenly lucid. "The other two...?"

"Seems the gunman shot three men when they stepped off the Red Line at Thirty-Fifth. Two of them were his intended victims. Drug dealers from Bridgeport. Your son was...well, an innocent bystander, I'm afraid."

Innocent? There was no better word for Jake Stauros.

"Will he...regain consciousness?" his mother asked, gnawing on her lip, stray wisps of hair matted to her forehead damp with sweat.

"He's coming around a bit now." The doctor turned fully toward them, momentarily blocking their view of Jake, and lowered his voice to a whisper. "I can't offer you much hope, ladies. He was struck several times. The bullets did a great deal of damage internally, and his bleeding is extensive. We're doing what we can, but I want you to prepare yourselves."

He turned back to his patient, his gaze assessing Jake's battered form. "He's headed to surgery next, then we'll move him to a private room as soon as he's stabilized. Sorry the news isn't better. I'm sure he's a nice young man."

Nice? There were much better words for Jake Stauros.

Godly. Pure. Wise. Righteous. Kind. Loving. Sacrificial.

"May we…speak with him?" Jake's mother sounded bruised and beaten, as though she herself were the one bleeding internally.

Like me, seven years ago. Wanting to die in Luna's place. Wanting to save her.

Mary Margaret, who knew only too well the pain of losing a child, wanted no such grief to come to her new friend. She cupped the woman's elbow, offering silent support as they both stepped closer to the side of the gurney.

"Jake, it's Mom."

"And Mary Margaret," she added softly, praying he would open his eyes so he might see them. And they might see him.

His eyelids fluttered, then opened. With great effort, he tried to speak. "Don't…" He swallowed and tried again. "Don't…cry."

"I'm…s-sorry," his mother sputtered, her sobs increasing.

"We love you, Jake." Mary Margaret felt the hope inside her struggling for air. "The doctors are doing everything they can to help you."

He shook his head ever so slightly, his gaze focused on her. "My turn."

"Your turn?" *Father, what does he mean?*

He let his eyes roam around the room, then land on Mary Margaret.

"Oh! Your turn to be in the ER, you mean." *Of course.* The last time they'd both been in this room, it was she who lay bleeding on the gurney and he who was looking down, praying for her to live.

Mary Margaret Delaney would give anything to trade places with him now.

A minor commotion not far behind them brought Little John and Marijane rushing to Jake's bedside before a nurse intervened, her words a terse whisper. "This is not a hospital room, and there are no visitation hours in the ER. Immediate family only. If you'll wait in the reception area, we'll have him admitted to a private room after surgery and you can visit him there. One at a time. Are we clear?"

They meekly backed out of the busy ER, waiting for what felt like hours instead of minutes while Jake was wheeled to an operating room. Mary Margaret gave John and Marijane what little information she had. When Sallie Mae came stumbling through the door ten minutes later, Mary went over it all again.

"Mrs. Stauros?" A nurse approached the group, clipboard in hand. "Your son is in surgery. It should take about an hour. There's a waiting area outside the OR. It might be easier if you used the regular hospital entrance half a block down."

They were there in minutes, traveling in a huddle, daring anyone to get in their way. Others soon joined them, passing out tissues and cold sodas from the machine, making phone calls, speaking in hushed tones. Two detectives came, asked questions, and left. So did reporters from the *Tribune* and *Sun-Times*. It wasn't until a nurse appeared with a progress report that the noisy waiting room abruptly grew quiet.

"Mr. Stauros survived the surgery, but his condition is still grave. We're moving him from recovery to a private room." She looked at his mother, seated on a tan couch, one of the Sisters on either side. "Are you ready to see him, ma'am?"

Mary Stauros stood. "Of course."

She was only gone for a few minutes before she returned, her eyes swollen and red. "I can't do this alone," she whispered. "I want all my Sisters"—she glanced at Little John, who was looking more forlorn than all of them—"and my brother to be with me. To be with Jake. Look, if he's in as bad shape as they say, surely it can't matter at this point."

Flagrantly ignoring hospital rules, the six of them tiptoed into the room and clustered at the foot of his bed. The sheets were clean, the wounds were dressed, yet patches of blood still appeared here and there, grim reminders of his fragile mortality.

Little John's voice was missing its usual bravado. "Jake, we're here for you, buddy."

"Yes, we are," his mother echoed, her voice faint.

Jake's slowly opened his eyes. The expression of love on his face was so pure it stung Mary Margaret's eyes to look at him.

"John," he whispered. He struggled to swallow, then spoke again. "Take care of my mom, okay?"

John reached out a beefy hand, enveloping Mary Stauros's shoulder in a firm squeeze. His voice, however, was not nearly as steady. "I will, Jake."

Jake closed his eyes for a moment. Recovering his strength, Mary Margaret imagined. She folded her hands tightly together so she wouldn't break every rule in the place and touch him. He was in too much pain and she too full of germs for such a thing. She would touch him with her heart, then, and speak to him with her eyes. That was all she could do.

It would have to be enough. *Lord, let it be enough.*

He opened his eyes again. "Others?"

"He means the other two men who were shot," Mary Margaret guessed, not surprised when he gave a small nod. Minutes earlier she'd heard two reporters in the waiting area, comparing notes. The news was not good. Was it fair to keep it from him? Did he really have to know?

Mary thought of the Jake she knew and had her answer. He would want the truth. "I'm sorry to tell you this, Jake, but both of those men died."

A cloud of sorrow covered his face. She was sorry she'd told him, sorry to make him suffer further, sorry to steal his own hope of recovery.

Did he harbor such a hope? Or did he know the truth?

Mary gazed into his brown eyes, muddy with pain, and in them recognized the certainty of death. *He knows.*

She could not stop him from bleeding, let alone from dying. But she could help him prepare his heart for the journey ahead. Yes, she could do that.

His jacket lay forgotten on a bedside chair. Mary eased her way across the room as the others offered words of comfort. She wanted to give him the encouraging words he needed most. Mary slid her hand inside his pocket and smiled. *Yes!* Her red Bible was right where he'd put it. Could that have been only hours ago? When all was well. When Jake was still whole.

She bit her lip, sensing another wave of tears coming. *Let me read to him, Lord. Store my tears in your bottle, and let me read.*

Mary Margaret opened the Scriptures to the psalms, to the one she had learned by heart but did not trust herself to remember at this dark hour. She began to read. "'Out of the depths I cry to you, O Lord.'"

She watched his eyes flicker, then focus on her. *Yes,* he seemed to be saying.

"'O Lord, hear my voice. Let your ears be attentive to my cry for mercy.'" The word stuck in her throat, and Mary Margaret had to stop. *Mercy, Lord. Have mercy on Jake.*

She swallowed and pressed on. "'If you, O LORD, kept a record of sins, O Lord, who could stand?'" *Grace, Lord. Jake needs it, right now.*

The others had grown silent, listening as she read.

Little John finally spoke, his eyes on Jake. "We're standing with you, brother."

Jake blinked to acknowledge John's words. Already he'd grown too weak to shake his head.

Mary Margaret, fighting down panic, kept reading. "'But with you there is forgiveness; therefore you are feared.' I know what that means now, Jake. Not fear, but awe." She wet her lips, then realized they were already salty with tears.

Taking a deep breath, she read the final verse. "'I wait for the LORD, my soul waits, and in his word I put my hope.'" Mary Margaret closed the book and held it against her chest, pressing it hard against her breastbone, trying to hold the sobs inside. Of all the emotions churning inside her that terrible day, hope was not among them.

Jake had closed his eyes again, then opened them. His brown eyes said what his parched lips could not. *Hope, Mary Margaret. Hope.*

What could she do but nod? *Yes. I'll try.* She was failing miserably, but she would try to hope, try to see the purpose in his suffering. Try to understand why Jake—Jake, of all the people in Chicago—should have to face death because of the evil that ran amuck in the world around them. The world he wanted to help. The world he wanted to change. The world he wanted to *love.* That world had put a bullet in his chest and called him worthless.

Jake, who was worth everything to her, who had saved her life and pointed her back to God. That Jake, worthless?

"Mary Margaret, can you read some more?" Sallie Mae's voice was small and tinny, her eyes huge, filled with pain, as she knew her own must be.

"I can try."

They took turns reading all through the middle of the day. By noon, the sky had darkened, and the threat of rain seeped into the room. Mary Stauros turned on a bedside lamp and smoothed his brow with her mother's touch. The head nurse, knowing they were ignoring hospital policy, mercifully looked the other way. Doctors came and went, checking Jake's wounds, making no promises. Their faces were grim.

As it neared three o'clock, Jake managed to say only one thing: "John 12:25."

Little John, confused, pointed to his watch. "No, brother, it's later than that."

"He means the Scripture verse," Mary Margaret said as kindly as she could. Poor John was on the edge. They all were. She quickly turned to the verse, reading silently, then looked at Jake. "Here's what it says: 'The man who loves his life will lose it, while the man who hates his life in this world will keep it for eternal life.'"

Jake smiled for a moment, then clenched his jaw as though seized by a horrific pain they couldn't begin to fathom.

"Jake! Jake, are you okay?" At John's shout, the nurses came running.

"Out!" one small woman ordered, nearly pushing them through the door. More of the nursing staff hustled in the room behind her, while Mary Margaret and the others hovered in the hallway, distraught at being separated from Jake at the moment he needed them most.

They could barely make out Jake's voice, strained to the limit. "Don't... leave. Don't leave me, Father!"

Mary Margaret couldn't bear it. "We're here, Jake. We're right here."

Seconds later a loud cry of pain filled the air. Then silence.

Jake Stauros was no more.

"No-o-o!" His mother's sobs echoed down the sterile hallway outside Jake's room where medical personnel whispered in confidential tones. They came and went with soft-soled movements, averting their eyes from the small huddle of mourners.

Mary Margaret gripped his mother's hand, comforting the grieving woman with meaningless words. Inside her a hard knot was forming. *Why, God? Why Jake?*

The image of Jake's gentle features twisted in agony hung before her like a cruel painting. Jake Stauros was the last person on earth who deserved such a terrible death. *Where were you, Lord? How could you let your servant die like that? How could you watch and not intercede?*

There was no other word for that bitter knot inside her but *anger.* A tiny fist of rage tightening in her gut. *You did nothing to stop that gunman, Lord. Just as you did nothing to stop Luna.*

Gritting her teeth to maintain control, Mary Margaret steered Jake's mother to an empty chair down the hall. *Only the good die young.* Another one of her mother's pet phrases. Jake was thirty-three. *Too young, Lord. Fifty years too young.*

"Mrs. Stauros?" An intern not much older than Jake approached them. His eyes were kind, but the news he bore was not. "The attending physician has pronounced your son dead of internal injuries. No bones were broken, but his wounds proved fatal, and his blood loss was..." He lowered his gaze to the green tile floor. "I'm very sorry, ma'am. Might I have one of the nurses call a funeral home for you?"

Jake's mother turned to Little John, a blank look on her face.

"I'll take care of all that, Mary." He mentioned a funeral director on Southport Avenue. When she nodded listlessly, he took off down the hall in search of a phone, his long stride resolute.

Mary Margaret envied him the assignment. Was there nothing she could do but weep? No practical way she could help? Mary needed her, of that she was certain. And Jake needed her to be strong for all of them.

A question gnawed at her. *Who will be strong for me?* Jake, the one who had saved her from her own death, was gone. There would be no one to support her, encourage her, teach her. No one to fend off her anger.

No one to drive away her demons.

"They won't come back," Jake had assured her whenever she'd broached the subject. "You belong to God now, Mary Margaret. Nothing to worry about."

And she hadn't worried, not since Ash Wednesday, not since God had revealed himself to her and those taunting nuisances had disappeared. Jake's words still echoed in her heart: *"Love the Lord, Mary. Listen to his voice. Hold fast to him."* She loved God but felt no love in return at that dire moment. She was listening, but God wasn't talking. And how could she hold on to something she couldn't see?

"Ja-a-ake." His name came out on a moan before she could stop it.

Sallie Mae bent to hug her, wrapping her slender arms around her shoulders, pressing her soft cheek against Mary's, both of them wet with tears. "I know, Mary Margaret, I know. It's so unfair."

It was several minutes before Mary Margaret could pull herself together, dabbing at her nose with a much-used tissue. She had to think clearly, had to address the issues at hand, if only to keep herself from falling apart. "Sallie Mae, I need you to call the elders and make arrangements for Sunday."

Her eyebrows lifted slightly. "Sunday?"

"Easter," Mary Margaret reminded her, then turned to Jake's mother. "What if we have our Sunday morning service at eleven as usual, Mary, then follow it with a memorial service for Jake at one? Would that please you?"

Mary Margaret watched Jake's mother, waiting for some sign of approval, but the woman was staring at her hands, not paying attention. "Jake would surely applaud the simplicity of it, don't you think, Mary?" Suddenly she wasn't certain. What right did she have to be making such decisions? *Because you're here, Mary Margaret. Because you care.*

Finally, Mary Stauros nodded her consent, then slumped forward in a fresh spate of tears. Sallie Mae spoke softly to her for a moment, then gathered the others who hovered nearby, their eyes red, their faces blotchy. "We'll be at the church if you need us," Sallie Mae murmured as they turned to go. "Keep an eye out for the under...the...uh..."

Mary Margaret lifted her hand, holding the word at bay. *No need to say it.* The one who would take Jake's body and put it in the ground. The one who would arrive shortly wearing a plain dark suit and a somber expression. The one who would manage the next three days, then fade quietly away. *That one.*

"I'll watch for him," Mary promised, waving the Sisters on their way.

The funeral director walked up minutes later, looking exactly as she'd imagined.

"My name is Vincent Romano," he said in a voice that could calm anyone's nerves. Even hers. "I was told to ask for Mary."

"I'm Mary Margaret Delaney, a friend of the...of Jake's." She patted Mary's limp hand. "And this is Mary Stauros, his mother."

"Is there a Mr. Stauros?" he asked.

Both women shook their heads.

"I see. Will you be making all the decisions then, Mrs. Stauros?"

Her tear-streaked face looked up, sorrow and grief etched on her features. "Ask Mary Margaret."

"Fine." His relief was unmistakable. "My associates are handling all the details here."

Mary grimaced at the euphemism. *He means the body.* The men would be handling Jake's body. Like they handled Luna's body. In a bag. Then a box. *Lord, give me strength.*

She managed to ask, "Shall we follow you to the funeral home?"

"If you would, Mrs....ah?"

"Delaney. Though 'Mary Margaret' will do; that's what everyone calls me." She lowered her voice and bent toward Jake's mother. "Come, Mary, let's walk back to church and get your car. The fresh air will do us good."

She helped Mary to her feet, distraught to find her friend had aged twenty years in the hour since Jake's death. Hunched over, her face gray, her features slack, Mary Stauros looked ready for the grave herself. *Just as I looked seven years ago.* Long-forgotten memories were starting to surface, few of them good, none of them welcome.

Mary Margaret made sure their coats were buttoned, then steered Mary through the winding corridors and out into the chilly day, headed for the church. "Are there other relatives we need to contact?"

"No." Mary dropped her chin a notch further. "Jake always said the people at Calvary Fellowship were his family."

Mary Margaret paused at the curb and squeezed her elbow. "He was very much loved, Mary. I don't understand any of what happened today, but I know this much: Jake loved the world, and most of that world loved him back."

"Most, but not everyone."

They looked up to discover a grim-faced Charles Farris marching across the parking lot, waving his cane. "Is it true? Was the poor fool shot?"

Mary Margaret skidded to a stop, appalled by his words. "Charles, for heaven's sake!" She slipped her arm around Mary's shoulder as though to protect her from his cruel verbal blows. "He…he died, Charles."

"Sorry to hear that, Mary." He banged his cane on the pavement, his gruff voice rising. "But the truth is, he brought it on himself. Going to that part of the city, thinking he could somehow change those people."

Those people. Looking at poor, bitter, misguided Charles Farris, Mary Delaney felt her own anger dissipate. If that's what it looked like, she wanted no part of it. "Charles, this is neither the time nor the place for this discussion. If you'll excuse us, I'm taking Mary to the funeral home. See if you can't make yourself useful at church."

While he stamped off in the opposite direction, Mary Margaret guided Mary toward the cramped space behind the church where the woman's Toyota sat parked, a few stray lily leaves still strewn across the backseat. "Can you drive, or shall I call Suzy?"

Mary Stauros shook her head, clearly agitated. "I'll drive. I'd like…" She glanced over, her cheeks stained with red. "I'd like it to be just the two of us this evening, if you don't mind. I know it will be so…so chaotic later." She pulled out her keys. "It isn't far. I'm okay to drive. Really, I am."

Friday afternoon traffic was heavy, so Mary Margaret sat quietly on the passenger side, letting Mary concentrate on her driving. The silence between them was a safe cocoon, shutting out the pain. Maybe if they didn't talk about it, their heartache would subside enough for them to function, to go through the motions of living.

When they arrived at the funeral home, two familiar cars were parked in the lot. *Joe and Nick.* As expected, the men were waiting inside, talking in subdued tones with Vincent Romano.

The funeral director greeted them with a slight nod. "Mrs. Stauros, Mrs. Delaney. Thank you for coming."

Joe and Nick both offered stoic condolences, though their eyes had a distinct sheen, and their chins were none too steady. "We're here for you, Mary," Joe said, patting her arm.

"There are some decisions to be made," Mr. Romano reminded them. "If you'll step in here, we'll make this as quick and painless for you as possible."

There was nothing painless about choosing a casket. "Jake would want the simplest, plainest one available," Mary Stauros said, grieved by the display of expensive woods and rich velvets. "You're going to put the casket in a grave, aren't you, never to be seen again?"

Mr. Romano shrugged in understanding. "We do have an alternative container. It's an unfinished fiberboard box. Not on display, of course, but if that is your preference…"

"Yes, yes. Please."

"You might want to reconsider if there is to be a viewing."

Mary Stauros shook her head. "No viewing. No graveside ceremony. Only a funeral ceremony at Jake's church this Sunday at one."

His pen hovered over the paper. "Easter Sunday?"

Mary Margaret nodded. "Odd as it may seem, it could not be more appropriate for those of us who love him. Loved…loved, I mean."

"I see." He made a notation on an important-looking form. "Do you have a family plot?"

Jake's mother's eyes flew wide at that. "N-no. No, we…I don't."

"I can help there." Both Marys turned to find Joe pulling a sheaf of papers from his jacket pocket. "I took the liberty of calling Graceland Cemetery this afternoon and making some…arrangements."

Graceland. Mary swallowed repeatedly, holding back the bile that stung her throat. *Not another grave at Graceland.*

Joe handed Mary Stauros the papers, his kind expression like salve on an open wound. "If you want it, this plot is meant for Jake."

She took the papers with trembling fingers. "We…I can't possibly afford to buy this."

"No need to." He pointed to his signature. "It's already been paid for, in full."

"How generous," Mr. Romano murmured, smiling. "That will ease the funeral expenses for you considerably, Mrs. Stauros."

Nick, always a quiet man, patted his shirt pocket where a checkbook stood at attention. "I'll be taking care of all the other expenses. Including the…preparation of the body and the…uh…um…"

Mary's eyes widened. "We don't have to do that, do we? Embalm him, I mean?"

"Not if there will be no viewing, no. Suppose we sign a few papers, and then we'll be ready to proceed."

Mary Margaret could bear it no longer. "Where *is* he? Where is Jake right now?"

For the first time that afternoon, Mr. Romano looked shocked. "Why, he's…he's in the preparation room. Surely you don't want to see him now?"

Mary Margaret nodded emphatically. "Yes, I do." A quick glance at Mary confirmed it. "We both do."

Joe and Nick stepped back, ill at ease. "We paid our respects when Jake arrived," Joe explained. "If you ladies will forgive us, we'll let you have a moment alone with him while we get back to church, see how we can be useful there." He touched Mary Stauros on the shoulder. "Will you be all right this evening by yourself? You are more than welcome at our place. Karen can fix up the guest room…"

"You've been more than generous already, Joe. Thank you." She reached up and patted his hand. "We'll talk in the morning."

The two moved toward the front door while Mr. Romano led them back through a maze of hallways, stopping short of a door marked EMPLOYEES ONLY. "If you would kindly wait in this room, I'll have his body brought out to you."

Nodding, they stepped into the small, windowless room. It was chilly and sterile, the walls unadorned. Not a public room. A utility room. *A room for saying good-bye.* Mary shivered as she heard a door glide open and a table being wheeled into the room.

Without a word, he was there, among them.

Jake was scrubbed clean. Not a drop of blood remained, though his wounds still gaped, ragged and surreal looking. His face had lost its grimace. "He seems…peaceful," his mother said, then turned away.

Mary Margaret closed her eyes, fighting a fresh round of nausea. That's what people always said, wasn't it? *He looks so peaceful.* Jake's death was anything but peace filled. But perhaps now, as he stood in the presence of God, his expression was not misplaced.

She opened her eyes again, took a deep breath, and laid her hand gently on his arm.

It was a mistake. He was colder than the room.

Jake is dead. Jake is dead.

Reality hit her full force, like a runaway freight train. Jake was alive in heaven, but he was dead on earth. She snatched back her hand, shoving it into her pocket to warm it. *He's dead, Mary. Dead.*

She would never hear his voice again, never hear his laugh. Never hear him say her name. *Mary.* Why hadn't she paid more attention the last time they were together? Had he said it then?

"I didn't know it would be the last time," she moaned, hardly noticing the concerned looks on the faces of those around her. "I didn't know."

"None of us knew, Mary Margaret." His mother gently led her away, back into the warmer hallway, away from the cold room where a shell of a man lay in eternal sleep.

They moved into the undertaker's office, furnished in subtle tones of navy and gray. *Just like his suit. Just like his eyes.* Mary Margaret sank into an upholstered chair, suddenly aware of how exhausted she was. Every muscle ached; every joint groaned in protest.

"So," Mr. Romano was saying, pulling out yet another form. "Let's take care of a few more details, and then we'll be finished for this evening."

Finished. The word rang like a death knell in her heart.

Chapter Eight

THE DEWY MORN

The morn is up again, the dewy morn...
And living as if earth contained no tomb.
GEORGE GORDON BYRON

Sunday could not dawn soon enough for Mary Margaret.

It had rained overnight, leaving the ground soggy and the atmosphere laden with a heavy mist. Standing on her front steps at barely past six, she drank it in like a thirsty woman, letting the cool, damp air fill her lungs. Since Jake's death she was keenly aware of the simple gift of breath. Of sensation. Of *life*.

Luna had thrown her life away.

Jake had his life taken from him.

Mary, you are not to blame for either one.

She slowly exhaled, a burden of guilt rolling off her shoulders into the thick morning air. Perhaps the Lord had called out to Luna, but she'd refused to listen. That was so like Luna, to push away love. And Jake? He'd told them over and over: *For to me, to live is Christ and to die is gain.* Their earthly loss was his gain in glory.

Mary Margaret pulled her raincoat tighter around her neck, looking at the overcast skies above. Bad weather or good, she had one important task left. Yesterday she'd found Jake's red tie looped over the coatrack in his office. His favorite tie—his only tie. Surely he would want to be buried wearing it. The casket would be sealed shut by the time it arrived at the church for the memorial service. Hours later it would be buried under the fertile soil of Graceland Cemetery.

If she was ever going to manage this final preparation, it had to be now.

A car turned onto her street. The sight of JoAnn's battered Dodge lifted her spirits. *Bless you, Sisters.* She walked down the steps and toward the curb, smiling as their faces came into view. Marijane, Sallie Mae, and JoAnn had agreed to join her on her unorthodox morning venture. Jake's mother had begged off, weary from all the pressures since Friday, media intrusions among them. Even in an urban area the size of Chicago, murders in broad daylight were so rare they made the front page. The memorial service would no doubt be a circus.

All the better to have this time alone with Jake. *Hurry, girls.*

JoAnn pulled her car up to the curb, waving her forward. Mary yanked open the door, wincing as the metal groaned in protest. "Good morning, Jo." She slid in the front, then reached around to greet each one with a touch on the shoulder, a pat on the hand. "Thank you for doing this. Before this day is done, we'll be glad we got an early start."

They were a subdued group, driving through the foggy streets of the sleeping city. "Turn here," Mary suggested, an idea forming in her mind. "It's a bit out of our way, but let's swing by Graceland Cemetery first. I'd like to see…" She swallowed, then started again. "I'd like to find Jake's burial plot." *Plot* was such a horrible word, though *grave* was hardly an improvement. "Would you mind? I have the location."

"Sure, Mary Margaret," JoAnn agreed, stepping on the gas. "Who knows when the funeral home will open its doors anyway?"

Mary blanched. She hadn't even thought of that possibility. What if they didn't allow Sunday visitors? What if she couldn't see Jake at all? *Easy, Mary.* She took a deep breath to calm herself, watching familiar landmarks as they passed in and out of sight. Lincoln Park gave way to Wrigleyville, and soon the ballpark loomed on her right.

Everything she saw reminded her of Jake. His treasured Cubs cap with the trademark red *C.* Tickets for the first home game of the season, waiting untouched on his desk. Friday afternoon when the opening pitch had sailed across the plate, Jake had been fighting for his life. And losing. *Oh, Jake.*

A fresh wave of grief rolled over her, flattening her. Mary sank deeper in her seat under the sheer weight of it. She would forget for a moment that Jake was dead, and then the terrible truth would overwhelm her all over again. The taunting voices of her past remained blessedly silent, but God was silent, too, as though in mourning with her.

JoAnn nudged her gently with her elbow. "We're coming up on Irving Park Road, Mary Margaret. Tell me where to turn once we're inside the cemetery."

An icy finger of fear slid down Mary's spine. She straightened, hoping to make it go away, but the images were too strong. There was the vine-covered Victorian statue of a woman embracing a cross, her long hair so like Luna's had been. Elaborate mausoleums of myriad styles and fashions—Greek, Roman, Egyptian—stood watch over the smaller graves, belittling them even in death.

She'd practically lived here on many a moonlit summer night, hiding behind the headstones, hoping no one would see her lingering around the one with the intricate floral carvings and the simple name: *Luna Delaney.*

"Turn here," she said, her voice strained. The bronze-robed figure, *Eternal Silence*, guarded the path to Section A, where Joe had purchased a resting place for Jake. She turned away from the ominous statue and pointed farther down the winding road where a square tent straddled a dark patch of dirt. "That's it, on the right."

The four of them climbed out of the car without a word, picking their way across the wet grass until they stood in a semicircle at the foot of the grave. It was covered with a board, but they all knew what waited beneath it: a yawning hole in the earth, a gaping wound waiting to be stitched closed with dirt.

Perhaps it was the eerie silence of the hour or the way the mist hovered about the graves that drew them closer together until they were tightly joined, arm in arm. The women took turns praying, then weeping, then comforting one another, until Mary Margaret tugged at Sallie Mae's sleeve. "We have to go." She heard the urgency in her tone, felt the pounding of her heart. "I need to see him, don't you?"

Sallie met her gaze. "Yes. We need to make sure things have been done...properly. That he's..."

"Ready." Mary nodded, hurrying them toward the car.

Minutes later they were speeding west on Diversey Parkway, ignoring the speed limit, talking all at once. The open grave had somehow opened them up as well, and their questions tumbled over one another.

"What if the door's locked?"

"It's nearly seven, isn't it?"

"Surely there's a doorbell?"

When they pulled into the small parking lot adjacent to the funeral home, theirs was the only car on the premises. That and a hearse, its curtains closed tight against prying eyes.

Mary led the four of them to the front entrance, lifting a finger to her lips. "Shh, Sisters." The windows were dark. The place looked deserted. Mary rang the bell and heard it echoing through the unseen interior. But no one opened the massive door; no footsteps sounded through the empty hallways.

"Try the door," Marijane whispered.

Mary squared her shoulders, determined to be brave, to risk setting off an alarm and bringing the Chicago police bearing down on them. She *had* to see Jake, had to see that he was properly dressed in his red tie. Not trying the door was not an option. Her fingers wrapped around the cold brass knob, then turned.

It opened. It was unlocked. *Unlocked!*

Swallowing the last of her apprehension, Mary pushed the door open and stepped across the threshold, her eyes adjusting to the early morning darkness. Within the last hour the sun had risen, but the thick clouds hid any evidence of it. "Hello!" she said, raising her voice, loath to move much farther. Shadows filled the foyer and waiting area. The rooms on both sides of the hall were dark.

Not a sound greeted them.

"Hello?" All four of them began calling out, giving one another courage as they moved deeper into the funeral home. "Anybody here?"

All at once a figure appeared from a side room. The four of them gasped in unison, falling back as though struck.

"Oh!" Mary wet her lips, longing for a drink of water for her parched mouth. "I'm so sorry. We didn't see you."

A blond young man gazed at them. He was dressed in white, head to toe. A brand-new lab uniform, it seemed. Spotless, with the creases still showing. Even his teeth were white as snow. "Didn't mean to scare you. Are you looking for Jake Stauros? The young preacher who was murdered?"

Mary's swallowed. "Y-yes. We are." Who *was* this man? She'd never laid eyes on him before.

The stranger spoke again. "Why are you looking for him here?" He tipped his head, studying her. "He's already gone."

"Gone?" Sallie Mae blurted out, her eyes blue saucers against her pale face. "What are you talking about? We've been to his grave. We know he's not there. Where else…?"

"I can't tell you where he is, ma'am. I can only tell you where he *isn't*." He gestured toward the darkened viewing rooms. "Look for yourself."

The Sisters exchanged wary glances, then Mary shook her head. "We believe you. It's…well, we were hoping to…see him." Her cheeks warmed. How foolish the whole thing seemed now! Showing up at the crack of dawn to dress a dead body. *What were you thinking, Mary?*

JoAnn checked her watch. "Surely they haven't already taken him to our church?"

The young man shrugged. "That would seem the most likely place to look."

Pete and Little John were already at Calvary, placing bulletins on the seats, when the four Sisters arrived, breathless and agitated. They hurried into the sanctuary, tossing aside purses and coats. "We've been to the funeral home," Mary managed between gulps of air. "Jake's body isn't there—"

"What?" Pete threw down a handful of bulletins and turned toward them, fists on hips. "Don't tell me the funeral director has taken him to the wrong church."

"He's not at Graceland Cemetery either," JoAnn volunteered.

"You went to the cemetery?" Pete looked more than a little put out with them. "Ladies, why didn't you call my cell phone? You're saying the casket wasn't at the funeral home?"

"Right." Mary's throat tightened. "We haven't seen the body since Friday.

I don't know where they've taken him. Maybe you should go over there with me, fellas, and talk to this young man—"

"Yes!" Sallie Mae jumped in. "He was dressed in white, right down to his shoes—"

"What young man?" Pete looked exasperated. The stress of the last three days had taken its toll on all of them. "Look, I'll call the place right now and straighten things out."

Mary followed him into the office to track down the number for him. As she'd feared, there was no answer. "Look, suppose *you* go over there, Pete. I'll come with you." She glanced behind her where the others were gathered, their faces filled with concern. "Not to worry, we'll get all this straightened out. Little John, you're driving."

Minutes later it was John who cautiously opened the unlocked door but Pete who walked through first, leading with his chin. "Well? Where is this guy? The one in white Sallie Mae was babbling about."

"I...don't know," Mary confessed, her spirits sagging. Had they hurried there for nothing?

Pete pointed to a book resting on the table in the foyer. "Isn't that Jake's?"

Mary blinked. *His Bible.* The large study version he used Sunday mornings, bound in white leather. His preaching Bible, Jake had called it, always jammed with notes and reminders. How had they missed seeing it earlier?

She picked it up, her hands shaking. It felt warm, as if someone had just put it aside and walked off. A slim ribbon marked Jake's passage for the day. She let it fall open there, surprised to find it pointing not to last week's sermon text, but this morning's: *John 20.*

John's eyes widened. "How did *that* get here?"

"I dunno." Pete shrugged, consulting his watch. "All I know is, we have a body to find, a sanctuary to prepare, and the biggest crowd we've ever had coming to Calvary in a couple of hours. I say we head back, and I'll make the necessary phone calls from there. This undertaker has a cell phone, doesn't he? I'll find him."

Pete stomped out the door, John close behind him still scratching his head. "Sorry, Mary." He paused and glanced over his shoulder. "Do you want a ride back to the church?"

"No," she whispered. Another wave of grief was headed her way. She could feel it building inside her, threatening to crash against the shores of her heart. "I think I'll wait here. Send Marijane for me a little later, would you? I'll let you know if I find out anything here."

Little John waved, then disappeared down the steps, swallowed up by the morning mist.

Mary sank into a nearby chair, feeling her momentary hopes sinking as well. Tears dropped onto the white Bible clutched in her hands. She quickly wiped them off with her sleeve, but they kept falling like rain, faster and faster. *Why aren't you here, Jake?*

"Surely you're not still looking for Jake?"

She whirled around, one hand pressed against her throat to hold back a scream. "Who…?"

The young man in white had returned, this time with a partner in similar attire.

"Do you two work in the…?" She couldn't find the words for what she was picturing in her mind. A room where they prepared the bodies, draining them of fluids, arranging their features. Mary sensed her own face draining, her cheeks growing cool.

She brushed away her tears, too embarrassed to look at the men any longer. "They've taken my pastor's body, but I don't know where." Maybe this time she'd get an answer. *Please, Lord.*

Mary felt a prompting inside. *Turn around.*

And so she turned, not knowing who or what she might find.

A man she had never seen before stood behind her. Not dressed in white, as the others. Dressed like a man who carried a spade on his shoulder. A gardener. *A gravedigger.*

"Ma'am," he said. "Who are you looking for?"

"Oh! I…" She spun away from him, feeling foolish talking to yet another stranger. Had there ever been a more difficult morning in all her life? "If you've taken him someplace, tell me where, and I'll see that things are taken care of."

Then he said the last thing she expected.

He said her name.

"Mary?"

A chill ran through her bones as she glanced up. The two men in white were gone—how had they slipped away so quietly?—leaving her alone with a man she did not know, yet who seemed to know her.

The dimly lit waiting room of the funeral home offered little comfort. His voice, though, was soothing as an Irish lullaby.

"Do you know who I am?"

Mary turned around in her seat to face him once more, clutching Jake's Bible as though it had the power to save her, to protect her from calamity. The man who stood before her now was in his thirties, she guessed. Ruddy complexion, dark hair, dark eyes. Something about his demeanor reminded her of Jake. *Calm. Reassuring. Confident.*

Her heart rate slowed, and she took a deep, full breath, the first in many minutes. "I'm afraid I don't recognize you," she confessed, genuinely sorry that this kind-looking young man was a stranger and not a friend. On such a somber morning, an old friend would be a welcome sight. "Have we met?"

"Yes…and no." When he smiled, the resemblance became more obvious. Did Jake have a brother? She couldn't recall him ever mentioning such a thing.

Mary studied his face, looking for clues. "Where did we meet?"

"Graceland Cemetery."

Mary shrank back. Was the man mad? Oh, she knew what *that* looked like only too well. He seemed lucid enough though. "I'm sorry, but in all the times I've been to Graceland, I don't remember running into you there."

"You *have* been there, Mary. Many times. At all hours."

He knows too much. He knows the truth.

She glanced out the window at the gloomy morning, feigning indifference. "So I have. My daughter is buried there."

"Luna Delaney."

Her head snapped back. "Did you…?"

"No, I didn't know her, ma'am." He shifted his weight to the other leg, his dingy work clothes hanging loosely around his muscular frame. "I know her grave." He held out his hands, the creases faintly stained with dirt and grass. The hands of a gardener. "I'm one of the groundskeepers at Graceland."

Oh. "And you…saw me…there?"

He nodded, and his smile widened. "You're not an easy woman to miss, Mrs. Delaney. All that wild hair and that big coat." His kind eyes appraised her. "Seems you've changed a bit."

Mary touched her hair, pulled back into a smooth twist, then glanced down at her tailored black dress and heels, her new dress coat, her simple gold jewelry. It was as though she were seeing herself for the first time. She *had* undergone a rather remarkable transformation. When had that happened exactly? Could she point to a week, a day, an hour, a single moment? Was it at Lincoln Park? In Jake's office? At Saint Clement? In Luna's bedroom that moonlit night?

The when and where don't matter, Mary. It's the who. Who changed you?

Jake Stauros had been her teacher, her guide, her friend, her mentor.

But Jake hadn't changed her.

Jesus had.

Mary's face stretched into a smile. *Yes!* He was the one who had made her whole, made her new, set her free.

She stood, wanting to be eye to eye with this young gardener so he might see the difference for himself. "Yes, I have changed. I'm…I'm glad it shows."

He ducked his head, eying Jake's Bible. "What's that you've got in your hands?" As he said it, he reached over and turned on a table lamp, filling the shadowy waiting room with warmth and light.

Mary held up the book pressed between her palms. "My pastor's favorite Bible. I'm not sure how it ended up here, but it's a blessing to have it, today of all days."

The gardener nodded. "He was a fine man, Jake Stauros was."

Mary's throat tightened. "Did you know him?"

"Yes…and no." His smile disarmed her. "Couple of his church members were buried at Graceland over the last year or so. He handled the graveside services." Glancing down at his thick work boots, he tapped one heel against the other. "I handled the graves."

"I see." Mary checked her watch, surprised to find it was almost nine. "What brings you here this morning?"

His dark eyes lost their sparkle. "There's been some confusion about the time we're to expect Jake's…to expect him at the cemetery. When I called here to confirm, I didn't get an answer. Since I was on my way home to change for church, I thought I'd stop by, see if anyone was around."

Mary nodded sympathetically. "We're a little confused as well. He's to be delivered to Calvary Fellowship by noon. The service is at one. Then I imagine he'll be at Graceland sometime after two."

"No graveside service?"

She shrugged, uncertain how to explain it. "His mother insists Jake never wanted that. They'd talked about it after every funeral, how the body in the ground was meaningless. It's the resurrected body that matters."

He nodded at the Bible in her hands. "Is that what it says in there?"

"Let's find out." She sat down again and opened to the concordance, as Mary Stauros had taught her.

"Look up 'resurrection,'" he said in that gentle voice that reminded her so of Jake. Leaning over her shoulder, he watched her turn to a passage in the New Testament. "Go ahead, read it."

She held the small text closer to the light. "'So will it be with the resurrection of the dead. The body that is sown is perishable, it is raised imperishable; it is sown in dishonor, it is raised in glory; it is sown in weakness, it is raised in power.'"

Mary Margaret paused, letting the words sink in. "So our resurrected bodies will be *better* than our earthly ones?"

His laugh was a great, warm, rumbling thing. "Decidedly better, Mrs. Delaney. Keep reading."

Swallowing the tears that were gathering in her throat, she forged on. "'When the perishable has been clothed with the imperishable, and the mortal with immortality, then the saying that is written will come true: 'Death has been swallowed up in victory.'" The book fell into her lap as she stared at the page, incredulous. "*Victory?* How is death victorious?"

"Because it doesn't win, Mary. 'Where, O death, is your victory? Where, O death, is your sting?'" He sighed expansively. "When the body is set free from mortal death, the spirit soars with eternal life."

She closed the Bible slowly, staring up at him in amazement. "Who *are* you?"

He chuckled, moving toward the door. "Just a gardener, ma'am. A groundskeeper at a cemetery." Turning back toward her, he studied her with compassion in his eyes. "You do understand, don't you, Mary? Jesus is alive...and so is Jake. His spirit is alive in heaven. And he's alive in you."

"What...? In me?"

"The truth he planted in you is like a living seed. And it's growing, Mary. I can see it in your eyes. Jake taught you well."

"Yes, he did." A fresh wind of hope blew through her, filling her, lifting her out of her chair. "He was my teacher." She reached out her hand, tentatively touching his sleeve. "Like you. You've taught me something this morning."

"Jake hasn't left you to fend for yourself, Mary." He glanced at the grandfather clock in the corner. "Gotta go, ma'am." His wink was playful. "It's Easter, remember? You have somewhere you need to be as well."

"I guess I do." She reached for her purse, forgotten on a side table. "I need to get to church and—"

"Tell the others," he said firmly.

Her eyebrows shot up. "Tell them what?"

"What you've learned. That Jake is alive in Christ." He waved a leathery hand at the Bible. "Everything you need is in there, Mary. You're having a memorial service this afternoon, right? Somebody better remind them what this day is all about."

He backed toward the door, keeping his eyes on her. "Seems to me, with all the changes you've been through, you're the perfect woman to do it."

As he turned to leave, she thrust out her hand. "Forgive my manners. I haven't even asked your name."

"Paul." His handshake was warm, enveloping. "Paul Didaskalos."

"You're Greek then. Like Jake." Her eyes lit up. "Are you two...related?"

He laughed and released her hand. "In a manner of speaking. Now go, Mary. Go tell your church what you've learned this morning."

Mary barely heard him leave, so full were her emotions. Joy and sorrow fought for the upper hand, finally blending into one overflowing, overwhelming sense of peace.

Yes, Lord. I will tell. I will!

"Mary?"

Startled, she looked up to find Marijane in the doorway, car keys in hand, a look of astonishment on her face. "Pete said you needed a ride back to church. Are you...okay, Mary Margaret? You look as if you've seen a ghost."

"A holy one maybe." Laughter poured from her like a fountain bubbling over, spilling over her whole being. "Let's hurry, Marijane." Still laughing, she linked arms with her friend and headed for the front door. "I have so much to tell you, sister. So much to tell everybody. It's been quite a morning."

"No kidding." Marijane pulled the door shut behind them. "I've been pulling my hair out trying to decide what music to use for Jake's memorial service. Got any suggestions?"

Mary, who never thought of herself as a singer, all at once felt a hymn rising to her lips, preparing to float above the misty morning air. Poised at the top of the steps, she threw out her arms and sang with her whole heart, "I know that my Redeemer lives!"

THE STUDY

Chapter Nine

HER INFINITE VARIETY

HER LEGEND

Age cannot wither her, nor custom stale
Her infinite variety.
WILLIAM SHAKESPEARE

Take a deep breath. Our story has only begun, beloved.

If you found yourself rooting for Mary Margaret Delaney, you'll cheer yourself hoarse for the real Mary Magdalene. And if you were drawn to the character of the late Jake Stauros, wait until you meet the One of whom even Jake the Good would confess "the thongs of [his] sandals I am not worthy to stoop down and untie."[1]

His name is Jesus, the star of Mary Magdalene's transformation story and millions of others' stories, including my own.

> After this, Jesus traveled about from one town and village to
> another... *Luke 8:1*

"After" what exactly? Did we miss something?

A few things. Forty days in the wilderness with Satan, a startling church announcement in Nazareth, a ton of miraculous healings, the gathering of twelve disciples, the raising of a young man from the dead in Judea.

Your basic everyday life with the Master.

Mind-blowing, life-changing, earthshaking stuff.

We meet him here following "a period of fairly settled ministry,"[2] when his traveling salvation show had kicked into four-wheel overdrive. Jesus was busy meeting, greeting, and preaching around Galilee, determined to visit both the urban centers and the two-donkey towns. This itinerant teacher who didn't "confine himself to one place, but diffused the beams of his light"[3] wanted to make sure the whole Galilean world heard the good news.

> …proclaiming the good news of the kingdom of God.
> *Luke 8:1*

What "good news" exactly? Forgiveness. Mercy. Eternal life. "Glad tidings to the world that there was hope of its being reformed and reconciled."[4] We still need that good news, sis. We need to hear afresh the promise that we can reconnect our hearts with God, the one who made us and loves us no matter what sort of devilry we've foolishly gotten ourselves into.

Jesus' love for people was written all over his face and all through his words. Already a dozen men were on his ministry team.

> The Twelve were with him… *Luke 8:1*

You know…the twelve apostles. I never can keep those boys straight, so in case this ends up as the million-dollar question on *Who Wants to Be a You-Know-What?* here they all are. (I've added numbers for those among us who are math impaired.)

> (1) Simon (who is called Peter) and (2) his brother Andrew;
> (3) James son of Zebedee, and (4) his brother John;
> (5) Philip and (6) Bartholomew; (7) Thomas and
> (8) Matthew the tax collector; (9) James son of Alphaeus,
> and (10) Thaddaeus; (11) Simon the Zealot and (12) Judas
> Iscariot, who betrayed him. *Matthew 10:2-4*

I want you to notice something about these twelve: They were called, but they weren't cured. None of them was healed of an illness or delivered of demons. They left their day jobs behind them—not a pile of discarded demons, as their spiritual sisters did.

> ...and also some women who had been cured of evil spirits
> and diseases... *Luke 8:2*

"Some women," eh? It wasn't only the Twelve who kept Jesus company. Some *women* followed him too.

MEET THE SISTERS

Luke—bless him—mentioned more women in his gospel than Matthew, Mark, *or* John included in their accounts.[5] He didn't hesitate to show Jesus openly and unashamedly associating with women, even the Bad Girls. *Especially* the Bad Girls. Those of us who *know* we're in trouble (and know we need help) often respond to his offer of grace with more gusto. Jesus said to the chief priests and the elders, "I tell you that crooks and whores are going to precede you into God's kingdom."[6]

Bet *that* got their attention! Whores in heaven? What *is* the world coming to?

It's coming to *grace.*

That grace was manifested in Jesus of Nazareth, a man who valued women. More important, he forgave them. And in the case of these particular female followers mentioned in Luke 8, he delivered them—emptied them, washed them clean, made them whole—doing away with both evil spirits and physical illnesses.

Is there a doctor in the house or *what?!*

Check out his list of patients.

> Mary (called Magdalene) from whom seven demons had
> come out; Joanna the wife of Cuza, the manager of Herod's
> household; Susanna; and many others. *Luke 8:2-3*

Tons more on Mary coming up, naturally, and we'll meet Joanna and Susanna, too. "Some women" could account for those three, but look at the end of the sentence: "and many others." We're talking *lots* of sisters set free from bondage. One woman in a company might be overlooked, but "several women cannot be ignored."[7]

There *is* strength in numbers when you're a bunch of disease-packin', demon-totin' women, the most famous of whom appeared first on the list.

Mary (called Magdalene)... *Luke 8:2*

It's not by accident that Mary Magdalene is mentioned before the others. In her world, "the order of naming indicated the order of importance."[8] Whenever two or three women are mentioned by name with her, Mary Magdalene is listed first *eight* out of nine times. She was clearly a woman of prominence, not to be confused with any other Mary. Everybody knew which woman you were talkin' about when you said "Mary Magdalene."

Wonder *why* they knew her? Because she was wealthy? powerful? famous? beautiful? mad? Or because she was Magdala's busiest harlot?

Keep reading, babe.

HOW A GOOD GIRL WENT BAD

Just as the nefarious name *Jezebel* has become part of our language, so you'll find *magdalen* defined as "(1) a reformed prostitute (2) a house of refuge or reformatory for prostitutes."[9] The image is very clear: long hair, long face, long history of sin.

Most people might sum up her story like this: "Mary Magdalene has gone down in history above all as an attractive and very sinful woman, who thanks to Jesus was converted and repented."[10]

Does that about cover it?

One problem: *None of those elements are true!* Nor can those statements about her be found anywhere in Scripture. Except the "thanks to Jesus" part.

Surprised? Then why *do* we think of Mary Magdalene as a Bad Girl? Habit mostly. And two thousand years of bad press. Put more elegantly, "Legend is very willing to fill the gap left by factual records."[11]

One source of the confusion is simply this: too many Marys. (Sorry,

Lord, but it's a fact.) More than 50 percent of the women in Palestine in Jesus' day were named either Mary or Salome.[12] In Scripture we find Mary the mother of Jesus, our own Mary Magdalene, Mary the wife of Clopas, a chick called (now *this* is helpful) "the other Mary,"[13] plus that New Testament biggie, Mary of Bethany.

Bethany, "the village of Mary and her sister Martha,"[14] sat on the eastern slope of the Mount of Olives, a mile and a half southeast of Jerusalem (and nowhere near Magdala).[15] The apostle John described Mary of Bethany as "the same one who poured perfume on the Lord and wiped his feet with her hair."[16] More descriptively, she "massaged the Lord's feet with aromatic oils" (MSG).

The perfume part is easy enough to imagine—I've never known a man whose feet wouldn't benefit from a sprinkling of Estée Lauder—but wiping his feet with her *hair?* Outrageous as the idea sounds, in the first century it was customary for masters to dry their hands on (gulp) the heads or hair of their servants.[17] (I must confess, in my apartment-decorated-by-Goodwill years when towels were scarce, I once dried my hands on my *cat.*)

Mary of Bethany had a much higher purpose in mind, one that Jesus applauded: "I tell you the truth, wherever this gospel is preached throughout the world, what she has done will also be told, in memory of her."[18] As long as we remember the good name that goes with that fragrant story is Mary of Bethany and *not* Mary of Magdala.

I know what you're thinking: Didn't Mary Magdalene also anoint the Lord's feet with perfume somewhere, somehow? That's what the medieval paintings show, that's what the movies show, but believe me, that was *not* Mary Magdalene's show! That moving story belongs to a woman with no identity at all…except a sinful one.

HOW A BAD GIRL WENT GOOD

When a woman who had lived a sinful life in that town learned that Jesus was eating at the Pharisee's house, she brought an alabaster jar of perfume… *Luke 7:37*

This was not a demon-possessed woman, like Mary Magdalene. This nameless woman was a Sinner with a capital *S.* Big difference, since demonic possession "has nothing to do with badness of character."[19] Nor should this story be confused with Mary of Bethany's perfume pouring at the home of Simon the Leper in Bethany. The town in *this* story remains unnamed, like the sinner herself. It's possible that her story takes place in Nain, mentioned earlier in the chapter,[20] but it's almost certainly *not* in Bethany, nor in Magdala. And the host at this gathering is Simon the Pharisee, not Simon the Leper.

(I know, I know. Too many Simons.)

One scholar after another has made it clear that "there is no solid basis for identifying Mary of Bethany with the Galilean sinner or Mary of Magdala."[21] Okay, but how do we know the unnamed Galilean sinner wasn't Mary Magdalene (as most folks assume)? Because Mary M. is introduced by name in the next chapter of Luke "as if she had not before been spoken of."[22]

Another clue: The Lord's last, gentle command to this unnamed sinful woman in Luke 7 was to "go in peace,"[23] *not* "come follow me." Jesus healed people, shared meals with people, delivered people, but he invited only a few of them to follow him as his disciples. Mary Magdalene chose to do so and was not turned away, which means the sinful woman of Luke 7 and our Mary Magdalene of Luke 8 "have as little to do with each other as Peter and Judas."[24]

In every camp, liberal to conservative, commentators defend Mary Magdalene, insisting she "was *not* the woman of ill repute...the identification does her an injustice,"[25] especially since the Bible gives us "absolutely no indication that she was either a prostitute or the town tramp."[26]

Okay, all right, we get it. Time to see Mary Magdalene as a "woman with her own personal history, rather than being the prototype of the sinful woman."[27]

The Bible tells us Mary Magdalene was delivered of seven demons.

Period.

We simply don't *know* what her life was like before Christ appeared and turned her world right side up. "Poor Mary is the victim of untruth in labeling."[28] Come to think of it, those other women listed with Mary—Joanna,

Susanna, et al.—weren't accused of being harlots simply because they were delivered of demons. With the right lawyer, "Mary of Magdala could have sued for libel."[29]

More than one observer has moaned, "Mary's myth is too deep to uproot."[30] Well, sister, I intend to give it my best shot.

Mary Magdalene deserves an honest bio. And we deserve a gutsy role model.

MYTH-UNDERSTOOD MARY

If you want to pinpoint one day in history when the Bad Mary myth took root, you'll need to go back to the Middle Ages. Gregory the Great—think Gregorian chants—preached a homily (or *sermon,* for the Protestants among us) in A.D. 591 that lumped together three women described in three different gospel accounts—the "sinful woman" of Luke 7, Mary of Bethany of John 11–12, and Mary Magdalene "of whom Mark affirms that she was delivered of seven demons"[31]—and turned them into *one* woman.

Ta-da! Bad Mary.

This composite of a decidedly sinful Mary Magdalene blossomed like a hothouse flower until 1969—fourteen *centuries* later—when the Second Vatican Council described *Saint* Mary Magdalene as "the one to whom Christ appeared after the resurrection,"[32] and *not* Mary of Bethany nor the sinful woman.

Finally. Somebody send out a memo.

Ah, but we're a few epochs too late. Once the medieval pronouncement was made, artists began to interpret and embellish the story of Mary Magdalene the "reclaimed courtesan,"[33] until the real Mary got lost in their scarlet pigments. Hundreds of voluptuous Mary Magdalenes were splashed onto canvases, bosoms pouring out of their dresses, lips protruding in a permanent pout.

As Kathleen Turner, the sultry voice of Jessica Rabbit in *Who Framed Roger Rabbit?* put it, "I'm not bad; I'm just drawn that way."

Mary Magdalene's image in art "waffled between being a visual witness to Christian spirituality and an excuse for depictions of the female nude."[34] I found that out the hard way when I took my eleven-year-old daughter to a much-touted religious exhibit at a local art museum. "Mom!" she gasped, averting her eyes. "None of these women have any clothes on!"

A very observant girl, my Lilly.

For centuries, religious artwork *was* the gospel for those who couldn't read. Gregory called art "the Bible of the illiterate."[35] *Think* about that. No words, only pictures. No wonder centuries of Christians embraced the image of Bad Girl Mary Magdalene. That's all they saw! Art was, for the medieval masses, what movies are for us today: a way of not only defining culture but also shaping it.

BOO, HISS FOR HOLLYWOOD

Without question, Hollywood has shaped Mary Magdalene into a curvaceous 36-24-36 dish. In the 1960s the movie *King of Kings* filled the silver screen with an exotic Mary M. Draped in fake turquoise jewelry, she ran onto the set, pursued by men and women with stones in their hands, prepared to punish her for her sins. They cruelly taunted her with every name—and every sin—in the book.

"She's a harlot!"

"She's an adulteress!"

"She's a sorceress!"

Make up your mind, people. Better yet, read the Bible. The woman caught in adultery was never identified by any name, let alone our famous Mary's name. And while the adulteress was caught "in the very act," at no point was she accused of charging for her sexual favors nor of practicing witchcraft. One sin at a time, okay? Though the movie trailer for *King of Kings* identified this sinful woman as "Mary Magdalene, the fallen who found forgiveness," that was also a figment of the scriptwriter's imagination. Once again, another biblical Bad Girl's story has been woven into the mythical tapestry that is the Magdalene.

When Andrew Lloyd Webber and Tim Rice unleashed *Jesus Christ Superstar* on the world in 1970 (I was sixteen, girlfriend, and must confess I knew *all* the words by heart), it was very clear when the Mary Magdalene character sang "I Don't Know How to Love Him" that she had something other than pious devotion in mind. Not only did the movie's interpretation of Mary Magdalene include a lurid past, but Mary's present didn't look too respectable either.

One motion picture that *is* centered on the truth of the Bible is the *JESUS* film, which has been viewed by four billion people, translated into more than six hundred languages, and billed as "the most accurate film ever made about Christ." Even that wonderful production showed the same actress anointing Jesus' feet with her tears at Simon's house, then appearing as Mary Magdalene in the next frame.[36] In no way does that diminish the life-changing power of the film. No way. But it does reinforce a misconception about Mary Magdalene that the church seems reluctant to put to rest.

Here's the big question, babe: Are *you* willing to see her as she was—a woman possessed by Satan, then repossessed by Christ? The fact is, "Mary was only a sinner in the sense that we all are."[37] As her real life unfolds, you'll see the truth is actually more awful—and more wonderful—than any "sinner saved by grace" tale.

But first we need to let go of the Hollywood version.

And that's easier said than done.

Those of us who are Former Bad Girls—FBGs—loved the idea of a sinful but repentant Mary Magdalene. Even if we never knew much about her, we knew she was somehow bad, which made us feel somehow good. "Look, one of our own became a close friend of Jesus!"

For the Good Girls among us, a supposedly sinful woman like Mary M. gave us someone to point at. "Hey, at least I'm not *that* bad." Although our heavenly nature calls us to focus on all that is good, pure, and uplifting, our natural person still revels in hearing about someone's badness. (Except our *own,* of course...)

There are plenty of women in Scripture to fill those needs, but not Mary Magdalene. She's a category unto herself, "an articulate, generous woman of ability, courage, and faith,"[38] not the "fallen woman" who "loved too much."[39]

While we're on the subject, what *is* the deal with "fallen women"? You never hear people talk about "fallen men."

Then again, we don't speak of "fallen women" anymore either. More's the pity. We've all sunk lower than a snake's belly. Satan fell from heaven,[40] Eve fell from grace,[41] and "all have sinned and fall short of the glory of God."[42] We are all "fallen women." In relationships with fallen men.

All sinners. *All.*

Yes, including Mary Magdalene.

DESPERATELY SEEKING MARY

If she didn't look like a fallen woman, what *did* Mary Magdalene look like? History doesn't tell us if she was a young thing or an old crone, a pretty maid or plain as a post. If only those ancient papyrus scrolls had included a few portraits! Not only could we have sorted out the seven different Marys in a jiffy, but we could also get a clearer mental image of Mary of Magdala—her age, her body type, her hair, her features, her sandal size, *something.*

Not that those things define a person. You *know* I'd never go that route. It's her heart, her mission, her message that are eternal, not her makeup or the measurement of her waist...not hardly. Still, my curious nature dug deep into the soil of her story looking for visual clues and came up empty-handed.

Over the years students of the Bible have guessed at Mary M.'s appearance. One wrote, "Mary, perhaps thirty years of age, is thought to have been beautiful and gracious."[43] Another insisted, "We can be sure she was...young and pretty, well-favored.... [P]robably in her late twenties, she possessed beauty of face and form."[44]

Once again, none of those details appear anywhere in the Bible. Common sense, though, points to a woman not quite so young or so attractive. Here's my reasoning:

1. Age over Beauty

Since she's almost always listed first when Mary the mother of Jesus and the others are mentioned, it's clear that Mary Magdalene was a leader among these women. Generally we look to someone older and wiser for counsel and direction, yes? In Mary's era especially, older was better (fathom that!), and seniors were honored as a tribute to the Lord. "Rise in the presence of the aged, show respect for the elderly and revere your God. I am the LORD."[45]

2. Do the Math

If Jesus was about thirty years old when he met Mary (coulda been older), his mother was a minimum of forty-four, assuming Jesus was conceived when she was thirteen (oh my). In order for Mary M. to lead a group that included this esteemed woman, Mary Magdalene would no doubt have been the same age or older than Mother Mary—in her midforties at least and possibly a good bit older. She'd certainly be past the childbearing years, perhaps a widow, giving her the freedom to leave Magdala behind and follow Jesus, which is precisely what she did.

3. Just Plain Beautiful to God

As to her appearance, I'd gently place her in the category of a woman who had a beautiful soul rather than a picture-perfect face and curvaceous figure, because outward appearance never impresses God: "Your beauty should not come from outward adornment.... Instead, it should be that of your inner self, the unfading beauty of a gentle and quiet spirit, which is of great worth in God's sight."[46]

4. R – E – S – P – E – C – T

To serve well, a woman who leads must have the trust and respect of women *and* men. A more mature woman has left the fleeting concerns of youth in the dust as she picks up her bifocals, touches up her roots, gathers her sisters about her, and forges on—wearing sensible shoes, of course. With both genders, several decades of life experience would be to her credit.

Honey, I didn't make up this middle-aged-Mary idea just because that's what I'm lookin' at in the mirror—honest! Another writer suggested, "Perhaps she was already aged, had a marriage behind her which provided the means with which she was able to help the Jesus movement."[47] Or how 'bout the reference to Mary Magdalene and company as "matronly women"?[48] *Hmm.* Since *matronly* conjures up images of small-print dresses and large bosoms, suppose we say "well seasoned" instead. That allows for the dash of pepper I suspect ran through Mary's veins.

What we *do* know, absolutely, is from whence she hailed: Magdala. Mary is always associated with her hometown. The only time she was called simply "Mary" was when Jesus addressed her in that very personal manner at the tomb. In all other cases, she's Mary (the) Magdalene, well known to the followers of Jesus the Nazarene.

So what do we know about Magdala?

BIG-CITY GIRL

"Magdala"—from the Hebrew *migdol,* meaning "a tower or watch tower"[49]— was one of nine cities on the western shore of the Sea of Galilee with more than fifteen thousand inhabitants.[50] Not the size of Chicago with its Sears tower, but a big city for its time.

Magdala stood along the ancient road from Nazareth to Damascus[51] and not far south of Capernaum—all familiar spots. We're talking the very heartland of Jesus' ministry. Though it's not on modern maps, look for "el-Mejdel, a few miles from Tiberias,"[52] which is right about where Magdala used to sit.

A prosperous place, Magdala bragged about its dye works and eighty (*eighty!*) woolen factories. People passing through town en route to one synagogue or another also took advantage of the town's trade in turtledoves and pigeons offered for purification.[53] In the Talmud, Magdala is called *Migdal Nunya,* or "fish tower," which tells us the fishing industry was a big part of its economy as well.[54] Salted fish in particular, not unlike the kind Jesus used to feed the multitudes.

Fine. Now we've got Magdala figured out: fabric, feathers, fish.

There was one more thing the town was famous for: fallen women.

Rabbinic literature paints the town in dark colors, its unsavory reputation due to "corruption brought about by excessive wealth."[55] No wonder Mary M.'s reputation became unfairly tainted. "Magdala even had its own hippodrome for entertainment, to the disgust of the nearby Jewish population."[56] Hippodromes had nothing to do with hippos but everything to do with horses, chariots, violent men, and wild animals—think *Gladiator*. The Talmud explains why Magdala isn't on the map anymore: "because of the harlotry practiced there," it was destroyed.[57]

But a bad town doesn't make a Bad Girl.

Since respectable rabbis from Mary's locale are also mentioned in the Talmud—"Rabbi Jehuda the Magdalene," for one—the identification "Magdalene" can hardly "imply immorality in one case and not in the other."[58] In fact, Mary Magdalene's in some pretty good company. It was said of Jesus' hometown, "Nazareth! Can anything good come from there?"[59] Most definitely.

Now that we know who she was—and what she wasn't—it's time to wade into her devilish past. Because where Mary Magdalene used to reside isn't nearly as important as the identity of those who used to reside in *her*. That's what really grabs our attention.

Since Mary Magdalene was once possessed by seven demons who were bound to do the bidding of the Adversary, maybe—just maybe—this smoke screen of "myth-understanding" about Mary was inspired by her former master's attempt to cover up the gospel truth about this powerful, grace-filled woman.

Get lost, Bad Boy. The smoke is about to clear.

What Lessons Can We Learn from Mary Magdalene and Her Legend?

Let go of labels.

Mary Magdalene is neither the first nor the last woman in history to suffer from a bad—but false—reputation. Even if she had committed every sin she is reputed to have committed—prostitution, adultery, sorcery—the fact that Christ honored her by doing away with her demons should give us a clear picture of what he thought of her—and of what he thinks of us now.

> Do not call anything impure that God has made clean.
> *Acts 10:15*

Put a lid on gossip.

No doubt the rumor mill added a third shift when Mary Magdalene and her seven demons showed up. Things haven't changed much. We can't resist swapping stories about so-and-so, and bad news travels ten times faster than good. The best way to undo gossip, slander, and hurtful misinformation is to stop it in its tracks when we hear it being whispered down the lane. How? Throw a wet blanket on the conversation, offer a positive comment about the person, or change the subject. The yuck stops here, girl.

> Without wood a fire goes out;
>> without gossip a quarrel dies down. *Proverbs 26:20*

Dress your age.

I've got a bunch of clothes in my closet that don't fit anymore or are so out of style they just scream, "Stuck in the '80s!" And my cosmetic drawers…I mean, get serious. Navy blue mascara? Mary Magdalene would know better. She'd choose something that suited her age, that demonstrated her *new* life, not her old one. In the same way, I've got some old habits—okay, *sins*—that are hanging around, taking up space, keeping me from maturing in Christ. You, too? Time to get rid of them for good, sis. Cast them out. Let Christ dress you in a whole new wardrobe of grace, one that suits the mature you and never goes out of style.

> [Y]ou have stripped off your old evil nature and all its wicked
> deeds. In its place you have clothed yourselves with a brand-
> new nature that is continually being renewed as you learn more
> and more about Christ, who created this new nature within
> you. *Colossians 3:9-10, NLT*

Do your homework.

When society at large portrays a biblical character—in print, in art, on film—those of us who are Christians need to take an honest look at their labors and offer praise wherever merited. But our first point of reference should be the source of truth itself, the Bible. Is the media depiction accurate?

If not, what story are they trying to tell? More to the point, what message are they trying to *sell?* Before we sound a war cry, let's be sure we have all the facts...*and* the truth.

> Do your best to present yourself to God as one approved, a
> workman who does not need to be ashamed and who correctly
> handles the word of truth. *2 Timothy 2:15*

GOOD GIRL THOUGHTS WORTH CONSIDERING

1. Some of Jesus' followers, like the Twelve, were called. Others, like Mary Magdalene, chose to follow. Would both groups be equally valuable to him, do you suppose? Why might he have needed both men and women to support his ministry?

2. Before you read this chapter, what was your concept of Mary Magdalene? Did you think she was one of the women who anointed Jesus' feet? A prostitute? The woman caught in adultery? Or simply a faithful follower of Christ? Can you recall where those ideas came from? Is it important to have an honest understanding of Mary? Why or why not?

3. Is Hollywood at all responsible for keeping the Bad Girl myth alive? Have you seen any of the movies mentioned here? Are there others that come to mind—or television programs or books? What should be the Christian's response to the media's mishandling of biblical stories? Do we raise the roof, refuse to support their advertisers, or hope they just go away? What are some redemptive alternatives?

4. Why *do* we say "fallen women" and not "fallen men"? Does society expect more of women, morally and spiritually? Is there a double standard in the body of Christ? Should there be? Why do you think we have several stories in the New Testament about "Bad Girls" who were pardoned by Jesus but relatively few about morally "Bad Boys" who sought his forgiveness?

5. What age do you imagine Mary Magdalene might have been when she was part of Jesus' ministry team? What makes you say that? Does it change your perception of her—and identification with her—if she was indeed middle-aged or older? What should our attitude be toward those around us who are "well seasoned"? Does it matter what age Mary Magdalene was?

6. Magdala was a town with a bad reputation. What cities in America do we think of as "evil"? Do we make assumptions about the people who live there—that everyone in Las Vegas gambles or that everyone in Boulder is part of the New Age movement? Have you ever made disparaging comments about "those pushy New Yorkers" or "those lazy Southerners"? How can we overcome our geographical prejudices?

7. If indeed the Adversary *is* to blame for our misunderstandings about Mary Magdalene, to what purpose? Has blurring the truth about Mary's life hurt Christian women? Might revealing the truth bring about some good? Are you (be honest) disappointed that she wasn't *that kind* of Bad Girl? Are you willing to wipe the slate clean and meet the real Mary Magdalene? What do you hope to learn about this ancient sister?

8. Read again chapters 1 and 2 of *Unveiling Mary Magdalene*. What did you feel toward Mary Delaney when you read it the first time? Did those feelings change on this second reading? If so, how? and why? Who might Charles Farris represent from biblical times? (Hint: On the church roster, his name is listed as "Farris, C."!)

Chapter Ten

MOONSTRUCK MADNESS

HER DEMONS

Demoniac frenzy, moping melancholy,
And moon-struck madness.
JOHN MILTON

Two thousand years ago Mary Magdalene wasn't a Bad Girl…she was a Mad Girl.

> Mary (called Magdalene) from whom seven demons had come
> out… *Luke 8:2*

Demons. *Ick.*

Described as "the forces of evil infesting the universe,"[1] those demons didn't come out willingly. They were "expelled" (AMP), and thank goodness. But how did they get *in*?

Scholars tell us demons were "able to take up their abode in a man, apparently without him having any choice in the matter."[2] *Poor Mary!* Since demons are evil spirits, and therefore invisible, how did people know they were inside her? Here's a checklist, as it were, of evidence that might indicate "demonic affliction."

a compulsive desire to curse the Lord by name

a revulsion against the Bible

thoughts of suicide or murder

bitterness and hatred

deep depression and despondency

horrific nightmares

violent, uncontrollable rage

superhuman strength

self-inflicted injuries

restlessness and insomnia

anguish and torment[3]

In other words, demons on the inside looked like madness on the out-side.

One writer called it "terminal abuse."[4] Our Mary would have been "grievously tormented, and rendered, doubtless, insane by the power of evil spirits."[5]

Mad Mary indeed.

Check out what's *not* on that long list: prostitution.

Few customers would be attracted to a woman who was prone to violent rages, murderous thoughts, and self-mutilation. Not unless they were truly kinky (and let's not go there).

One important note before we explore Mary's dark side. I believe her demons were just that—evil spirits—not merely a first-century word for something we might call an illness today. Having said that, we need to "avoid two extremes when it comes to the matter of demons: (1) seeing a demon behind every tree; and (2) treating the doctrine of demons with disdain or contempt."[6] Let's shoot for a balanced and biblical view of what tormented Mary.

Turn on a few more lights if it'll make you feel better.

And don't confuse *temptation*—which happens to all of us—or *obsessions*—which happen to some of us—with demonic *possession*, which involves total control of an individual by a demon, an "oppression that he or she could not successfully withstand alone."[7]

The Seven Deadly Demons

To say Mary Magdalene's rights were violated is an understatement. We, who consider personal freedom a birthright, cannot fully imagine the terror of having no choice whatsoever about how we look or behave, what we say or how we say it, where we go, who or what we see, all that. She was, in a word, a *demoniac,* a woman created by God, then "strangled by Satan."[8] The indwelling was such that the possessed "mistook the thoughts of the fiends for his own."[9]

Oh, Mary.

And not just one demon...*seven.* Mary Magdalene is the only demoniac in the Bible whose multiple invaders are precisely numbered. It's seen as "the ultimate number,"[10] representing not simply the finite number seven but "the idea of totality itself"[11]—in this case "the worst possible state of corruption."[12] I'll say! Cherishing control as much as I do, I can't fully grasp the horror Mary M. must have gone through when seven demons "completely possessed her body and mind."[13] *Oh, Mary.*

All this time we thought Mary was just a typical Bad Girl, a woman who made poor choices as many of us have, maybe dated a Bad Boy or hung out with the wrong crowd. Some crowd, woman. *Seven!*

Gregory the Great—you remember, the sermon that turned three women into one—said that Mary Magdalene's seven demons "were to be understood not only literally but also morally as the seven deadly sins."[14] Great, Greg. More bad press for Mary. No wonder she became known not as demon possessed but *sin* obsessed, though "there is not one word in the Bible that indicates that she was other than a pure, though deeply afflicted woman."[15]

It's the *demons* that were bad. "Morally perverted,"[16] to be exact. The poor possessed person was considered a "helpless victim."[17] None of the demon possessed in Scripture "were rebuked or even scolded for it. [Jesus] never associated demon possession with sin."[18] Further proof? Not once in the biblical record does Jesus set someone free of demons and then say, "You are forgiven" or "Go and sin no more."

This distinction is important because there are those in the body of

Christ who suggest that believers can bring demon possession upon themselves: "As one constantly repeats a particular sin, then Satan takes up his abode. As this happens, then the individual is possessed or oppressed in the area that was yielded to Satan."[19]

Now *that* is a scary thought. "Repeating particular sins" would sum up life as most of us know it. Wonder *how many times* we'd have to repeat said sin before Satan moved in? Seven? (Sorry, couldn't resist...) Even if I *did* manage to get all my sins under control, I can guarantee which sin would rear its ugly head next: pride.

THE GIRL CAN'T HELP IT, SHE JUST CAN'T HELP IT

See if this pattern sounds familiar, sis: We're challenged in a particular area of our lives, like trying to quit smoking. We try patches, we try classes, we try hypnosis (*not* recommended), we try prayer, we try gum, we try special filters, we try quitting cold turkey, we try cutting down, we finally give up and light up.

And beat up ourselves unmercifully.

"What is *wrong* with me?" we moan. "Why won't God help me?" At a loss to explain our dilemma, we look in every corner of our lives in search of *some* valid explanation.

Maybe it's that addictive nicotine. Blame the cigarette manufacturers.

Maybe it's too many years of seeing pretty people on billboards puffing away. Blame the advertisers.

Maybe it was all those years of watching Mom smoke herself to an early grave. Blame our mothers.

Then someone comes along and whispers, "You have the demon of smoking."

That's it! we decide, breathing a sigh of relief. *It's not my fault after all!*

Ringin' any bells? Girl, we have been deceived—again, still. In a society that is loath to accept responsibility for anything, we find it easier to blame something "out there" or something that sneaked "in here" rather than confess that our own stubborn, rebellious pride couldn't say no to temptation.

We have a hard time—Let me make this more personal. *I* have a hard time confessing, "I love this sin of mine." It's easier to wail and wring my hands and blame demons. I'm singing Eve's song all over again: "The devil made me do it." Yet the Bible reminds us, "If we claim we have not sinned, we make [God] out to be a liar and his word has no place in our lives."[20]

But Lord, your Word is the centerpiece of my life! Help me accept responsibility for my sins and not give Satan credit for being more powerful than he is, when you assure me "the one who is in you is greater than the one who is in the world."[21]

I'm not a repository for demons; I'm a sinner saved by grace. I could list my sins for you and call them demons—the spirit of lust, the spirit of vulgarity, the spirit of gluttony—but in these cases and many others, I cannot play Pin the Pitchforked Tail on Satan's Donkey.

I have sinned. I am sinning. Wretched woman that I am!

Here's the good news. When I ask God to forgive me, he does. Seventy-seven times and that's just for starters.

Welcome to *grace.*

It's the last place a demon wants to hang out.

DON'T BE AFRAID OF THE DARK

When Jesus came, he changed the rules. He conquered Satan for us, "first in the wilderness, and finally on Calvary."[22] The work is finished. Our personal deliverance comes at the moment of salvation, just as for Mary, whose "soul's deliverance from the seven devils was simultaneous with her heart's conversion to God."[23]

When we invite Christ into our hearts, his dwelling place, *he will not share his lodging with demons.* Demons love darkness. But "God, who said, 'Let light shine out of darkness,' made his light shine in our hearts."[24]

No way could evil spirits and the Spirit of Christ cohabit the same heart. No way.

Can demons torment, tempt, mislead, and confuse Christians from the outside? Oh yes, and very well! But they cannot take over a heart where

Christ is King. The most they can do is whisper lies and make accusations. An external menace? Absolutely. An internal force with dominion over us? Absolutely not.

How I long for you to rest in that truth, beloved.

Demon possession à la Mary Magdalene is only a concern for those who reject the lordship of Christ.

> The Spirit clearly says that in later times some will abandon the faith and follow deceiving spirits and things taught by demons.
> *1 Timothy 4:1*

But for those who honor Christ as King, no demon, not even Satan himself, can prevail against the matchless grace and boundless love of Jesus.

> For I am convinced that neither death nor life, neither angels nor demons, neither the present nor the future, nor any powers, neither height nor depth, nor anything else in all creation, will be able to separate us from the love of God that is in Christ Jesus our Lord. *Romans 8:38-39*

Have no fear of demons separating you from your Savior, my sister in Christ. It simply can't be done. Send them packing at the first knock on your door. "Hit the road, jackals. This heart's spoken for."

It's a Mad, Mad, Mad, Mad World

There are those, then and now, who shy away from the supernatural notion of demons and prefer to see demon possession as "the customary explanation for any baffling physical or emotional condition."[25] Not demons—diseases. They weren't evil spirits, the argument goes, they were "mental illness, perhaps manic depressions or epilepsy."[26]

No need for Jesus. A good psychiatrist could have handled things just as well, eh?

Maybe not.

Mary Magdalene appeared mad, all right, but it wasn't genetic, and it wasn't learned behavior. It was demons. Seven demons, name them one by one. It may be fashionable, even politically correct, to conclude that the gospel writers' "demons" would today be labeled mental or emotional illnesses. But then you'd have to explain away these three facts:

1. Jesus himself called them demons and evil spirits (Matthew 12:28; Luke 11:24).

He was certainly capable of calling them sins, if they were such, or an evil spiritual inheritance from the victim's parents, if that applied, or a bad trip on a mustard seed. He called them demons.

2. Jesus spoke to the demons (Matthew 8:31-32; Mark 9:25).

He addressed them as though separate from the victim. Rebuked them. Sent them running. I've never had a physician talk to my illnesses, have you? Wouldn't be likely to go back if I did. But Jesus was speaking to entities, not illnesses.

3. The demons spoke back to him (Luke 4:41).

Boy, that'll get your attention. Illnesses don't talk. Madwomen don't make sense. But these demons spoke in full sentences, knew the Lord's identity, and begged for mercy.

When it came to demons, there was "no subject on which [Jesus] expressed himself more clearly, or acted more uniformly."[27] Demons were real, and Jesus had dominion over them since "they are not sovereign, nor are they God's equals."[28] Yahoo!

Since "mental derangement…seems invariably to have accompanied Satanic possession,"[29] it's hard to know which came first—the demons or the derangement. Symptoms included "intense depression and morbid melancholy…ill-temper and a persistent nervousness."[30]

Yeah, I guess that sort of behavior would stand out in any social gathering.

This may be the best description yet of how our Mary Magdalene was viewed by others before Christ appeared in her life: She was the "town crazy woman."[31]

I think I met her at church last Sunday.

The lights had dimmed, and the worship team was already singing when Bill and I slid into two empty seats near the aisle and tucked our coats around us. There was one seat left in our row, next to Bill. A few minutes later someone landed there.

And I do mean landed, with a noisy *whoosh.*

She was a woman of uncertain age. Fiftyish. Could have been younger, older, hard to say. Her clothes were oddly mismatched. Her voice was loud, too loud for church or any other quiet place, and her movements seemed jerky and uncoordinated.

But it was the words she spoke that gave me pause. When she recognized me and said my name several times, my mouth went dry. She pointed out people around us and muttered outrageous, nonsensical things about them, then bent over to jot something down on the fistful of notebooks stuffed in her huge, messy purse, all the while fuming, "It's not a game! It's not a game!"

Dear one, I can't be less than honest with you. While I felt great pity for this poor soul, I also felt uncomfortable. Uneasy. Scared, even. What else might she say? What might she *do?* Was she dangerous? *What* was "not a game"? Did we need to help her? Avoid her? Calm her down? Turn her in?

That's when my eyes met Bill's, and he mouthed two words: *Mad Mary.*

Oh, my. The enormity of that truth hit me with gale force. *Of course.* That's how people would have looked at our sainted Mary Magdalene.

Not "people," Liz—*you.* That's how *you* judged, categorized, evaluated, sized up, and otherwise held at arm's length this woman at church, who was no more in charge of her mind than she was her bulging purse and its unruly contents.

A dozen different emotions churned inside me that morning. Sad to say, "unconditional love" was not among them.

Forgive me, Father.

Such was the world in which Mary Magdalene lived. A world where supposedly good people couldn't bear to share their pew with a madwoman, a "dark and desperate age" when there were "forms of madness which owed their more immediate manifestation to evil powers."[32]

Then the Light appeared and dispelled the darkness forever.

Maybe you saw the banner headline in the *Magdala Daily News*…

Local Madwoman Set Free
Seven Demons Flee to Galilean Hills
Nazarene Preacher at Scene

If only we had such a story in print! Considering she's the "only demo-niac who bears a name,"[33] it's surprising that Mary Magdalene's deliverance wasn't recorded. We know it *happened*. But we're missing a few details—like when, where, and how. We know the answer to the most important question though: We know *who* did the delivering.

Perhaps Jesus was alone when he delivered her. Although both Mark and Luke clearly state the reality of her deliverance, if the disciples weren't there to serve as witnesses, that may explain why we get no description of this sacred moment. Maybe this one was kept on the q.t. because the most important appearance of the Christ in Mary's life was the *second* time he showed up unexpectedly and rocked her world forever.

Whatever the reason for the silent treatment, when we meet Mary, her seven demons are history. Done deal. Past tense. If we wanna see how it might have happened, we'll need to look at a handful of other deliverances and learn what we can from them.

Deliverance 101

After returning from forty days of being tempted by Satan in the desert, Jesus began his ministry by hanging out his shingle: "The Doctor Is In."

> …people brought to him all who were ill with various diseases,
> those suffering severe pain, the demon-possessed, those having
> seizures, and the paralyzed, and he healed them. *Matthew 4:24*

Two things are obvious here: One, demon possession was treated sepa-rately from diseases and seizures and such. And two, the demon possessed did not come under their own steam. They were "brought," probably by loved ones. But the casting out, the healing, was God's work alone.

Luke described another evening when Jesus busied himself healing the sick and delivering the possessed.

> When the sun was setting, the people brought to Jesus all who
> had various kinds of sickness… *Luke 4:40*

Why wait until sunset? The close of the day. And the cloak of darkness. We're talking about miracles here, not a trip to a twenty-four-hour clinic or a mad dash to the ER with the faint hope of seeing a George Clooney look-alike.

Without medicine or scalpel, with only his holy hands, Jesus made demoniacs whole.

> ...and laying his hands on each one, he healed them.
> *Luke 4:40*

Notice, "on each one." Not mass healings. Individual touches. Don't miss that lesson, sis! Jesus knows our hurts and comes to us personally, one at a time.

His method of healing people "was neither magical nor medical...it was transcendental."[34] Yes, it was utterly "out of the bounds of decorum and reason; it was extravagant; it was dangerous."[35] Dangerous for the demons, that is.

> Moreover, demons came out of many people, shouting, "You
> are the Son of God!" *Luke 4:41*

Not just one demon in one person but lots of 'em in lots of folks. In fact, "demons left in droves" (MSG) and made plenty of noise in the process, "screaming and crying out" (AMP).

> But he rebuked them and would not allow them to speak,
> because they knew he was the Christ. *Luke 4:41*

Wow! The demons *knew* who he was? It seems "they knew too much, knew him to be the Messiah" (MSG) and so "he stopped them and told them to be silent" (NLT).

The Day the Devil Came to Church

A Sabbath crowd at Capernaum had barely settled down to listen to Jesus of Nazareth, a new preacher on the scene, and were "amazed at his teaching, because his message had authority"[36] when—*bam!*—here came the village madman to stir up things.

> In the synagogue there was a man possessed by a demon, an
> evil spirit. *Luke 4:33*

This wild man "who had an evil spirit from the devil inside him" (ICB) and was "demonically disturbed" (MSG) sure sounds like a kindred spirit (pun intended) with our Mary Magdalene. One physician observed, "Madmen of this sort are extremely prone to crimes of horror and bloodshed. Probably this man was already known in Capernaum as a dangerous character."[37] No kidding. You wonder how he managed to get into the synagogue in the first place. I'm reminded of the old joke "Where does an eight-hundred-pound gorilla sit in church?" The answer, of course, is "Anywhere he wants to."

"Where does a murdering demoniac sit in the synagogue?"

You got it.

> He cried out at the top of his voice... *Luke 4:33*

The man was not only dangerous, he was disruptive. He "shrieked" (NEB) with a "loud (deep, terrible) cry" (AMP). Sure would bring communion to a halt at our church.

> "I know who you are—the Holy One of God!" *Luke 4:34*

How did he know? It's a spirit-world thing. The attributes of a demon include possessing "a supernatural knowledge of things unknown to ordinary men"—yet another reason why demons "cannot be rationalized away" as mental illness.[38] This demon was speaking directly to Christ, ignoring his host, because for demons "the issue is not between them and their captives, but only between them and the Deliverer."[39]

Mary and her seven demons must have presented quite a cacophony of voices shouting at Jesus, calling him names. Notice they didn't yell out bad names; they used his righteous names—Son of God, Holy One. Much as demons must have longed to blaspheme his name, in the presence of the Christ they were powerless to do anything but acknowledge who he is.

Don't you love it? God wins every time.

But for the moment, Jesus had to turn down the noise.

"Be quiet!" Jesus said sternly. *Luke 4:35*

In other words, "Jesus rebuked him" (NEB); that is, he "cut him short" (NLT). Yes indeed, he "shut him up" (MSG).

The fact that "Jesus rebuked it almost as if it were a person"[40] gives us a further clue to the unique nature of this evil personality. Not that Jesus intended to waste any time getting to know the nasty thing.

"Come out of him!" *Luke 4:35*

That makes my hair stand on end. The all-powerful pronouncement, the not-to-be-ignored command: *"Come out!"* No tricks, no hocus-pocus, no waving of wands, no smoke and mirrors. It was the Son of God's power—not man's clever rituals—that drove the demons out. He did it with his word— his irrefutable, spoken word. God, who said, "Let there be light"—and there was—said, "Let there be no darkness inside this man." And there wasn't.

Then the demon threw the man down before them all…
Luke 4:35

Why did the demon throw his victim on the ground, I wonder. So he could disappear into the bowels of the earth? To humble the man one last time? Or was the demon himself humbled, wanting to distance himself from the Holy One?

Whatever the reason, everybody in the synagogue saw this miracle go down. And they thought Jesus spoke with authority when he preached a ser-mon? The man got *seriously* authoritative when he delivered a demon.

…and [it] came out without injuring him. *Luke 4:35*

An exit "without hurting him further" (NLT) means all the fight went out of these demons when the Christ showed up. Throwing their host on the ground was their last hurrah before they were history.

At the demon's demise, the worshipers in Capernaum were wide-eyed.

All the people were amazed and said to each other, "What is this teaching?" *Luke 4:36*

They came for a sermon and got more than they bargained for! Can't you hear the buzz as they asked one another, "What does this mean?" (ICB) and "What kind of talk is this?" (AMP) and "What is there in this man's words?" (NEB).

There was no denying what they'd seen with their own eyes.

> "With authority and power he gives orders to evil spirits and they come out!" *Luke 4:36*

Does it sound to you as if they'd never seen such a thing before? Perhaps casting out demons was a fairly new phenomenon, and so they marveled, "Even evil spirits obey him and flee at his command!" (NLT).

> And the news about him spread throughout the surrounding area. *Luke 4:37*

Honey, you just try to keep a story like that quiet. Like a match to dry kindling, this spark "spread like wildfire" (NLT) until Jesus "was the talk of the whole district" (NEB).

Oh, I'll just bet he was!

JUST SAY THE WORD

Soon folks were lined up with their demon-possessed loved ones in tow. As was becoming customary, they waited for the cover of night.

> When evening came… *Matthew 8:16*

Surely there was a sense of shame about having a demoniac in the family. As to Mary, "she could only have been a daily grief, anxiety, and terror to her relatives."[41] Better to seek out this demon chaser when the shadows fell long across the desert.

Or maybe that's when the demons manifested themselves. The particularly bright moonlight of this Middle Eastern world had "a curious stimulating effect" on those who suffered from madness.[42] Indeed, one of my dozens of resource books titled the chapter on Mary Magdalene, "The Restored Lunatic."[43]

Well, Jesus was in the restoration business.

> ...many who were demon-possessed were brought to him...
> *Matthew 8:16*

"Many" now, not just one at a time. People were lined up to meet this Nazarene who seemed to be their long-awaited Messiah incarnate, the embodiment of the psalmist's words: "From the LORD comes deliverance."[44]

The crowds got what they came for, in a hurry.

> ...and he drove out the spirits with a word... *Matthew 8:16*

The Greek words for "the spirits" are *ta pneumata*. The root word, *pneuma*, is also used to refer to the Holy Spirit and angels,[45] so this definitely means creatures from the spirit world, *not* depression and headaches.

And look how he kicked them out: "with only a word" (CEV).

A word!? Just *one*?

That's right. One word. Doesn't matter if that word was "Go!" or "Out!" or "Scram!" or "Vamoose!" What matters is *who said it.*

His spoken word had the authority, the energy, the ability to change everything. Death to life. Creation to recreation. "In the beginning was the Word,"[46] and when that Word came to earth, he took on the prince of darkness with his most powerful weapon: his words.

What word was it, dear Mary? Did you hear it? Did you feel its power?

One demon or seven, it only took *one word* for him to bring Mary back to her right mind, tearing down those demons exactly the same way he upholds everything else—"by the word of His power."[47]

In his hymn *A Mighty Fortress Is Our God,* Martin Luther wrote of Satan, "For lo, his doom is sure! One little word shall fell him!"[48] Yes, indeed, "as long as that word is Jesus."[49] Sister, you *know* that's right!

Jesus was unique in that he didn't use "incantations, religious rites, or magic formulas as others did. He delivered the demon-possessed by a simple and direct command to the demons to come out—and the demons obeyed."[50]

Two things are worth noticing about these high-powered displays: (1) Jesus never asked for money, nor is there any record of payment being offered. It was a gift freely given. Like faith. Like grace. No wonder our grateful Mary was willing to follow him anywhere! And (2) it was done for the benefit of others, not merely to bring glory to his name, though that was profit enough.

Unlike the Egyptian magicians who mimicked the miracles of God to please Pharaoh and confound Moses,[51] Jesus performed his mighty deeds of deliverance to heal the afflicted and make them whole. It was for *their* benefit, not for his ego. "Not just works of mercy" but "part of the all-out attack of the Messiah on every kind of evil in God's world."[52]

Back up, Bad Boy! Our Deliverer has come.

WHEN PIGS FLY

Jesus had a full-scale military battle on his hands when he met a man who, like Mary Magdalene, had more than one demon driving him mad.

> They sailed to the region of the Gerasenes, which is across the lake from Galilee. *Luke 8:26*

Depending on which translation you use, this name could be spelled "Gerasenes" (NIV, NLT, MSG), "Gadarenes" (KJV, NKJV), or "Gergesenes" (NEB). Don't panic. It's probably the same place. Think of it as a first-century typo of sorts, since there were spelling discrepancies among the earliest manuscripts and two towns with very similar names in the area—Gadara and Gerasa.[53]

> When Jesus stepped ashore, he was met by a demon-possessed man from the town. *Luke 8:27*

Some greeting party! A "madman from town…a victim of demons" (MSG), meaning he didn't choose this state of mind. Let's look at his behavior and see what clues it might give us about Mary Magdalene's suffering.

> For a long time this man had not worn clothes… *Luke 8:27*

Well, there you are. If Mary did the same, no wonder people thought of her as a Bad Girl! To run around "naked" (NLT), "clothed only in sunlight or starlight,"[54] would surely make people talk…and gawk.

For this troubled man, tearing off his clothes wasn't about exhibitionism; it was possibly discomfort from "uneasy cutaneous sensations" (his clothes itched) or could be it was "sheer destructiveness."[55]

Not only did he have no shirt on his back, he had no roof over his head.

> ...[nor] lived in a house, but had lived in the tombs.
> *Luke 8:27*

Was this man no longer able to afford housing? Did he feel more at home with the wild beasts, whose behavior he seemed to imitate? Or had his anguished family thrown him out into the darkness rather than suffer his torment along with him?

Whatever the case, his last resort was living in the "graveyard" (CEV). A place of suffering, mourning, and death. Ideal spot for evil spirits. Terrible location for their human hosts. Because of the proximity of corpses, this demon-possessed man would have been "ceremonially defiled"[56] and therefore unwelcome at the synagogue...or anywhere else.

> Night and day among the tombs and in the hills he would cry
> out and cut himself with stones. *Mark 5:5*

If he was shrieking around the clock, then sleeplessness was part of the misery of possession. Insanity would be the only possible escape, the only way to mentally disconnect oneself from the agony. Unfortunately "slashing himself with sharp stones" (MSG) kept this man awake and painfully aware of his existence. Self-mutilation wasn't done in penance. No doubt he found a deluded source of momentary pleasure in the pain. Demons are all about destruction. His body was powerless to resist the malevolent command to cut, cut, cut.

It's unlikely any good Samaritan passing by could have confiscated those rocks. Not from this man, not from Mary Magdalene. The superhuman strength of demoniacs, powered by subhuman resources, made them untouchable.

> Many times [the demon] had seized him, and though he was
> chained hand and foot and kept under guard, he had broken
> his chains... *Luke 8:29*

Oh, Mary.

Were you chained too? Your hands, your feet?

Did you writhe and twist and yank on those noisy chains?

It makes my wrists ache to think of the metal tearing into Mary Magdalene's tender skin, drawn tight against her bones from malnutrition. In the same way nails pierced the innocent body of Jesus—his hands, his feet—demoniacs were pierced and imprisoned by their madness.

If the resurrected Jesus carried the scars of those nails, you know Mary M.'s skin was marked forever.

> ...and [the demoniac] had been driven by the demon into
> solitary places. *Luke 8:29*

The isolation alone would have made me a madwoman.

By no choice of his own, "completely under the demon's power" (NLT), this demoniac was forced to live in "lonely places" (CEV). Was our Mary driven by her seven demons to the remote corners of Galilee?

For Jesus, there was no wilderness too bleak, no landscape too barren to keep him from reaching out to a person living on the lunatic fringe. The Lord was fearless, but the demoniac in the desert was plenty afraid.

> When he saw Jesus, he cried out and fell at his feet, shouting at
> the top of his voice... *Luke 8:28*

Are you seeing a pattern here? Fall down, shout out? An act of submission. But when the Bible says "every knee will bow...every tongue will confess,"[57] it does not mean they will do so by choice. Demons trembled on their knees before the lordship of Christ, yet we humans stubbornly refuse to bow our heads in prayer, let alone our hearts in submission. Have mercy on us, Lord!

That's what this demoniac begged for: mercy.

> "What do you want with me, Jesus, Son of the Most High
> God?" *Luke 8:28*

Another translation puts it, "What have we in common?" (AMP). Best I can tell, absolutely nothing. It's the Light of the World versus utter darkness and depravity.

> Jesus asked him, "What is your name?" *Luke 8:30*

Because of the answer Jesus received—"Legion"—most people assume he was asking the *demon* what his name was. If so, it's the only time recorded in Scripture that Jesus requested a name from a demon. I think he was speaking directly to the fella himself, hoping to "recall the man to a sense of his own personality apart from the demon,"[58] because, as you see, the man was the one who responded.

> "Legion," he replied, because many demons had gone into
> him. *Luke 8:30*

"Legion" would definitely qualify as "many," since a legion was the main unit of the Roman army, made up of "3000 to 6000 foot soldiers."[59] Gives a whole new meaning to "spirit filled"…

This translation is dead-on: "Mob. My name is Mob" (MSG).

That unruly mob jumped in and started yammering.

> And they begged him repeatedly not to order them to go into
> the Abyss. *Luke 8:31*

Personally, I vote for the Abyss.

That "deep" (KJV), "bottomless pit" (AMP) of "eternal darkness" (ICB) sounds like a perfect fit to me, a "place of confinement for demonic forces which, though hostile to God, are ultimately under his control."[60]

Let's face it, what *isn't* under God's control?

A nearby herd of pigs gave those cowering demons an idea.

> The demons begged Jesus, "Send us among the pigs; allow us
> to go into them." *Mark 5:12*

Acknowledging his supreme power, the demons threw themselves at his mercy.

So he threw them at the pigs.

> He gave them permission, and the evil spirits came out and
> went into the pigs. *Mark 5:13*

Possessed pigs. Would that be…deviled ham?
Okay, okay, I'll behave.

> The herd, about two thousand in number,… *Mark 5:13*

Two thousand?!? Yikes. That's a mob all right.

> …rushed down the steep bank into the lake and were
> drowned. *Mark 5:13*

It is for Mary of Magdala's sake that we spent time with this demoniac's story, because I want you to see the incredible change Jesus made in this man's life once he tossed out those demons. Believe me, the townspeople were about to be blown away.

> When they came to Jesus, they saw the man who had been
> possessed by the legion of demons, sitting there, dressed and in
> his right mind… *Mark 5:15*

You mean this raving lunatic was transformed on the spot? Instantly?
Yes he was.
This was not simply a case of the guy getting well because somebody cared enough to send the right Hallmark card.
This was a drop-dead *miracle!*
Now that he was "no longer a walking madhouse of a man" (MSG), he was sitting quietly instead of running around barking at the moon. He was fully dressed instead of stark naked, cutting his exposed skin. And he was in his right mind because he had left his old mind behind!
Without saying a word, this man struck terror in the hearts of those who showed up, probably to complain about getting swindled out of their swine.

> …and they were afraid. *Mark 5:15*

Not afraid of the demons, babe. Afraid of the One who had the power to cast them out. They coulda been a little leery of the former madman, too. Think of the cruel things they might have done to this poor soul. The chains, the beatings, the name calling, the house burning. Who knows?

> Then all the people of the region of the Gerasenes asked Jesus
> to leave them, because they were overcome with fear.
> *Luke 8:37*

To be specific, they were "suffering with dread and terror" (AMP), and for good reason. The supernatural had just thrust itself into their everyday lives. What might happen *next?* Besides, "if Jesus stayed yet other things might have to go."[61]

Girl, do I get *that.*

In those moments when I have a sudden awareness of God's supernatural presence crashing into my ordered and ordinary life, I feel my chest tighten and my heartbeat increase because I know from that moment on *nothing will be the same.* He never touches my life without leaving me a changed woman.

Changed, and grateful for it (eventually).

This demoniac—and surely our Mary Magdalene—felt exactly the same way.

> As Jesus was getting into the boat, the man who had been
> demon-possessed begged to go with him. *Mark 5:18*

The pigs begged to be set free; this freed man begged to be joined with Jesus. We can imagine him clinging to Jesus' robes, pleading, "Take me with you, Lord! What if the demons come back?"

> Jesus did not let him... *Mark 5:19*

Don't see this as a rebuke. The Lord just had a better plan in mind.

> [Jesus] said, "Go home to your family and tell them how much
> the Lord has done for you, and how he has had mercy on
> you." *Mark 5:19*

Of course! This man's family—for that matter, *everybody* who'd caught sight of the floating pig party—needed to see that this man truly was healed and made new and that the demons were gone for good. To whisk him away immediately might have left them doubting the rumors. Nor would the glory have gone to the Lord.

When I came to know Christ, people around me were convinced it was nothing more than Liz's latest obsession. They assumed "this, too, shall pass" and that my wild child would return. Rather than hiding in church 24/7, I needed to hang around and let them see a transformed life up close so they would grasp that indeed *something life changing had happened here.*

And all the people were amazed. *Mark 5:20*

Amazing grace, how sweet the sound of his voice must have been to the mad who became suddenly sane at his appearing.

The fact that Jesus did not allow this man to join him makes it all the more wonderful that he *did* let Mary Magdalene come with him! She didn't accidentally tag along, uninvited and unwelcome. Jesus wanted her by his side, or he would have gently refused her company. Instead, she left her demons behind and joined his disciples.

WHICH WAY DID THEY GO?

I can guess what you're thinking: "Why so many demons then and not now?"

We've all known people with serious, deep-seated problems but not many living in caves, breaking chains, howling at the moon, shouting out the name of Jesus. And since the crowd was always awe filled, it's clear they'd not seen these demons dealt with in such a way before.

Know what *I'm* thinking? I'm thinking that in the presence of the Messiah, demonic activity greatly increased. Satan was testing him publicly, just as he had in the wilderness one-on-one. "The coming of Jesus is a challenge to the kingdom of Satan."[62] Indeed, "all the forces of hell were let loose to raise havoc where the Redeemer of the world walked among men."[63]

Spiritual warfare and then some.

Good thing we have a mighty warrior to fight on our behalf.

The reason the Son of God appeared was to destroy the devil's work. *1 John 3:8*

Once the work of Calvary was finished and Christ ascended to the Father, sending the Holy Spirit to guard the hearts of his followers, the mention of demons in Scripture drops dramatically. Don't misunderstand me, demons are still out there—don't think they're not! But when it comes to those who profess Christ as savior, the demons are *out there*, not *in here*.

When Jesus met Mary Magdalene, he "transformed her into a strong tower."[64] A tower with the door shut tight. Jesus sealed her for himself. No one—and no thing—would ever stake a claim on Mary Magdalene again. He emptied her of seven demons, washed her clean, then filled her with his Spirit. "You are already clean because of the word I have spoken to you. Remain in me, and I will remain in you."[65]

Precisely what Mary Magdalene did. She remained. The demons did not.

I'm glad to leave those devilish dudes behind, aren't you? Not one-seventh as glad as Mary must have been. "No language can express the gratitude which she felt at her deliverance."[66] She expressed it, all right, through her unending devotion, for "she who was delivered from much loved much!"[67]

WHAT LESSONS CAN WE LEARN FROM MARY MAGDALENE AND HER DEMONS?

Let God fight your battles with the Bad Boy.
Why struggle to put the devil in his place when God is armed and dangerous and ready to do battle for us? We're never told the demon-possessed folks did *one thing* to help their deliverance process. It was all God, all the time. Same thing for the Christian trying to fight temptations. Let God go to war for you. Of course, that battle begins with total surrender to Christ. Wave the white flag, babe.

> Submit yourselves, then, to God. Resist the devil, and he will flee from you. *James 4:7*

Deliverance is all about God's worthiness, not ours.
More good news! The demoniacs we've met here weren't special in some way. They didn't earn their freedom or deserve it because of their good and righteous living. They were simply people in need. Not morally depraved, but not

sinless either. They were people like us, longing to be set free, loved by a Savior who pulled off their chains forever.

He will deliver even one who is not innocent. *Job 22:30*

Sometimes demons are smarter than we are.

The demons knew the Son of God when they saw him. They cried out his name at the top of their voices. Yet many who claim to know Christ won't whisper his name in public for fear of offending someone. If the demons are shouting his name, girlfriend, we'd better get with the program and shout first. Not just "God"—anybody can shout that. "Jesus Christ, Son of God"—that's the name that stakes the claim.

You believe that there is one God. Good! Even the demons believe that—and shudder. *James 2:19*

Guard your heart.

When Christ comes into your heart, give him the key and let Scripture serve as your guardian, holding the demons and their troublesome temptations at a safe distance. Reading God's Word is good, studying it is better, meditating upon it is better still, but *memorizing* God's Word—hiding it in your heart— is the best defense. When temptation comes aknocking, you'll be ready!

I have hidden your word in my heart that I might not sin against you. *Psalm 119:11*

GOOD GIRL THOUGHTS WORTH CONSIDERING

1. Were you aware, before reading *Unveiling Mary Magdalene,* that Mary of Magdala was demon possessed until she met Jesus? Do you think it's possible for her to have been so without somehow inviting those demons in? Why do you think the details of Jesus' casting out Mary Magdalene's seven demons were not included in any of the four gospels? Does that make you doubt the reality of it?

2. Do you believe in literal demons? Why or why not? If so, do you
    believe that you are demon free? How can you know for sure? Read
    Romans 8:38-39 aloud. Has any stone been left unturned—"death nor
    life," "height nor depth"—any possibility left uncovered? Is *feeling*
    separated from God the same as *being* separated? When we feel distant
    from him, where can we turn for assurance? According to these verses,
    from what will we *never* be separated?

3. Was it difficult to imagine the demoniac naked and shrieking and
    abusing himself in the desert? Do these same things happen today in
    mental institutions? In either case, were they to blame for their mad-
    ness? Is there hope for such people? How might you comfort a family
    member in that situation? Are you confident that Christ has the answer
    for *all* who are hurting?

4. What do you think was the "one word" Jesus used to cast out
    demons? Did the demons have a choice to obey or disobey? Does
    Christ give us the power to keep the Adversary at arm's length?
    What "one word" might you use, in Jesus' name, to be victorious over
    those pernicious spirits? What else do Christians have as ready
    weaponry?

5. What is your own understanding of the supernatural? Has there been a
    specific incident in your life, a particular moment, when you were
    aware of something happening outside the natural realm? Does it
    comfort you—or frighten you—to think of a spiritual world outside of
    our own earthly experience? Can you think of a scripture or two that
    assures us that a spiritual world does exist and that Christ has dominion
    over it?

6. Think of all the people Jesus delivered and healed during his min-
    istry...the blind, the mute, the leper. Why did these people not come
    forward in Jesus' defense in his last days? Are we always grateful for the
    Lord's work in our lives, or does an answer to prayer simply produce
    another request instead of the gratitude he deserves?

7. Why do you think Jesus would not allow the demoniac with the legion of demons to follow him, yet he allowed Mary and the other women to do so? Do you suppose the man was disappointed? Have you ever questioned why God seemed to have one calling on your life, another on someone else's? What would sending the man back to his community do for his family? For his community? For the kingdom of God?

8. Read again chapters 3 and 4 of *Unveiling Mary Magdalene*. How is Pastor Jake Christlike in his approach to helping Mary Delaney? What risks does he take on her behalf? What are his motivations? Why does Mary Delaney reject his ministry at first? Can you relate to her resistance—or his persistence—in some personal way?

Chapter Eleven

THROUGH THICK AND THIN

HER DEDICATION

Through perils both of wind and limb
Through thick and thin she follow'd him.
SAMUEL BUTLER

Now that Mary's demons are history, let's hit the road with Jesus.
Here's a reminder of who tagged along.

> The Twelve were with him, and also some women who had
> been cured of evil spirits and diseases: Mary (called Magdalene)
> from whom seven demons had come out; Joanna the wife of
> Cuza, the manager of Herod's household; Susanna; and many
> others. *Luke 8:1-3*

It's clear why Mary Magdalene wanted to be with Jesus and the other
women—they were the only ones who understood what she'd lived through.
They wouldn't judge her for her past or ask her to share painful details. If
you've been to Hades and back, beloved, you may find yourself drawn to
other women who've also seen the inside of a jail cell or the bottom of a shot

glass. Women who don't ask, "What was it really like?" or "How 'bout them demons?"

When they were traveling with their Savior, Mary Magdalene, Joanna, Susanna, and the other women felt whole, normal, and accepted. They knew that wherever they were headed, it was in the right direction. "We may follow Christ figuratively. Mary followed Him literally."[1] JoAnn and Suzy—make that Joanna and Susanna—followed too.

Going back to Magdala was *not* an option for Mary, even if she had a house waiting for her. Her old neighbors might have seen her as still a madwoman. And though she knew Christ had driven her demons out, perhaps she feared those dreaded devils might return—and bring friends. Ohhh no, she wasn't letting this Jesus out of her sight. And so she followed him, this holy man who'd saved her from the demons and given her a reason for living. This wasn't a job or a ministerial appointment for Mary. It was a commitment as binding as marriage, and it cost her everything.

We can only guess what she left behind—family, wealth, property, prestige. None of it is listed in Scripture because *none of it mattered.*

> And everyone who has left houses or brothers or sisters or
> father or mother or children or fields for my sake will receive
> a hundred times as much and will inherit eternal life.
> *Matthew 19:29*

You're thinking, *Oh, she's counting on that 'hundred times as much' thing. What a greedy so-and-so!* Not likely. Mary Magdalene would have turned right around and given it all to Jesus to support his ministry.

What about the others? Did they leave anything of value behind?

> Joanna the wife of Cuza, the manager of Herod's household…
> *Luke 8:3*

If you know the story of Herod Antipas from Mark 6, you'll remember his second wife, Herodias, and that grisly decapitated head of John the Baptist. (Sorry to mention it.) Well, Cuza was Herod's steward, or "business manager" (NLT), which was a position of prominence. His wife, Joanna, would have been a high-society dame for sure. Though Joanna outranked Mary Magdalene "socially, economically, and politically,"[2] Mary M. was given what is known as "pride of place" and was mentioned *before* Joanna. Forgive me for harping on that, but it really *is* significant. Mary Magdalene's contribution to Jesus' ministry flat *counted.*

Joanna's sacrifice is worth noting too. Tossing aside her comfortable way of life, Joanna followed Jesus, leaving behind "her mansion on earth for the mansion in Heaven she knew would be hers."[3]

And, oh, Susanna! What do we know about her?

> …Susanna; and many others. *Luke 8:3*

Her name means "lily,"[4] a lovely foreshadowing of the Easter story that looms on the horizon. She must have been a special servant of the cause to be included by name before the "many others."

How I wish the Bible told us more about these ancient sisters! Their names and their devotion to the Christ are the only glimpses we get of them throughout his three years of ministry, since "a veil of mystery hangs over the women."[5] We know enough though. We know they stayed beside him—in life, in death, and in life again—even if their voices do "become muffled whispers in the gospels."[6]

The Twelve followed Jesus because he called them.

The women followed Jesus out of sheer love and gratitude.

He healed them, delivered them, saved them, empowered them. And though it's not recorded in Scripture, he may have called these women to share the gospel publicly as well. It's clear he counted them among his closest disciples. He gave their lives meaning in a culture that did not always value women.

"Jesus broke the mold in His relationships with women,"[7] not only by welcoming them in his company, but also by including them in his parables. We think nothing of a woman being the central figure in a contemporary story, but back then, honey, it simply wasn't done. Jesus tossed that outmoded idea aside, making it "abundantly clear that his teaching, unlike that of other rabbis, was intended for both women and men."[8]

This did not go over well with the religious establishment.

Neither did the company Jesus kept. Soon the Pharisees started murmuring, "This man welcomes sinners and eats with them,"[9] to which Jesus responded with two familiar parables: (1) the shepherd who left ninety-nine sheep to find one lost sheep, and (2) the woman who lost one of her ten coins and so lit a lamp and swept the household looking for the missing coin.[10] Jesus concluded his stories—one with a male hero, one with a female hero— with the assurance that "there is rejoicing in the presence of the angels of God over one sinner who repents."[11]

Man. Woman.

Equally lost, equally forgiven.

We nod our heads in agreement today. But two thousand years ago Jesus' listeners probably dropped their jaws in shock or vehemently shook their heads in anger at the concept of men and women being equally worthy of God's attention.

Women had no honor of their own. Their primary role was to avoid embarrassing their husbands in public. They were taught to dress modestly, speak to men only when spoken to, and in general behave "in a positive, virginal manner."[12] When she left the house to go shopping, a wife had to be accompanied by a suitable male, "not so much to protect her, but to protect her husband's name from any slips she might make…through improper conduct. Any males who wished to address her had to do so through her chaperone, not directly."[13]

Can you imagine such a thing, my twenty-first-century sister? No question about it, "the place of the Oriental woman was in the rear."[14] *Ouch.* In fact, it was "politically incorrect to refer to the women being present" at all.[15]

These women who walked with Jesus were present all right. They were following, serving, supporting…and learning. Which was the most radical part of all. Women were allowed to listen to the words of God being read in the synagogue, "but they were never disciples of a rabbi unless their husband or master was a rabbi willing to teach them."[16]

Mary M. had no husband willing to claim her, no earthly master walking before her. But she had Jesus, both Bridegroom and Master to all his disciples, who taught her as they traveled side by side through Judea. Mary would have heard Christ proclaim the gospel at every turn—in the synagogue and the marketplace, at Martha and Mary's house in Bethany, and among the hills of Galilee. By the time of his death, Mary Magdalene would have been saturated with his truth. Immersed in it. Transformed by it.

Perhaps others who were not as physically close to Jesus tugged on her tunic from time to time, pressing her to share what she'd heard.

"Mary, we saw you talking with him. What else did he say?"

"*Psst!* Tell us, Mary. What did that story mean to you?"

And so, "delivered, Mary became a disciple,"[17] the simple definition of which is "one who learns from or about Jesus."[18] Having learned, she no doubt taught her sisters, for she was "a leader among the women comparable only to Peter among the men."[19] Today we'd find her heading up a Precepts class or serving as a Bible Study Fellowship teaching leader, qualified to teach the Word because she knew the One who spoke it.[20]

Makes total sense to us in the twenty-first century.

Made zero sense to the religious leaders of the first century.

Women were not permitted to pray, in public or at home. In the synagogue they were set apart from the men, hidden behind a screen. They couldn't bear legal witness, nor did their presence in the assembly count toward a quorum. Not to mention the fact that rabbis did not speak to women in public.[21]

Oops. Jesus broke that rule, too.

Those rabbis of old talked *about* women though. Two thousand years ago Rabbi Eliezer fumed, "Rather should the words of the Torah be burned than entrusted to a woman!"[22] Josephus, a historian of the time, chimed in, "The woman, says the law, is in all things inferior to the man."[23]

Time did not improve such biased opinions.

Origen, a second-century scholar, said, "It is not proper for a woman to speak in church, however admirable or holy what she says may be, merely because it comes from female lips."[24] Hang on, it gets worse. Jerome, in the fourth century, attacked women interested in religious service by snarling, "What do these wretched sin-laden hussies want!"[25]

We want nothing more—and nothing less, Jerome—than what Jesus gave us. The chance to hear and speak the Truth.

This much is very clear in Scripture: Mary Magdalene advanced the ministry of Jesus the Nazarene, not only by following him, not only by spreading his teachings, but also by providing something he needed: cash.

> These women were helping to support them out of their own means. *Luke 8:3*

"Means" as in money? Well! And they were "considerable means" (MSG) at that. This money was clearly theirs to spend—"private means" (NASB), "their own resources" (NEB). Whether money, food, or goods, they "used what they owned to help Jesus" (CEV).

How about *that!* The Lord's ministry was financed in part by *women!*

Now we know who paid for the meals all these good men must have eaten, whose silver denarii greased the palms of innkeepers to keep a dry roof over their heads on stormy nights, who paid for new sandals, kept their tunics from being repossessed by irate dry cleaners, and filled the animals up to their humps with Purina Camel Chow...*the sisters!*

A woman of independent means—meaning independent from a man—was a big, honkin' deal. Unlike the woman with the issue of blood who was penniless from going to doctors or the sinful woman with little more to her name than her alabaster jar of perfume, Mary Magdalene apparently had some sort of sizable nest egg. Furthermore, as a woman of substance, she no doubt enjoyed "the nurture and education suitable for a daughter of Israel."[26]

Mary was not only wealthy, she was *educated?* Suddenly we have before us yet another picture of Mary Magdalene, so different from the wanton seductress we'd once imagined or the demon-possessed woman slashing her skin with rocks in the wilderness and screaming like a banshee. Boggles the mind, doesn't it?

Now I'm more convinced than ever that Mary and her cohorts weren't a gaggle of teenagers dogging Jesus like groupies trailing a rock star. "Their ability to dispose of their money presupposes their financial independence, and possibly their maturity."[27]

As the Lizzie Revised Version calls it, "midlife mamas with dough."

Believe me, this large traveling band needed Mary M.'s help, since their visits were seldom the two-hour, glass-of-lemonade kind. Remember when it was time to feed the five thousand? His disciples fretted, "We have only five loaves of bread and two fish—unless we go and buy food for all this crowd."[28] Purchasing food, it seems, was one of their options, though it was out of the question on that particular day.

"Pizza for five thousand…to go!"

Not likely Mary M.'s budget could swing that.

How about lodging? When Jesus went down to Capernaum with his mother, brothers, and disciples, "they stayed for a few days."[29] Even if home-owners provided free rooms, several *days* of meals for a crowd would cost a bundle, yet "we never read of Jesus or His disciples taking up a collection or asking for money."[30]

In fact, he commanded his followers to do just the opposite.

> He told them: "Take nothing for the journey—no staff, no
> bag, no bread, no money, no extra tunic. Whatever house you
> enter, stay there until you leave that town." *Luke 9:3-4*

He received hospitality when it was offered, but Jesus generally traveled with nothing, expecting nothing. So when Mary M. and her company of women gave of their bounty, with "great humility…he accepted it."[31]

I'm beginning to wonder if one of the many reasons Jesus was despised by the Pharisees was this generous female financing. You can imagine what people thought of these women giving their substantial funds to a ragtag bunch of radicals. Nothing but "another form of lunacy."[32]

Yes indeed, I get that.

Nothing makes people sit up and take notice like a woman giving her money away.

Even *I* thought I was going a little mad that morning long ago when the offering plate went by and I slipped in *five dollars* instead of one. Not much, I know, but I was a brand-new Christian and had only *six* dollars in my wallet at the time and nothing in the bank! It was a big leap of faith for a young woman who once counted every crumb-covered quarter in her waitress apron to pay the rent.

There's also the possibility that Mary wasn't overly wealthy, just willing to share along with the others—"not rich women, but generous women."[33]

The point isn't the dollar amount but the percentage—*100 percent*, girl. All of it.

In those days new believers thought "it was proper to give *all* up to him—their property as well as their hearts."[34] They heard Jesus' teaching on this and responded accordingly because more than anything else they wanted to follow and support him.

> In the same way, any of you who does not give up everything
> he has cannot be my disciple. *Luke 14:33*

Mary and her spiritual sisters showed 'em how it was done. They left "home, family, relations, their village, their everyday life, and stayed with him, listening, speaking, traveling, offering goods and services, living with him, in short."[35]

"Living with him"? *Uh-oh.* No wonder Jesus was seen as such a trouble-maker. Men without their wives! Women without their husbands! People forsaking family for faith! It simply wasn't done. "We do find instances in the Talmud when women gave support to rabbis and their disciples out of their own money, property or foodstuffs, but for her to leave home and travel with a rabbi was unheard of."[36]

It seems Mary was as willing to go against convention as Jesus was.

By the way, resist the urge to tie an apron around Mary Magdalene's waist and to slip Playtex Living Gloves over her hands. Her service to him "was more than just cooking and serving meals."[37] Remember, Jesus and company were on the move, traveling all over Galilee. Cooking would have been minimal—ever been to Girl Scout camp for Primitive Week? And clothing meant loose tunics that were wash-and-wear—wash once, wear until worn out.

So yes, the women served Jesus, but it was "in no way a 'lesser' role and in fact had very much to do with Jesus' interpretation of witnessing for him."[38] Today we'd say they "walked their talk." The key is they had servants' *hearts,* whether or not they performed the chores that fit a servant's job description.

What Mary Magdalene was definitely *not* was Jesus' better half.

You'll find a handful of books on store shelves now that look for mystic connections between ancient Egyptian goddesses and biblical sisters, written by authors who speak of "the sacred union of male and female, of Bride and

Bridegroom…embodied in the intimate relationship of Jesus and Mary Magdalene."[39]

The intimate *what?*

Read on.

In 1945 an Arab peasant at Nag Hammadi in Upper Egypt stumbled upon an ancient jar containing papyrus books buried around A.D. 400. Before they found their way into safer hands, some were burned, some lost, some sold on the black market. Fifty-two remaining treatises are now housed in the Coptic Museum in Cairo,[40] and they contain some eye-opening material.

The *Gospel of Philip* states, "the companion of the [Savior is] Mary Magdalene."[41] So far, so good. *Companion* meaning a friend, someone who kept him company. No problem there. After all, "the fact that Mary Magdalene was one of the closest followers of Jesus is far from implying 'sexual intercourse.'"[42] Very far. Very, very far.

This ancient text continues, "[But Christ loved] her more than [all] the disciples, and used to kiss her [often] on her [mouth]."[43]

On her *what?* Don't panic, babe. Those brackets indicate a lacuna—that is, "a blank space or missing part."[44] So "kiss her on her [ ]" doesn't really tell us much.

One author explained, "We must not understand this 'kissing' in a sexual sense, but in a spiritual sense."[45] Yet people leap to conclusions, filling in brackets and blank spaces with whatever their fertile imaginations can come up with.

On the A&E *Biography* episode "Mary Magdalene: The Hidden Apostle," one New Testament professor sighed, "We would love to think that Jesus and Mary Magdalene were lovers. It's so romantic."[46] The Son of God a fornicator? That's not romantic; that's blasphemous. She quickly went on to call it "unlikely," but her take on our culture is revealing…and heartbreaking.

We shouldn't be surprised, beloved.

> For the time will come when men will not put up with sound
> doctrine. Instead, to suit their own desires, they will gather
> around them a great number of teachers to say what their

itching ears want to hear. They will turn their ears away from
the truth and turn aside to myths. *2 Timothy 4:3-4*

Despite the fact that most scholars insist "there's absolutely no historical
or biblical evidence that Mary Magdalene and Jesus were anything other than
very good friends,"[47] our itching ears perk up at the scandalous notion of
Jesus and Mary being one in flesh as well as in spirit. Female writers seem
especially eager to focus on Mary as his lover, which reduces Mary Magdalene
to a sexual being. Wasn't the whole idea of feminism (last time I checked) to
move women *past* such limitations?

Even Martin Luther declared that Mary Magdalene had a "hot, lusting,
rutting heart" for Jesus.[48] Goodness, Martin! Now who needs reforming?

Yes, Jesus was "the throb of Mary's heart, the lover of her soul,"[49] but
that's where it ended. Nothing else was throbbing, babe. The rest is pure conjecture based on our oversexed modern viewpoint.

Jesus loved Mary Magdalene, certainly. He knew her well. But he used
the same words for all of his disciples—to love, to know. Same Greek words,
same emotions. In a sense he knows us all "very well." The psalmist confessed
for all of us: "You know when I sit and when I rise; you perceive my thoughts
from afar. You…are familiar with all my ways."[50]

He knew Mary. He loved Mary.

But not like *that*.

She knew Jesus. She loved Jesus.

But not like *that*.

In evangelical lingo, we talk about having a "personal relationship with
God." Well, that's exactly what Mary Magdalene had. "This kind of friendship would be unheard-of in conventional Judaism, and would suggest a clear
break with custom."[51] But not a clear break with the biblical mandate to
remain sexually pure. Mary and Jesus were friends, not lovers. "Jesus Christ is
the same yesterday and today and forever."[52] He would not have been one
man in public and another man in private.

Perhaps to curtail such advances, God made very sure his Son wasn't
physically attractive. The prophet Isaiah wrote, "He had no beauty or majesty
to attract us to him, nothing in his appearance that we should desire him."[53]

Women like Mary were drawn to his love and his grace, not his form and his face. There's "no reason to doubt that she was a woman of spotless character and high social standing,"[54] a woman who felt a "brave, eager love" for this Jewish rebel,[55] rather than a shameful attraction.

Mary Magdalene devoted her life to his ministry. Whatever wealth she might have once owned, it was surrendered to Jesus. By choice she lived a life of poverty, harsh simplicity, and sacrifice. And whatever carnal relationships she might have had in her pre-demon past (and we can't rule out that possibility), it's clear that following Jesus "meant abstaining from sex."[56]

There it is, the unvarnished truth.

When I fell in love with Jesus—as you did perhaps, and as our delivered Mary Magdalene clearly did—there were a whole slew of sins and bad habits and ungodly behaviors in my life that needed to go. Some went quickly and (thank you, Lord) permanently—the Southern Comfort, the marijuana, the six nights a week on a barstool, the cocaine. Some departed, then circled back for a second go-around. Language issues (much victory there, sis, but don't pull out in front of me in traffic, just in case!). Materialism (always a struggle in our culture). And food. (*Groan.* Can I save that for another book?)

Of all the issues that needed immediate attention, my sexual promiscuity was obviously the one to begin with. The very afternoon I was baptized— February 21, 1982, if you're curious—the guy I was dating at the time came by for a visit. He arrived at my apartment expecting...well, you *know* what he was expecting. What he *got* was a woman in a slinky black nightgown, bubbling nonstop about Jesus, doing her best to cover everything from Genesis to Revelation while he was doing *his* best to uncover anything in reach or, at the very least, to change the subject.

Are you picturing this? *Good grief.*

He finally got the message and left. My life of celibacy began.

Women, especially younger women, corner me at conferences or send me heart-tugging e-mails: "I want to remain pure, but how do I live without sex?" An honest question. In our culture we assume it's impossible, if not unhealthy and downright un-American, to remain celibate. We look the other way when divorced couples at church take long weekend trips together.

We ask our children to wait until marriage yet expect the worst because, after all, "everybody's doing it."

Mary Magdalene wasn't doing it. Nor were the other disciples. Nor was Jesus.

Don't fool yourself into thinking "Well, that was a long time ago. Things were different then." Sex has always been popular. That's how every generation since Adam and Eve got here, including yours.

I believe, absolutely, that our Mary was able to serve the Savior with a pure heart—and everything else. It can be done. Is done all the time, in fact. The only time a pastor/parishioner story makes the news is when the two give in to the desires of the flesh. We never hear about the thousands of positive relationships, the solid friendships, the dedicated ministry partners who walk worthy of their calling.

Remember, Jesus was in his early thirties. If Mary Magdalene truly was his mother's age or older—perhaps much older—she no doubt treated him as a son, and the whole thing was a nonissue. Not because older women aren't attractive, but because the Word says he lived a life "without sin."

No further debate needed.

Now that we have a clearer picture of Mary Magdalene's healthy relationship with Jesus, her role as a servant-leader among the disciples, and her generous contribution of her resources to keep things moving, what did she *do* all day?

The Lord knows. But he's not telling.

Perhaps she and the other women were on hand when he shared the parable of the sower with the multitudes. Maybe she watched as the fishes and loaves turned into a multiplication table or saw him stretch out his hand to calm the raging sea.

Whatever her day-to-day life included, it surely included a lot of *walking*, because everywhere the Shepherd went, his sheep were sure to follow. Look at this quick travelogue (the italics are mine, for emphasis):

> Then he got into the boat *and his disciples followed him.*
> *Matthew 8:23*

Hearing of this, *the crowds followed him on foot* from the towns. *Matthew 14:13*

Jesus went to a town called Nain, *and his disciples and a large crowd went along with him. Luke 7:11*

Jesus went out as usual to the Mount of Olives, *and his disciples followed him. Luke 22:39*

Peter summed it up: "We have left all we had to follow you!"[57] Follow, follow, follow.

I can't think of anything harder for a natural leader like Mary Magdalene (or a take-charge chick like me) than to follow someone around, putting aside any agenda of her own. To follow, not knowing the final destination or how long they might be staying. To follow, instead of running ahead and saying, "I'll clear the way for you, Lord! I'll make the reservations, hit the market stands, call Foot Washers to Go, start supper…"

To follow, leaving everything behind, worries included.

Many among the hoards of listeners wanted to follow Jesus but had one excuse or another that stopped them.

"I will follow you, Lord; but first let me go back and say good-by to my family." *Luke 9:61*

Seems a reasonable request, doesn't it? But not to Jesus, who asked that those who sought after God be willing to leave their families.

"If anyone comes to me and does not hate his father and mother, his wife and children, his brothers and sisters—yes, even his own life—he cannot be my disciple." *Luke 14:26*

It shouldn't be surprising that the day finally came when some people stopped following. Once Jesus explained that "no one can come to me unless the Father has enabled him,"[58] a goodly number of his crew jumped ship.

From this time many of his disciples turned back and no longer followed him. *John 6:66*

His disciples—not the teeming masses, but his own people—"returned to their old associations" (AMP), "deserted him" (NLT), and "were not walking with him anymore" (NASB).

And the masses wrote him off as a madman, every bit as mad as Mary.

> Many of them said, "He is demon-possessed and raving mad.
> Why listen to him?" *John 10:20*

They stopped listening and started criticizing: "He's crazy, a maniac—out of his head completely" (MSG). Well, he *was* saying some pretty outrageous things. He called himself the "light of the world,"[59] "the way and the truth and the life,"[60] and the "long-awaited Messiah."[61]

What do you do with a man like that?

Kill him. Or follow him to the death.

"Either Jesus was a megalomaniac madman, or he was the Son of God. There is no escape from that choice."[62] Some chose wisely, perceiving that his words, his actions, and his miracles all pointed to God the Father.

> "These are not the sayings of a man possessed by a demon."
> *John 10:21*

Ask Mary Magdalene! She knew exactly what *that* was like. She knew the teachings of Jesus weren't "the words of a crazy man" (MSG). But not everyone was convinced. They saw him as worse than crazy. They saw him as *dangerous*.

Dark clouds were beginning to fill the skies above Jesus. Bloodthirst was in the air. As Jesus would say to his accusers, "This is your hour—when darkness reigns."[63] This righteous rebel had attracted enemies in powerful places, men who watched with glee as his disciples began to fall away.

Not Mary Magdalene. While others fell, she followed. "She has counted the cost, she has taken up her cross, and through astonishment, sorrow, and fear, she still advances."[64]

We get no stories of Mary Magdalene's doubting like Thomas[65] or getting involved in petty power plays about which of them was the greatest.[66] Nor is it recorded that she ever denied him. Pastor Luke didn't write, "I tell you,

Mary Magdalene, before the rooster crows today, you will deny three times that you know me."[67] Nope. Jesus was speaking to Peter, not Mary.

Though one cannot teach from silence, I think if there was something negative to be said about Mary M., or any of these women, it would have come out in one of the gospel accounts. Instead, "when the Master was on earth no woman's hand did Him harm and no woman's voice was uplifted against Him."[68] Think about that! Herodias asked for the head of John the Baptist...but not for the head of Jesus. While Pontius Pilate held the Lord's life in the balance, his wife, Claudia, sent a note begging her husband, "Don't have anything to do with that innocent man."[69]

Women could defend him, support him, follow him...but they could not save him. Mary's Deliverer was about to deliver himself into the hands of his adversaries.

And where were the male disciples? They got outta Dodge the minute Jesus was arrested. After a brief altercation during which a servant was rudely separated from his ear—temporarily, of course, since with a touch Jesus healed him[70]—the Lord's support team suddenly realized their leader was going to die. They had no intentions of facing the same gruesome end.

...all the disciples deserted him and fled. *Matthew 26:56*

That's right, they "cut and ran" (MSG). Only John appeared by name on the day Jesus was crucified. "The cowardly defection of the male disciples contrasts sharply with the calm presence of the women."[71] Especially that former devil woman, Mary Magdalene, who calmly, quietly followed her Savior to the cross one very dark Friday in Jerusalem.

WHAT LESSONS CAN WE LEARN FROM MARY MAGDALENE AND HER DEDICATION?

Jesus cuts across the bias.

The Lord is color-blind, gender neutral, and unimpressed with class distinctions. He delivered women, forgave women, healed women, taught women...and men. We are not better than men, sister, but we are not less valuable either. In the economy of Jesus Christ, everyone counts. May his people go and do likewise, starting with us.

> There is neither Jew nor Greek, slave nor free, male nor female,
> for you are all one in Christ Jesus. *Galatians 3:28*

God has always loved a cheerful giver.

Mary Magdalene gave all she had—all her money, all her possessions, all her time, all her talents, all her faith, all her hopes for the future. All were poured into the pockets of this man Jesus. She humbles me, big time, because I hold stuff back. "Can't I keep this stray trinket, Lord? How 'bout this little habit—it's not *that* bad, is it?" If we want all that Jesus has to offer us, we gotta be willing to give him everything first.

> "Give, and it will be given to you. A good measure, pressed
> down, shaken together and running over, will be poured into
> your lap. For with the measure you use, it will be measured to
> you." *Luke 6:38*

Stick to the Truth.

Ten minutes on the Internet should convince you that, when it comes to options in spiritual pursuits, there are plenty to pick from. How's a girl supposed to figure out what's true and what's false? Is something true just because it's ancient? No—Satan is old as the hills and still peddling lies. Is something true just because it's intelligent sounding? No, there's a difference between *sounding* right and *being* right. Unless we compare every teaching to the revealed Word of God, we run the risk of being pulled in the wrong direction, which is any direction that doesn't lead to Jesus, the lover of our souls.

> But I am afraid that just as Eve was deceived by the
> serpent's cunning, your minds may somehow be led astray
> from your sincere and pure devotion to Christ.
> *2 Corinthians 11:3*

Follow the leader.

First on the list, that's our Mary M. Pretty impressive for a woman whose spoken words during the earthly ministry of Jesus weren't recorded in Scripture, with the exception of her Easter morning conversations. Maybe her new demon-free life was testimony enough. Maybe her generous actions spoke for her. Maybe her walk served as her talk. Maybe people followed in her footsteps because her toes trod so closely on the heels of Jesus. Maybe we can learn from this woman, this former prisoner of Satan who played Follow the Leader better than anyone I've ever known.

> Set me free from my prison, that I may praise your name.
> Then the righteous will gather about me because of your
> goodness to me. *Psalm 142:7*

GOOD GIRL THOUGHTS WORTH CONSIDERING

1. Mary Magdalene hung out with other demon-delivered women— Joanna and Susanna, to name two. Do you find yourself drawn to other sisters who have similar backgrounds to yours, whether strait-laced, sin filled, or somewhere in the middle? If so, is it by intent? Do you feel more comfortable and less judged by those who are like you? Are there advantages to surrounding yourself with women who have very different spiritual backgrounds? Disadvantages? What might you teach one another? Can you imagine having a woman with Mary Magdalene's past as your Bible study leader? Why or why not?

2. Why do *you* think Mary left the life that she knew in Magdala? Was she running away from her past—or toward her future? Have you had to leave anything behind in your pursuit of Christ? Was it difficult? Was it worth it? What have you learned in the process?

3. The restrictions for women in Mary's time and place sound extreme to us two thousand years later. Why do you think there were so many rules about what women could do? Were any of them valid for that era?

Do you see any social restrictions like that today? Why do you suppose Jerome and others so vehemently opposed women serving as leaders in the church? Do you think men and women in ancient Judea and Galilee responded differently to Christ's equal-opportunity ministry? And what about people today?

4. We've met Mary the demon-possessed madwoman, Mary the educated woman of means, and now Mary the woman who gave it all up for God. How do you juxtapose such different personas? Can each be accurate? Have you known women who've lived very different lives like that? What changed them?

5. Before reading *Unveiling Mary Magdalene* were you familiar with the Nag Hammadi papyrus books unearthed last century? Do such things challenge or threaten your faith? Why or why not? Should we give ancient texts like these equal weight with Scripture? Why or why not? How might you respond to someone who believes differently than you do? What might Jesus have to say on the subject of additional texts that are not part of the biblical canon?

6. Was it ever your understanding that Jesus and Mary were more than friends, that they were attracted to one another or were, in fact, lovers? Or perhaps that it was a one-sided attraction on Mary's part? Whatever the case, where did that idea come from? If you've not heard of such a theory, does the conjecture surprise you? disgust you? intrigue you? Does it seem even remotely possible? Could you honor, respect, and worship a Christ who was sexually active? Why or why not?

7. Mary Magdalene was both a follower and a leader. How is that possible? What do those words mean to you? Do you lean toward one or the other—or demonstrate both, like Mary? Why did people stop following Jesus? Fear of death? Of looking foolish? Did he ask too much of them? Do any of those reasons mirror why people turn away from his message today? We have no record of Mary Magdalene's doubting or

challenging or denying the Christ. Why not, do you suppose? Is she a role model for you in that regard?

8. Read again chapters 5 and 6 of *Unveiling Mary Magdalene.* In what specific ways do we see Mary Delaney's behavior changing from madwoman to glad woman? Do you believe that Christ can make that dramatic a difference in a person's life? Were you fearful to keep reading Mary D.'s story, knowing what might be coming next? How do you feel now, knowing what will come next in this study of the life of Jesus...and of Mary Magdalene?

Chapter Twelve

PATH OF SORROW

HER DESPAIR

The path of sorrow, and that path alone,
Leads to the land where sorrow is unknown.
WILLIAM COWPER

On her darkest days with the demons, Mary Magdalene could never have imagined the pain and sorrow that awaited her at the foot of a heinous instrument of torture and death called a cross.

What, kill Jesus? Pure foolishness! Who would sentence such a man to die, a man who was the very definition of virtue?

That's the crux of it. He was too good for them.

> He was despised and rejected by men, a man of sorrows, and familiar with suffering. *Isaiah 53:3*

Long before the suffering began, the Lord had told his followers this day would come. But did they listen? Nah. They were too busy trying to figure out who was greatest among them or who would get to sit next to him at the heavenly banquet.

> Jesus began to explain to his disciples that he must go to Jeru-
> salem and suffer many things at the hands of the elders, chief

priests and teachers of the law, and that he must be killed and
on the third day be raised to life. *Matthew 16:21*

Jesus was so straightforward about it. What did they think he meant? Perhaps it was too much for them, too horrific to imagine. Peter hotly denied it—"This shall never happen to you!"[1]—to which Jesus shot back, "Get behind me, Satan!"[2]

Whoa.

It was clear Jesus knew his enemy well. Hadn't he spent the last three years tossing out Satan's minions from their human hosts?

When Jesus made the same prophecy about his death and resurrection six days later, it was as if the poor *duh*-sciples had forgotten that whole incident, because the Bible tells us, "And the disciples were filled with grief."[3] Bless 'em, they kept missing the exciting part about Jesus' being raised from the dead and focused only on the death itself. The end. *Finis.*

Perhaps the women listened more attentively when the Lord went on to explain what was expected of them.

> Then Jesus said to his disciples, "If anyone would come after
> me, he must deny himself and take up his cross and follow
> me." *Matthew 16:24*

And the women did exactly as he commanded. They came after him, denying their own safety, putting aside their own needs, willing to forfeit their own lives if necessary. No doubt in my mind, these sisters would have gladly carried his cross if anyone had let them. Instead that task fell on the shoulders of Simon of Cyrene,[4] while the women bore an equally heavy burden—their broken hearts.

> A large number of people followed him, including women
> who mourned and wailed for him. *Luke 23:27*

No doubt they followed closer than was prudent, "grief-stricken" (NLT) as they were, their vision blurred with "crying and weeping" (CEV). Many of the paintings of Mary Magdalene show her covered with tears. Even the word *maudlin*, taken from the French form of her name, Magdalen, is defined as "emotionally silly" and "weakly and effusively sentimental."[5]

"Weak," is it? Man, it's the person who *never* cries who worries me. Dry eyes at a tragic moment point to an uncaring attitude or a hardened heart. Mary Magdalene and the other women had neither of those.

Despite his agony, Jesus missed nothing. His gaze caught every tear.

> Jesus turned and said to them, "Daughters of Jerusalem, do
> not weep for me; weep for yourselves and for your children."
> *Luke 23:28*

The Lord knew something Mary and company did not: Calamity was about to fall on Jerusalem, thanks to their Roman rulers.[6] While these women "raised a death-wail for Jesus," he raised "a death-wail for Jerusalem."[7] Even facing his own demise, he thought of these women, these daughters of Jerusalem, and the misery that awaited them.

Alas, his own destruction would come first, also at the hands of the Romans.

> They came to a place called Golgotha (which means The Place
> of the Skull). *Matthew 27:33*

The ancient Phoenicians are credited with inventing crucifixion as a brutal means of execution around the time of David, a thousand years before Christ was crucified.[8] The horrors of the cross—in Greek, *stauros*—were well known by those who challenged the authority of Rome. Still, risking all, the women stood.

> Many women were there, watching from a distance.
> *Matthew 27:55*

The lists of women at Golgotha differ in the New Testament accounts, "probably because the audiences for whom [the gospel writers] were writing would have known some of the women better than others."[9] It seems everyone knew Mary M., for she's the only one listed in every situation.

> They had followed Jesus from Galilee to care for his needs.
> *Matthew 27:55*

Doing what they did best, "ministering to him" (RSV), the women continued to follow him on his journey of sorrow. The Greek word is *diakonousai,* from the same root as the word *deacon.* They were serving him, caring for his physical requirements and his emotional needs as well. They could hardly do otherwise, so great was their love for this Jesus.

> Among them were Mary Magdalene, Mary the mother of
> James and Joses, and the mother of Zebedee's sons.
> *Matthew 27:56*

"Among them" means this is not a comprehensive list, just the main players. Once again, Mary Magdalene goes to the head of the class.

We learn from Mark's gospel that the wife of Zebedee was named Salome.[10] No, honey, not *that* Salome, the dancing daughter of Herodias. A different Salome, the "mother of the Zebedee brothers" (MSG).

> Many other women who had come up with him to Jerusalem
> were also there. *Mark 15:41*

Mary M. led the way, but "many other women" were right behind her. There was precious little the female disciples could do, but they were there. Their purpose was simply to *be.* I am such a *doing* sort of woman, such a list-making, goal-setting kind of gal, that I stand in utter awe of women who risked their lives simply to walk and watch and support this condemned man with their love and prayers and tear-drenched faces.

> Near the cross of Jesus stood his mother, his mother's sister,
> Mary the wife of Clopas, and Mary Magdalene. *John 19:25*

Note this is the only time Mary is listed *last* among a group of women. Mom is mentioned first simply because Jesus is about to address her. All of them stood nearby but not *too* close! It was "very dangerous for family and friends of the crucified to be seen near a cross."[11] These women were beyond courageous to be there, willing to risk death to mourn his suffering, knowing that the "Romans did not hesitate to inflict the same death on relatives or followers of an enemy of the state."[12] Oh, the cruel perversity of it! Even women were not exempt from such torture.

Speaking of which, where were the male disciples? Curiously absent, it seems. Of the Twelve, one was dead by his own hand, having betrayed the

Christ,[13] and only one—the apostle John, the beloved disciple—was listed among those at the cross. In the midst of his agony, the Lord acknowledged John's presence.

> When Jesus saw his mother there, and the disciple whom he
> loved standing nearby, he said to his mother, "Dear woman,
> here is your son." *John 19:26*

To the last, Jesus was aware of the women standing nearby, including his mother. I can't begin to imagine how *she* must have felt, she who had carried the Son of Man in her womb and had watched him grow up from innocent childhood to innocent manhood. It's no surprise that we find her close by on that sacred day. She was his mother. Out of love, devotion, and maternal duty, she had to be there.

But Mary Magdalene *chose* to be there. However painful, however agonizing it was to watch him die, faithful Mary Magdalene wanted not only to see him, but also to be seen by him, offering her silent support.

Years ago, when my mother's life was slipping through her hands, I stood by her hospital bed at the age of twenty-three, crushed with grief. Nothing in my young life had prepared me for the horror of watching this gentle, creative woman slowly collapse into skin and bones as each week dragged by. I felt so helpless just standing there, knowing I could do nothing to ease her discomfort, nothing to stop emphysema's deadly grip on her lungs.

But I *had* to be there, had to communicate my love and support any way I could, even if it was little more than patting her hand and sneaking in the occasional Hershey's chocolate bar. (I was far from the perfect daughter, but I *did* know what my mother liked best.)

Then came the visit when she managed to scrawl on a piece of paper "Don't come."

Oh, Mom.

Was my presence making it worse for her? Now I was more distraught. Though it broke my heart to watch her suffer, I was certain it would be even worse to stay away. And so I continued to visit her, determined to be cheerful and not add to her concerns.

When the end came in the early hours of a gray May morning, only my father was at her bedside. Mom was probably relieved not to have all six of her adult children crowded into her sickroom, watching her struggle for her last breath. But I'll always regret that I was not there.

Always, Mom.

When the one she loved most breathed his last, Mary Magdalene was there.

We have no record of Jesus' asking his disciples not to watch him die. On the contrary, I believe he wanted them present for the crucifixion because it was the single greatest expression of love ever seen by humankind. As Catherine of Siena wrote in the fourteenth century, "Nails could not have held God-made-Man fastened to a tree, had not love held him there."

Mary Magdalene remained for the whole of it, every agonizing hour. She saw him stripped naked and exposed to the elements, his human form on display for all to see. Even his clothes no longer belonged to him.

> When they had crucified him, they divided up his clothes by
> casting lots. *Matthew 27:35*

Lord Jesus, it's so hard to watch. To see you like this. To think of your earthly body so blatantly abused. To see every gaping wound, to see the nails tearing at your skin.

Oh, Lord.

Mocking words from onlookers struck a deeper wound. Mary no doubt cringed at every blasphemy that was thrown at him like rotting fruit.

> Those who passed by hurled insults at him, shaking their heads
> and saying, "You who are going to destroy the temple and
> build it in three days, save yourself! Come down from the
> cross, if you are the Son of God!" *Matthew 27:39-40*

But you did not come down, Jesus. You stayed there. For us.

The passersby were cruel enough, but even those who professed to love God ridiculed Jesus on that cross.

> In the same way the chief priests, the teachers of the law and
> the elders mocked him. *Matthew 27:41*

To quite literally add insult to injury, the criminals who hung beside the Christ found fault with his innocence.

> In the same way the robbers who were crucified with him also
> heaped insults on him. *Matthew 27:44*

Pierced with words, pierced with nails, pierced with the pain of our sins, Jesus was lifted up on that cross only to be brought down to the lowest of human degradations.

> But he was pierced for our transgressions, he was crushed for
> our iniquities; the punishment that brought us peace was upon
> him, and by his wounds we are healed. *Isaiah 53:5*

It must have grieved Mary Magdalene to the point of utter collapse to see Jesus' tormented expression, hear his anguished cries, smell the blood and sweat all around her, feel the rude soldiers brushing against her as they taunted him, taste the bitter tears running along the corners of her mouth.
Jesus. Rabboni.
When the sun was at its zenith about noon, the land grew suddenly dark, as though creation itself was hiding its face from the holy passion of the cross.

> From the sixth hour until the ninth hour darkness came over
> all the land. *Matthew 27:45*

Three hours of darkness. This was no solar eclipse, nature's sleight of hand when the moon covers the sun. In an eclipse, the sky turns to twilight, not total darkness. And an eclipse is fleeting. Scientists measure the "totality" in mere minutes.
No, this darkness was what insurance attorneys call "an act of God."
Beyond human ability to control or intervene.
Or in this case, to comprehend.
We can guess what happened to the throng when the skies suddenly darkened without warning. People ran back to the safety of their homes in Jerusalem, filling the air with frightened whispers. Roman soldiers gripped the handles of their weapons, squinting into the darkness. The curious crowds who'd followed Jesus through the streets thinned to the faithful few.

But Mary Magdalene stayed.

She was there to hear his heart-rending plea, which surely tore her own heart asunder.

> About the ninth hour Jesus cried out in a loud voice, "Eloi,
> Eloi, lama sabachthani?"—which means, "My God, my God,
> why have you forsaken me?" *Matthew 27:46*

"Abandoned" (MSG) by his heavenly Father, he echoed the words of David from Psalm 22:1, asking the eternal "why"—why did the Father withdraw from his presence, "leaving Me helpless, forsaking and failing Me in My need?" (AMP).

Though necessary, his Father's absence was the hardest blow of all.

A deathblow, in fact.

> And when Jesus had cried out again in a loud voice, he gave up
> his spirit. *Matthew 27:50*

Luke recorded that the last words of Jesus were "Father, into your hands I commit my spirit," after which "he breathed his last."[14] According to John, the beloved disciple, Jesus also said, "'It is finished.' With that, he bowed his head and gave up his spirit."[15] His last human breath no doubt sounded like the lament of a man longing for the end to come quickly.

> For while we are in this tent, we groan and are burdened,
> because we do not wish to be unclothed but to be clothed with
> our heavenly dwelling, so that what is mortal may be swal-
> lowed up by life. *2 Corinthians 5:4*

He who was unclothed, then swathed in darkness, died at last.

Heaven and earth—and Mary Magdalene—took notice.

> At that moment the curtain of the temple was torn in two
> from top to bottom. *Matthew 27:51*

"Top to bottom"—a work of God, not of man, who would start at the bottom of the fabric and tear upward.

The earth shook and the rocks split. *Matthew 27:51*

I've been through three earthquakes, but none like this one. This was a God quake, strong enough to shake dead people awake.

The tombs broke open and the bodies of many holy people
who had died were raised to life. *Matthew 27:52*

Goodness. Hard to miss something like this.

Ask Lazarus, who came out of the grave after four days, already in a smelly state of decay: Resurrected bodies don't go unnoticed.

When the centurion and those with him who were guarding
Jesus saw the earthquake and all that had happened, they were
terrified, and exclaimed, "Surely he was the Son of God!"
Matthew 27:54

Yes, he surely was.

And yes, he surely is.

At this critical moment in history, Matthew's and Mark's accounts draw attention to the women who were present. Both list three women by name; both mention Mary Magdalene first, naturally.

A famous painting by Rubens, *Descent of the Cross,* shows Mary Magdalene helping to lower Christ's body.[16] Such a scene cannot be biblically proven, but in the sense that Mary M. was willing to do anything *except* depart from her Lord's side, it's a possibility.

After the darkness faded and the light of a late spring afternoon returned to the skies over Golgotha, someone stepped forward.

As evening approached, there came a rich man from
Arimathea, named Joseph, who had himself become a disciple
of Jesus. *Matthew 27:57*

The time is ambiguous. "Late in the afternoon" (MSG) or "some time after three o'clock,"[17] a rich man appeared on the scene. In a single sentence we know his name, his town, his allegiance to the Christ, and the health of his investment portfolio.

The man of sorrows who'd hung on a cross between two thieves was about to bring Isaiah's prophecy to life: "He was assigned a grave with the wicked, and with the rich in his death."[18]

Wealthy Joseph, a true believer, also believed in using his influence for the good of the kingdom. He took his request straight to the top.

> Going to Pilate, he asked for Jesus' body, and Pilate ordered
> that it be given to him. *Matthew 27:58*

Gutsy move, Joe! You see, bodies of executed criminals belonged to Rome, and "no one had a right to remove the body but by the authority of the magistrate."[19]

Joe brought along a little moral support.

> He was accompanied by Nicodemus, the man who earlier had
> visited Jesus at night. *John 19:39*

So we're thinking, *Nick at Nite?* Nick who? What night?

Nicodemus is introduced in John's gospel as a Pharisee, a "member of the Jewish ruling council."[20] The perfect guy to meet with Pilate. Plus Nicodemus was one of the followers of Christ, "one of their own number,"[21] convinced that Jesus was the Messiah. He had come "to Jesus at night and said, 'Rabbi, we know you are a teacher who has come from God.'"[22] (This word for *teacher* in Greek is *didaskalos*—hence, Paul Didaskalos, the gardener we met with Mary Delaney in the funeral home.)

To honor his teacher, Nicodemus brought more than an apple. He brought a fragrant offering fit for a king.

> Nicodemus brought a mixture of myrrh and aloes, about
> seventy-five pounds. *John 19:39*

This mixture was an "embalming ointment" (NLT), made of two substances Jesus was well acquainted with. Myrrh was acrid and bitter, with a "particularly unpleasant" taste, but useful to heal wounds or to sooth muscular pains.[23] As one of the gifts of the Magi, myrrh was a scent Jesus had known since birth.

Aloe was *not* the succulent plant you can find at any farmer's market, the bright green one with the cool, moist gel inside the leaves that makes a dandy salve. Rather, it was an aromatic substance made from the resin of the agallocha tree.

And seventy-five *pounds* of the stuff? You would have smelled Nick coming from miles away! This "very costly evidence of Nicodemus' devotion"[24] was just the right amount for a royal burial[25] and therefore the perfect choice for the King of kings.

> Taking Jesus' body, the two of them wrapped it, with the
> spices, in strips of linen. This was in accordance with Jewish
> burial customs. *John 19:40*

Jewish burial customs did not include true embalming—a removal of the brains and entrails—as practiced by the Egyptians.[26] *Ick.* Rather, the body was anointed with the myrrh and aloes mixture, then wrapped with strips of linen.

It seems they did this as soon as they were presented with the body of Jesus. Once the corpse—oh, I can't bear to call it that! Once his lifeless body was properly wrapped, they found him a resting place. The idea was that "bodies were placed on a shelf and allowed to decompose for a year. Then the bones were gathered and placed in a…'bone box,'"[27] or an "ossuary," a decorative depository for the bones of the dead.[28]

Not *these* bones. Not hardly!

For the next three days, his body simply needed a waiting room.

> At the place where Jesus was crucified, there was a garden…
> *John 19:41*

Ahh. How appropriate. Since Jesus said, "my Father is the gardener,"[29] a green haven was the perfect choice. Interesting that only John's gospel calls it a garden.

> …and in the garden a new tomb… *John 19:41*

Though we have no description of this grave in Scripture, excavations of the area suggest "a bench-like aperture with an arched ceiling hewn in the length of the wall,"[30] with about a three-foot square entrance.[31] You're right, that's not a very big space. It was, after all, hewn from the rock, not a natural cave. And it was designed for the dead, not the living.

> ...in which no one had ever been laid. *John 19:41*

Why is that significant? It means "Jesus' body was not brought into contact with corruption."[32]

> Because it was the Jewish day of Preparation and since the
> tomb was nearby, they laid Jesus there. *John 19:42*

Friday was the day to prepare for the Passover, and they were running out of time.

If his death occurred at approximately three in the afternoon and the Sabbath began at six, they only had three hours to give Jesus' body a proper burial, which Jewish law required: "If a man guilty of a capital offense is put to death and his body is hung on a tree, you must not leave his body on the tree overnight. Be sure to bury him that same day, because anyone who is hung on a tree is under God's curse."[33]

"God's curse," is it? I am haunted by the words, "But the LORD was pleased to crush Him, putting Him to grief."[34] Wrap your heart around this one, sis. God turned his back on his Son—by choice—rather than turn his back on us for eternity.

His body, now a fragrant sacrifice, lay in the tomb.

> [Joseph of Arimathea] rolled a big stone in front of the
> entrance to the tomb... *Matthew 27:60*

Not to keep Jesus in, of course—the idea of his leaving the tomb was preposterous—but to keep undesirables out, in particular the "wild animals and grave robbers,"[35] who frequented the tombs.

> ...and [Joseph of Arimathea] went away. *Matthew 27:60*

Arimathea was "about twenty miles northwest of Jerusalem on the border between Judea and Samaria,"[36] and sundown was fast approaching, so Joseph no doubt headed for a nearby inn or the home of a friend.

Not everyone left the scene though.

> The women who had come with Jesus from Galilee followed
> Joseph and saw the tomb and how his body was laid in it.
> *Luke 23:55*

Clearly they were close on Joseph's heels or they would have missed see-ing the tomb and the body, since a huge stone now blocked the entrance. And which women were they?

> Mary Magdalene and Mary the mother of Joses saw where he
> was laid. *Mark 15:47*

Since these two almost always traveled in tandem, we can imagine how closely knit their friendship must have been. Mary M. the leader and the "other Mary" as the supportive one perhaps. Or both may have had strong natures and shared the propensity for going where others feared to tread.

The Irish writer Eaton Barrett summed up the truth about courageous Mary Magdalene:

> She, while apostles shrank, could danger brave,
> Last at his cross, and earliest at his grave.[37]

More than duty brought our Mary to this gloomy place of mourning. Her heart was entombed there. Jesus not only understood her but accepted her "as is." How we all long for that! To be loved and not judged. To be wel-comed and not rejected. To have someone praise our strengths rather than point out our faults.

For Mary M., Jesus was leader and teacher, savior and sustainer, brother and friend—all in one humble man. For her, his death must have equaled the unimaginable grief of losing one's entire family in an afternoon. Maybe she couldn't leave because she couldn't move, so stricken was she with numbing, paralyzing grief.

When I buried my precious daddy just before my work on *Unveiling Mary Magdalene* began, the graveside service was very short at his request. A few lines of liturgy, a prayer, a reading from Scripture. Honestly, I don't remember any of it. My only clear recollection is standing there, staring at the freshly turned earth and the tiny stone box that held all that remained of my father.

How could so small a thing contain a man who'd meant so much to me?

One by one my brothers and sisters moved toward the cars scattered along the drive that meandered through the cemetery. I could not leave him. I felt my husband gently tugging at my elbow, but my feet were rooted to the spot, my heart unwilling to say what had to be said.

Good-bye, Daddy.

The two Marys would have understood. They, too, could not say farewell.

> Mary Magdalene and the other Mary were sitting there opposite the tomb. *Matthew 27:61*

There they sat "in plain view of the tomb" (MSG), their gazes no doubt glued to the huge rock that stood between them and their departed Lord. Were they simply mourning him or surreptitiously guarding his remains from man and beast? Or were they waiting expectantly for something miraculous to happen, inside or outside the grave?

We can only guess what they were thinking. But what Mary Magdalene demonstrated was incredible courage and unending devotion since being seen near "the grave of an enemy of the state was just as risky as being found in the proximity of the cross."[38] Plus, with her background, "hanging around tombs" was definitely "dangerous for her emotional stability."[39]

Might be demons skulking around those graves.

Might be Roman soldiers lurking behind those rocks.

Could be there wasn't much difference, danger-wise.

On the afternoon we've come to know as "Good Friday," the women would've had a few hours at most before the sun set and the Sabbath began. Eastern tradition tells us that the Sabbath officially begins in the last minutes of twilight when a black thread and a white thread appear the same color—gray.

At that gray moment in time, they trudged toward home as the Law required, their steps heavy, their hearts heavier still. "Never was a sadder Sabbath spent in the history of the world than that when the Son of God lay in the tomb."[40]

But they rested on the Sabbath in obedience to the command-
ment. *Luke 23:56*

Friday was the Day of Preparation because from Friday night until Saturday night was proclaimed "a sabbath of complete rest to you, and you shall
humble your soul…from evening until evening you shall keep your sabbath."[41]

Most churches don't address that sacred Saturday much. An Easter egg
hunt. A parade down Main Street. Shopping for a bonnet with all the frills
upon it.

In the Moravian congregation of my childhood, however, Saturday is the
Great Sabbath. The service at four o'clock in the afternoon is solemn indeed.
The music is somber, the tone is worshipful, and the mood is one of sorrow. I
distinctly remember a dear soul weeping softly in the pew behind me. I stole
a glance over my shoulder, wanting to catch her eye, to nod in sympathy.

But her grieving was beyond human comfort.

Her salt-and-pepper head was bent forward, a tissue pressed to her red-
rimmed eyes. It seemed her spirit was crushed with thoughts of her Savior
trapped in an earthly tomb. I desperately wanted to whisper what she—what
we—need to hear when all seems lost.

It will end soon.

When the Sabbath was over… *Mark 16:1*

Still not morning but getting closer. It's Saturday evening. The Sabbath
concluded, the marketplace is bustling once again. The women are—what
else?—shopping. Not for themselves. For the One who hasn't left their minds
for a single minute.

Mary Magdalene, Mary the mother of James, and Salome…
Mark 16:1

Our favorite trio. Note who is not mentioned here, nor was she included
among those at the tomb: Mary the mother of Jesus. No doubt she'd had two
sleepless nights, mentally revisiting her son's suffering on the cross, and so
remained at home in deep mourning. If so, none of the women buying spices
were blood relatives of Jesus. Usually family members were in charge of the

menial task of caring for a dead relative, though it would have been passed on to a lowly servant. A good Jewish girl touch a dead body? No, no, no. There were rules about that!

As usual, Mary Magdalene ignored convention and went with her heart.

> …[the women] bought spices so that they might go to anoint
> Jesus' body. *Mark 16:1*

While they might have kept a few ointments around the house, they surely wanted spices that were fresh and fragrant, despite the cost. But hadn't Nicodemus brought a truckload? Seventy-five-plus *pounds* of aromatic spices would have filled a *very* big alabaster jar.

Didn't the men do a good enough job? Perhaps the women didn't think so. As when I quietly clean the kitchen after Bill does the dishes. Women sometimes see details men don't. The sisters planned "to anoint the head and face, and perhaps the wounded hands and feet, and to scatter sweet spices upon and about the body."[42] Women's work, in the best sense of the term. Gentle. Caring. Purposeful.

Maybe the women simply wanted some time alone with the body and needed the spices as props, as justifiable evidence for any soldiers they might meet hanging around the tomb demanding, "Who invited you?"

No one invited her. Mary Magdalene simply came to anoint her Lord with her tears and her embalming ointment. Honey, don't you wish Mary knew then what we know now? That "weeping may endure for a night, but joy cometh in the morning."[43]

Yes, Lord! Let the morning come.

> Very early on the first day of the week, just after sunrise, they
> were on their way to the tomb. *Mark 16:2*

It's v-e-r-y early. The gospel of John says, "It was still dark,"[44] and the Greek literally means "deep twilight."[45] The predawn hour points to the urgency the women felt. *Something* drove them out the door before the full light of day. After all, sun*rise* and sun*shine* are two different things.

It wasn't common sense that drove them to a graveyard in that murky twilight. "A woman would scarcely have ventured outside the city alone at such an hour with Jerusalem crowded with visitors."[46] They were all brave, but Mary Magdalene in particular—this woman who had spent a season of her life in total darkness, separated from the light of truth and of Christ.

Bet she didn't sleep a wink Saturday night, waiting for the morning song of the birds, which chirp loudest just before sunrise. Perhaps she scanned the sky, looking for the "bright Morning Star"[47] to herald the dawn.

As solemn as the Great Sabbath lovefeast of the Moravians is, their Easter sunrise service is joy unspeakable. A trombone choir wakens the sleeping townsfolk long before the first streak of light enters the sky. Slowly but surely the worshipers make their way through the misty morning fog to gather in the dim sanctuary, anticipation the watchword of the hour.

Mary Magdalene would have been the first to arrive.

Love pulled her through the dark streets of Jerusalem.

Hope tugged at her skirts and urged her feet forward.

Devotion propelled her toward the tomb, pushing aside her fear.

She whose sacred love was "strong as death, its jealousy unyielding as the grave"[48] had a holy jealousy for the Christ who had saved her with his love. She would touch him one last time—she would!—and honor him with her tears.

The women were already on their way when one small, logistical issue reared its ugly head.

> …and they asked each other, "Who will roll the stone away
> from the entrance of the tomb?" *Mark 16:3*

Good question, girlfriend.

As "they worried out loud to each other" (MSG), you and I smile to ourselves, realizing that this practical touch of realism confirms yet again what an accurate account this is. That's *exactly* what women would do—get there first, work out the details later. The disciples were no doubt sleeping in, but when they rose, I'll bet you dollars to doughnuts Peter and John sat around over coffee and sketched out the best strategies for moving that rock.

Maybe they knew something the women didn't, like how these things were engineered. The burial chamber was "sealed with a cut, disk-shaped stone that rolled in a slot cut into the rock. The slot was on an incline, making the grave easy to seal but difficult to open: several men might be needed to roll the stone back."[49]

This fairly major hurdle didn't stop Mary Magdalene and company that morning. No sir. They'd been champing at the bit to return to Jesus' side. Just let a man—Roman guard or Jewish disciple—try to stop them! Let alone a stone.

They arrived to discover the first miracle of the morning waiting for them.

> But when they looked up, they saw that the stone, which was
> very large, had been rolled away. *Mark 16:4*

Make no mistake, "it was a huge stone!" (CEV).
But not too big for God, beloved.
No stone is too big for God.
And how did God move this particular stone? Dramatically, of course.

> There was a violent earthquake, for an angel of the Lord came
> down from heaven and, going to the tomb, rolled back the
> stone. *Matthew 28:2*

As on the day of his crucifixion, the women experienced another teeth-chattering earthquake. And just like on Friday, a tomb was emptied of its contents.

> ...but when they entered, they did not find the body of the
> Lord Jesus. *Luke 24:3*

Oh dear.
They were looking for a body, which means—how this grieves my heart to write it—they didn't believe Jesus was raised from the dead, although he'd made it clear that's what would happen. They'd believed everything else Jesus told them. Why not this? Perhaps because they didn't want to believe it,

didn't want to think about him leaving earth for good. At least in a tomb he was still a visible reality.

How often do we want a Jesus who stays put, who is manageable, predictable? Jesus who fits in a box—a tomb, if you will—who doesn't challenge us or call us to do anything beyond our comfort zone or ask us to risk selling out to him completely?

Those days are over, sis.

The tomb is empty.

It was the last thing Mary Magdalene expected. "The empty sepulcher filled Mary with grief when it should have made her shout for joy."[50] She's not thinking "risen Savior" though. She's thinking "missing Savior."

On the heels of their dismay at finding no body in the tomb, they had to contend with what they *did* find.

> ...they saw a young man dressed in a white robe sitting on the
> right side... *Mark 16:5*

We're supposed to figure out for ourselves that "the young man was an angel,"[51] though Matthew's gospel plainly calls him "an angel of the Lord."[52]

> ...and they were alarmed. *Mark 16:5*

Love the biblical understatement here. Even expanding it to "startled" (NLT) and "completely taken aback, astonished" (MSG) doesn't capture the full flavor of the thing.

These women were scared out of their minds!

No wonder! Angels don't show up every day. And his attire was, to say the least, showy.

> His appearance was like lightning, and his clothes were white
> as snow. *Matthew 28:3*

Among the Jews, the color white was a symbol of "purity or innocence,"[53] which certainly suits an angelic being. But it wasn't the color that blew their minds; it was when "shafts of lightning blazed from him" (MSG) that they got a little nervous.

Yeah, that would do *me* in.

These women weren't the only ones shaking in their sandals. The Roman guards who'd braved the early morning darkness to investigate were soon atwitter too.

> The guards were so afraid of him that they shook and became
> like dead men. *Matthew 28:4*

They not only "were agitated and they trembled" (AMP), they "fell down" (CEV) and "lay like the dead" (NEB). Our big tough Roman guards fainted. Swooned even.

Heavens, what a morning! The dead walked off, and the living acted like dead men.

> In their fright the women bowed down with their faces to the
> ground... *Luke 24:5*

Mary Magdalene, who'd already come face to face with the dark side of the supernatural, now saw the brighter members of the spirit world. But their angelic goodness didn't make them any less intimidating. Whether in homage or humility or simply to avoid meeting the angel's gaze, the women wisely hit the dirt.

Should you happen to notice that Luke's account mentions two angels instead of one, don't get in a dither. There easily could have been a second angel present yet only one who spoke for both of them. As an old maxim goes, "he who mentions a few does not deny that there are more."[54]

And what did our angel proclaim? The usual.

> The angel said to the women, "Do not be afraid..."
> *Matthew 28:5*

Oh, sure. Right.

Angels love opening conversations with "Fear not." It puts people at ease. Calms their hummingbird hearts. Quells the urge to run away. (Don't you wish the IRS began their phone calls that way?)

Check out these celestial visitors—as before, the italics are mine—and see how popular this phrase was for the Men in White:

But the angel said to him: "*Do not be afraid,* Zechariah; your
prayer has been heard." *Luke 1:13*

But the angel said to her, "*Do not be afraid,* Mary, you have
found favor with God." *Luke 1:30*

But the angel said to them, "*Do not be afraid.* I bring you good
news of great joy that will be for all the people." *Luke 2:10*

Come to think of it, what's so scary about angels? Demons, sure, but
why angels? Aren't they good creatures? Good, yes. Safe, no. They're bright
as lightning and often larger than life. And supernatural. In other words,
scary.

Notice in these verses that right *after* the "do not be afraid" part, always
comes good news. The angels were there to offer a comforting word at the
Lord's conception, at his birth, and at his resurrection.

At the tomb the angel first acknowledged why the women had come.

"…for I know that you are looking for Jesus, who was
crucified." *Matthew 28:5*

A statement of fact, a bit of foreknowledge.

In Luke's version, the angelic visitor almost sounds as if he's teasing the
women a tad, making them think, prodding them to greater faith.

"Why do you look for the living among the dead?" *Luke 24:5*

Indeed, girls. "Why are you looking in a tomb for someone who is alive?"
(NLT). C'mon, Mary! "Throw off your grave clothes of fear and come forth
from your [own] tomb."[55]

Then the angelic messenger delivered news that must have seemed terribly obvious.

"He is not here;…" *Luke 24:6*

The women could see that much for themselves. By Roman law, the
stone being rolled away meant Christ had "a legal discharge, and leave to
come out."[56] Yet it was God's law that held sway that morning and God's law
that released him from the grave.

The stone couldn't hold him.
Death couldn't hold him.
Satan couldn't hold him.
And the angel couldn't hold the good news one more second.

"...he has risen!" *Luke 24:6*

He has risen indeed!
Sing hallelujah, praise the Lord!
The Son has risen in our hearts, dear sister. Every day we acknowledge his resurrection he rises anew within us to conquer our fears, to roll away our stones, to give us new life in him.

There have been great men in history—but they have not risen from the dead. There have been great ideas that have lived beyond the grave—but only once in history has God gone into the earth a dead man and come out a living Christ.

And it was God's work. *All God's.*

> God raised him from the dead, freeing him from the agony of
> death, because it was impossible for death to keep its hold on
> him. *Acts 2:24*

Yes indeed, "Death was no match for him" (MSG). The angel nudged the women's memory banks (after all, these were midlife matrons) and reminded them of what the Lord had once said to them.

> "Remember how he told you, while he was still with you in
> Galilee:..." *Luke 24:6*

It was a very gentle rebuke: "Sisters, this shouldn't come as a surprise. Weren't you listening to the Rabbi's teaching?"

They were, truly. But could you tell them again? Once more, slowly?

> "'The Son of Man must be delivered into the hands of sinful
> men, be crucified and on the third day be raised again.'"
> *Luke 24:7*

Mary Magdalene must have grabbed Salome and Mary by their hands and squeezed tight. Suddenly it all made sense! Jesus *had* been manhandled by sinners—hadn't they been there, hadn't they seen it for themselves? He *had* been hanged on a cross—oh, the agony of it! They'd watched every dreadful minute, for six long hours.

And now—today, the third day!—he *must* be raised from the dead! They had yet to *see* him, but the tomb was empty, wasn't it? *Empty!*

Then they remembered his words. *Luke 24:8*

And remembering, Mary Magdalene and company were changed forever.
He has risen!
He has risen indeed!

WHAT LESSONS CAN WE LEARN FROM MARY MAGDALENE AND HER DESPAIR?

Drive out the darkness.
We all experience despair from time to time, that stifling fear that the darkness around us will last forever. But it will not prevail—the Resurrection is our absolute assurance. The sun will shine again. Birds will sing. Love will bloom like a rose. In the meantime, through those shadowy twilight hours, we must cling to the promises of God, who will love us through our despair. Love is all about happy endings, sis. Read to the end of the Book and believe in his undying love for you.

Perfect love drives out fear. *1 John 4:18*

Venture into the light.
Ever find yourself entombed in old habits, old pathways, old belief systems? I discovered a term paper from my sophomore year of college: "Why I Don't Believe in God." Lizzie, who thought she was enlightened, was truly in the

dark! It would be another six years before I saw the Light of the World, shining in all his glory. From the moment we take our first gasp of air until we breathe our last, God is calling us to walk in the light of his Word. Whatever "tomb" might feel like security to you is really a deathtrap. Morning has broken, child. The stone has been rolled away.

> Live as children of light (for the fruit of the light consists in all
> goodness, righteousness and truth) and find out what pleases
> the Lord. *Ephesians 5:8-10*

Look who's in charge.

My precious father never read the obituaries in the newspaper. "Too depressing," he confessed. And, as he grew older, too many friends were listed there. Death was a thing to be dreaded. And yet for the Christ, hanging in agony on the cross, death must have been the one thing Jesus longed for. Not only because it would relieve his suffering, but also because it would relieve *our* suffering forever. Death is not in charge of our reality anymore. I love life too much to say that I look *forward* to death, but I can say absolutely I look forward to meeting the One who mastered it!

> For we know that since Christ was raised from the dead, he
> cannot die again; death no longer has mastery over him.
> *Romans 6:9*

Stand on his promise.

Here's why death—even the fear of death—no longer has any power over us. Those of us who believe absolutely in Christ's resurrection, who stand in spirit with Mary Magdalene and stare at the empty tomb in amazement, know that if God did that for Jesus, he will do the same for us. Death is our beginning, not our ending. We get new bodies (a personal joy for me), we get new names, and we get a fabulous full-time job: worshiping the all-powerful God who made eternity possible.

> By his power God raised the Lord from the dead, and he will
> raise us also. *1 Corinthians 6:14*

GOOD GIRL THOUGHTS WORTH CONSIDERING

1. Jesus made it very clear that his death—and resurrection—were a fore-
    gone conclusion. Why didn't his disciples listen? Or if they heard the
    words, why didn't they believe them? Might they have begun to doubt
    that Jesus was the true Messiah? Or did they simply love him too much
    to let him go? Has a loved one ever told you he or she was facing
    certain death? Was your reaction like Peter's—"never happen!"—or
    were you willing to accept it? What might the disciples have said to
    show their understanding and support? And what might we do when
    we're facing such a situation with someone we love?

2. What might Jesus have meant by "take up your cross and follow me"?
    Could it be that only by suffering will we have true fellowship with
    him? That we are to welcome burdens and cares? That we should be
    willing to die for our faith? Or do you find a completely different mes-
    sage in this teaching? How might we live out this challenging verse in
    our everyday lives? Since someone else physically carried the cross for
    Jesus on the road to Golgotha, does that alter the meaning or signifi-
    cance of this statement he made before that desperate day came to pass?

3. What brought the women to the foot of the cross? Were they there for
    Jesus? For themselves? For one another? As an example to those who
    didn't believe? Think through all their possible reasons, motivations,
    and emotions. Why are the male disciples—other than John—not
    mentioned? Do you think they were there, just not in the forefront? If
    they truly weren't there, why not? And if they were there, why do you
    suppose they weren't mentioned?

4. Why, on the way to the cross, did Jesus point to the destruction of
    Jerusalem to come in A.D. 70, some forty years hence? To direct their
    mourning away from him and toward themselves? To encourage them
    to prepare accordingly? To affirm his prophetic anointing? Do you
    think they missed this prophecy, just as the disciples did his promise of
    a coming resurrection? How do you think this word from Jesus
    impacted their faith when Jerusalem eventually fell?

5. Jesus' excruciating death must have been the longest six hours in Mary Magdalene's life. How do you imagine Mary M. spent those hours? Crying? Praying? Offering an encouraging word to the Christ, to the other women? Planning for the future? Reliving the past? Have you ever watched someone die? What are the emotions that surface at such a sorrowful moment? What regrets come to mind at a time like that? What regrets might Mary Magdalene have had? Was there anything you said that made it easier for the dying person? Anything he or she said that made it easier for you? What is the role of one who stands by the dying?

6. We know the darkness was an act of God, not a mere fluke of nature. Why do you think it spread "over all the land"? Did that mean the whole earth? What was God covering, and to what end? Do you think it was for God's benefit, his Son's benefit, the crowd's benefit? Are some things too holy to be seen by man? Or might the darkness have signified the total—though temporary—separation of God from his Son? Think of all the things that "darkness" represents in God's Word. Which might apply here?

7. What motivations—love? curiosity? hope?—brought the women to the tomb Sunday morning? And why such an early hour? What made this anointing so important to them, or was it simply a way to see him one last time? What do you suppose they expected to find? What does the empty tomb signify to you?

8. Read again chapter 7 of *Unveiling of Mary Magdalene*. What parallels can you find between the contemporary scenes and the biblical ones? Did vicariously experiencing Mary Delaney's grief via fiction help you understand Mary Magdalene's suffering so long ago? What are some major differences between Mary Magdalene's watching the death of the Christ and Mary Delaney's bedside grieving for her dying Pastor Jake?

Chapter Thirteen

THE TRYSTED HOUR

HER DISCOVERY

O Mary, at thy window be!
It is the wish'd, the trysted hour.
ROBERT BURNS

History has never known such a morning, before or since. The stone was rolled away, the tomb was empty, and the angels had just announced that the Christ was risen...oh, happy day!

Mary Magdalene and company couldn't *wait* to tell the other disciples what they'd seen and heard.

> So the women hurried away from the tomb, afraid yet filled
> with joy... *Matthew 28:8*

They were not running *away* from the tomb so much as they were running *toward* Jerusalem, about half a mile away, "with fear and great joy" (AMP) and "deep in wonder" (MSG). Apprehension and unspeakable joy produce some of the same symptoms—a lump in the throat, tightness in the chest, butterflies in the stomach, clammy hands, a sense of awe. Imagine our sisters tripping over their tunics in their haste, laughing and crying in amazement, delight, relief. What news they had to tell! Hurry, hurry, hurry...

> ...and ran to tell his disciples. *Matthew 28:8*

The sun was rising, and they were making tracks. Mary Magdalene's personality shines through in this breathless dash back to Jerusalem. We picture her as "an energetic, vivacious, outgoing extrovert" here, leading the charge.

As Luke described it, several women were involved in sharing the startling news.

> It was Mary Magdalene, Joanna, Mary the mother of James,
> and the others with them who told this to the apostles.
> *Luke 24:10*

Can you picture how this must have unfolded? Half a dozen women, maybe more, all talking at once, interrupting one another, wiping their eyes, gasping for breath, while the confused male disciples tried to get a word in edgewise.

Girlfriends:	"The tomb's empty!"
	"And Jesus is risen!"
Disciples:	"It's *what?* He's *what?*"
Girlfriends:	"We didn't exactly *see* him…"
	"No, but we saw angels!"
Disciples:	"*Angels?* Are you…?"
Girlfriends:	"Of *course* we're sure!"
	"Tell 'em, Mary!"

Alas, their wide-eyed enthusiasm did not serve the women well. The men were not convinced that Mary and company were telling the truth.

> But they did not believe the women, because their words
> seemed to them like nonsense. *Luke 24:11*

Oh, puh-leeze! The male disciples wrote the story off as "an idle tale" (RSV) and as utter "madness" (AMP) and "thought they were making it all up" (MSG).

C'mon, fellas, Mary Magdalene was *there.* Plus the other Mary, and a couple more Marys and Joanna and…well, *lots* of people were there!

But they were all women. Female witnesses were "not convincing either in the Jewish or the Roman tradition."[1] Furthermore (much as it pains me to say this), a woman's words in a court of law were never trusted and had to be validated by two men.[2] *Sigh.*

Even allowing for the fact that a former devil woman, Mary of Magdala, was the primary witness, "one cannot but be amazed at the stupidity of these disciples."[3] Thanks, Reverend Henry. We couldn't agree more.

In fairness to the guys, the women returned with only two pieces of evidence—an empty tomb and an angelic announcement. They did not have at their disposal the most crucial evidence of all: *None of them had actually seen the risen Christ yet.*

But that was about to change, as we'll discover by jumping over to John's Easter morning account. There the story focuses on—you guessed it!—Mary Magdalene. Finally, her big moment is at hand.

> Early on the first day of the week, while it was still dark, Mary
> Magdalene went to the tomb and saw that the stone had been
> removed from the entrance. *John 20:1*

Was she on a solo mission *after* the first go-around, or is this the same story found in Matthew 28, Mark 16, and Luke 24 without any mention of the other women? My vote is a second visit by Mary alone because so many details differ, but it certainly *could* be the same visit, with only Mary's point of view presented.

This was typical of John's writing, "to drop unessential characters in order to heighten dramatic tension within scenes."[4] Especially in these scenes that are so crowded with characters, it makes sense to pick one person and present the whole thing through his or her eyes. In any case, both Mary Magdalene and John are main players in the first part of this scene, which is why it has "something indefinably first-hand about it."[5]

It's our kind of story, babe—right here, right now.

Let's rewind the tape and pick up where impulsive Mary Magdalene left the empty tomb and ran back to the disciples—my, "what a vivid impression we get of her vital personality!"[6] It's quite possible she ran ahead of the other women and got to John and Peter first or that this was a solo sojourn and she left the other women behind. Either way, she was on full-tilt boogie.

Feet, don't fail me now.

> So she came running… *John 20:2*

This Greek phrase is seldom used in the Bible, showing this runner "activated by a powerful emotion—consternation, in the case of Mary."[7] Now we get a different—and clearer—picture of what she was thinking: "Oh no! He's missing!"

You gotta love Mary Magdalene's let's-not-waste-time method of handling things. A high-spirited woman of action, she would rather run than wait, rather ask questions (at the risk of looking foolish) than wring her hands and wonder.

She was also smart enough to go to the top of the pecking order.

> …to Simon Peter and the other disciple, the one Jesus loved…
> *John 20:2*

Remember, the women as a group couldn't convince the male disciples that the tomb was empty. Now the most persuasive and vocal among them, Mary Magdalene, sought out the two leaders. We know how this works: Divide and conquer.

> …and [Mary Magdalene] said, "They have taken the Lord out
> of the tomb, and we don't know where they have put him!"
> *John 20:2*

Who were "they"? The angels? Roman authorities? Graverobbers? Apparently Mary was too distraught at the time to be more specific, even if she had known who "they" were, which she did not.

You're thinking, *Didn't she hear the angels say, "He is risen"?* You bet. But hearing the truth is one thing. *Knowing* the truth is something else again. Perhaps during that dash back to Jerusalem, Mary started to question the angelic announcement or wasn't totally sold on the resurrection story.

Oh yes, I get that. "Help me not to doubt!"[8] is ever the cry of my heart. On those occasional times I fall into doubting (sister, if you think I never question the whole shebang—Christmas to Easter—then I haven't shown you the depths of my dark soul clearly enough yet), I plead, "Where did God go?" just like Mary did.

Since the men were clearly skeptical, it's possible that Mary Magdalene wisely limited herself to a practical observation—a missing body—rather than to supernatural phenomena like angels and resurrections.

Sure would be a lot easier if we could read their minds, eh? Whatever her motives and emotions at this point, Mary Magdalene seemed convinced the body had been spirited away by an enemy of Jesus. She was persuasive enough that Peter and the "other disciple"—that is, John—took immediate action.

> So Peter and the other disciple started for the tomb. Both were
> running... *John 20:3-4*

Like a bunch of Energizer bunnies, they kept running and running and running...

This passage is known as the "'race' to the tomb,"[9] with Mary Magdalene, as we'll see shortly, hot on their heels.

> ...but the other disciple outran Peter and reached the tomb
> first. *John 20:4*

Well, John *was* younger, in better shape, spent more time on his Stair-Master, whatever. John got there first but then hesitated at the entrance.

> He bent over and looked in at the strips of linen lying there
> but did not go in. *John 20:5*

Think of what must have been running—figuratively, this time—through John's addled mind. A crucifixion, but no body. A tomb, but no body. Strips of linen, but no body. John's feet were glued to the ground, his gaze glued to the abandoned linen.

> Then Simon Peter, who was behind him, arrived and went
> into the tomb. *John 20:6*

How like Peter! The minute he got there, this bold, brassy, strong-willed disciple barged right past the more timid John.

He saw the strips of linen lying there, as well as the burial cloth
that had been around Jesus' head. *John 20:6-7*

We get another important detail now. Not just the linen but the burial
"napkin" (RSV) or "kerchief" (AMP) was also there. But the sacred head it once
encased wasn't anywhere in sight.

The cloth was folded up by itself, separate from the linen.
John 20:7

This cloth "had been wound around the head into the shape of a
sphere."[10] Rather than being neatly folded and put aside like a table napkin, it
was as though the head of Christ slipped out and the cloth simply dropped
flat, folding upon itself. Was it still fragrant with Nicodemus's myrrh and
aloes? Still stained with blood from the head wounds inflicted by the crown
of thorns? Still damp from the sweat that covered his brow on Calvary?

These discarded linens don't point to the work of graverobbers, who
would have been in too big a rush. Nor the Roman authorities, who had no
reason to unwrap his body in the first place.

Hmm.

Finally the other disciple, who had reached the tomb first, also
went inside. *John 20:8*

It seems Peter's chutzpa empowered gentle John to follow him into the
tomb.

[John] saw and believed. *John 20:8*

Whoopee!

This sounds thrilling, until I put my bachelor's degree in English to use
and realize it tells us nothing. Without a direct object after *saw* and *believed,*
we're left wondering: "saw *what?*" and "believed *what?*" "Ambiguity grows,"
wrote one commentator.[11] Got that right.

One thing's for sure: Neither male disciple saw an angel. It's hard to miss
a creature dressed like lightning. The heavenly beings were either invisible at
the moment or busy being angelic elsewhere.

Then, as an editorial aside, along comes this interesting bit of information in the next verse.

> (They still did not understand from Scripture that Jesus had to
> rise from the dead.) *John 20:9*

Aha! If the men didn't understand about the resurrection, then John simply "saw" that Jesus' body was gone and "believed" that the tomb was empty, just as Mary Magdalene had explained moments earlier. If John had truly believed Jesus was *alive,* this never would have happened next...

> Then the disciples went back to their homes. *John 20:10*

Honey, if they'd thought Jesus was raised from the dead, they would have done more than go home—they would have gone bananas and started looking for him! Instead, "puzzled but convinced that something unusual had occurred at the tomb," they returned to their lodgings in Jerusalem.[12]

Mind if we jump ahead? (Don't worry, we'll be right back. Mary's triumphant scene is right around the corner.)

Later that same day, when two disciples met Jesus on the road, not only did they not recognize their risen Lord, they shared their incredulity at what Mary Magdalene and the others had shared with them earlier that morning.

> "...some of our women amazed us." *Luke 24:22*

The translator was being generous. "Completely confused us" (MSG) sounds closer to the mark. "Drove us out of our senses" (AMP) is also dead-on.

> "They went to the tomb early this morning but didn't find his
> body. They came and told us that they had seen a vision of
> angels, who said he was alive." *Luke 24:22-23*

I think it was the mention of the angels that made the whole thing suspect for the guys, since the typical mind-set of the time was that "angels would have been sent to the apostles, not to the women."[13] Surprise, fellas.

That evening on the road to Emmaus, Jesus lost patience with those two disciples.

> He said to them, "How foolish you are, and how slow of heart
> to believe all that the prophets have spoken!" *Luke 24:25*

Our loving Jesus didn't mince words with those who were "sluggish in mind, dull of perception" (AMP) and "thick-headed!" (MSG). Tell it like it is, Lord. The disciples were positively clueless.

Know what? So was Mary Magdalene that morning long ago.

Know what else? I've been there too.

One spring afternoon a woman came to see me at a book signing in eastern Pennsylvania. She greeted me warmly and shared her name (which promptly vanished from my mind), then we chatted off and on while people stopped by for autographs.

Between customers she mentioned where she was from.

"Oh yes!" I gushed. (I'm a very *sincere* gusher.) "I just got a lovely letter from a woman who lives in your town." Off I went, babbling about the contents of said letter, the writer's name, where she worked, all that. How this woman kept a straight face I will never know, because I was talking about *her*.

Good grief.

It wasn't until I climbed into my rental car that I put two and two together and realized what a total nincompoop I'd been—*she* was the letter writer! *Duh.* Because I wasn't *expecting* to see her so far from home, I didn't recognize her name when she appeared in front of me, nor recall our previous connection, no matter how many hints she must have dropped, trying to help me save face.

The disciples had the same problem. They weren't expecting to find Jesus on the road to Emmaus and so didn't recognize him. After hours of walking and talking with this man, they broke bread with him and finally saw the light.

> Then their eyes were opened and they recognized him, and he
> disappeared from their sight. *Luke 24:31*

Whoosh!

Did God open their eyes? Or did watching Jesus handle the bread suddenly improve their vision? Whatever the case, these two disciples were transformed at his disappearing.

For Mary Magdalene, his appearing was every bit as unexpected and even more life changing. Returning to her story, we find John and Peter already on their way home and Mary M. lingering at the grave to grieve alone. How fitting that "the tender beauty of the garden scene is all hers."[14]

Mary stood outside the tomb crying. *John 20:11*

I suspect she waited until the men left to start leaking. I always feel strange crying around men, yet perfectly at ease crying around women or by myself. Her weeping "suggests frustration as well as grief,"[15] and no wonder. It gets old to keep coming back to the cemetery, only to find your beloved's body still missing and no one being helpful.

Truth is, "Mary has no home on earth without Jesus."[16] He has been the total focus of her life for months, years. How could she go on without him?

Every widow among us understands that sense of utter loss. The endless empty hours, the feeling of purposelessness, the unanswered questions, the unfinished business, the longings that threaten to crush us to dust. Mary Magdalene's heart surely felt as vacant and gaping as the empty tomb before her. Her tear-filled grief was like the faint fragrance of myrrh, scenting the air with sorrow.

Jesus was not her husband, but he was her Bridegroom.

Jesus was not her lover, but he was her Friend.

Nowhere is that more clearly seen than in the gospel of John, which describes "unparalleled intimacy between teacher and follower, lord and disciple, friend and friend."[17] She who loved much, wept much.

As she wept, she bent over to look into the tomb...
John 20:11

Maybe this is another reason why Mary Magdalene has been confused with the woman who wept all over the feet of Jesus. Like so many of us, Mary M. was a leaker. Her tears communicated what mere words could never convey. Alone in that shadowy garden, "she could weep as much as she needed to weep, and no one would think her mad again."[18]

Although, when people heard the news about what she saw next, they might have questioned her sanity or, at the very least, what she'd drunk for breakfast.

> and [she] saw two angels in white, seated where Jesus' body
> had been, one at the head and the other at the foot.
> *John 20:12*

We don't get a single word about Mary Magdalene's trembling in fear or falling on her face this time. A woman whose Former Bad Girl life included seven demons? No contest. At this point "she was not frightened or even surprised by the angels' appearance; she cared only about the body of her Lord."[19] Her calm reaction points to the strong possibility of this being her *second* visit of the morning. For our one-track wonder, what's yet another pair of angels?

Look at how they spoke to her, individually and specifically this time.

> They asked her, "Woman, why are you crying?" *John 20:13*

Musta been male angels. Guys, isn't the *why* obvious? The body of her Lord was missing! Yet the angels "have no word of comfort or encouragement to offer" her.[20] Perhaps they didn't intend to encourage her but were instead offering a "tenderly-phrased expression of disapproval,"[21] knowing that Mary Magdalene, of all his followers, should have remembered the Lord's promise of resurrection.

But, emotionally, Mary was still back at the cross, back at the burial with Joseph and Nicodemus, back at the mortally wounded form being placed in the grave. She'd appeared earlier that morning to care for his body, and, come angels or demons, she was going to finish her task. The Jews of the first century placed a heavy emphasis on correct burial practices and "regarded with abhorrence any disrespect paid to a corpse."[22]

This brave woman, who left demons in her wake years ago only to find herself now conversing with angels, wanted nothing more than to prepare his body properly. Even *that* humble task had been denied her.

Listen to the cry of her heart! Her words are personal, her devastation clear.

"They have taken my Lord away," she said... *John 20:13*

Note the distinction—*my Lord.*

Ahh. This was what Mary Magdalene wanted all along—time alone with the body of her beloved. I think of particular viewings I've attended and how, as I approached the casket, I prayed for a moment of privacy to say what needed to be said. Funerals serve many purposes, and that's one of them—a chance for the living to bring some closure to their relationship with the deceased, one-on-one. We know that these whispered words cannot be heard, but we still need to say them; we still need to look upon the earthly shell and make our peace.

How much more so for Mary, who had poured her life into this man's ministry!

Looking back across time with our Scriptures in hand, we know more than Mary Magdalene did at this point in the narrative, which makes the story a real page-turner. "Clue after clue is laid before her which she does not grasp; and, as the evidence mounts, so does our gleeful suspense: when will she know? why can't she see? how much longer before the light breaks through her tears?"[23]

Soon, but not quite yet.

"...and I don't know where they have put him." *John 20:13*

These words Mary spoke to the angels echoed almost verbatim the message she had brought to John and Peter a few minutes earlier: "They have taken the Lord out of the tomb, and we don't know where they have put him!"[24] And, as we'll see in a moment, she said them a third time to a certain unnamed gardener lingering behind her...

Was Jesus being cruel, making Mary Magdalene search for him, making her state her mission over and over, making her wait so long for his appearing?

Not at all.

Jesus wants us to grow in faith, and we grow only when we come to the end of ourselves. That point where proof gives way and hope kicks in, where we can do nothing but wait upon God even when we cannot see, touch, taste, smell, or hear his presence. "Every Christian in the process of maturing at times experiences the loss of Christ. There is no longer a sense of his presence. He has 'disappeared.' "[25]

That's when we must let go of the God of our own understanding.

And embrace the God Who Is.

Our neat and tidy God-in-a-box ideas about Jesus must be put aside as we seek after the real Christ, the one who won't fit in a tomb, who is both small enough to climb in our hearts and big enough to save the entire world.

Crushed in spirit that morning in the garden, Mary stared at the emptiness that loomed before her, mocking her loss, and wondered where else she might look, to whom she might turn.

Without warning, something or someone garnered her attention.

At this, she turned around... *John 20:14*

"At this..."? "This" *what?!*

What made Mary Magdalene turn around? Did she hear something? Did the angels bow in reverence, tipping her off? Or did she simply sense the presence of someone behind her?

My upstairs writing office has only one entrance, a narrow flight of wooden stairs fifteen feet behind my desk chair. I can't see someone climbing those steps, but I can hear them *clump, clump*ing up to my office. My son, Matthew, has a vile habit of sneaking up on me, climbing the steps on tiptoes and fingertips just to catch me by surprise.

Except he never gets past the top step. I can't see him, can't hear or smell him (unless he's fresh from gym class), but I can *sense* him behind me. A living human body is not a silent thing. The heart beats, the lungs expand and contract, the body warmth elevates the air temperature around it. Even though Matt holds his breath and doesn't move a muscle, I still feel the hairs on the back of my neck prickle.

"Maaaa-thew, is that you?"

He exhales with a noisy groan. "How'd you know?"

Same way Mary Magdalene knew. She intuitively felt someone behind her, then turned to discover if she was right.

...and [she] saw Jesus standing there... *John 20:14*

Oh, Mary! He *has* risen!

There he stood, "resplendently alive,"[26] appearing for the first time as his risen self for the benefit of Mary Magdalene alone. Mine eyes have seen the glory, girlfriend!

What I wanna know is, why didn't Jesus appear a few minutes ago when John and Peter were still there? I think the Lord wanted to honor and reward Mary Magdalene for her faithfulness. The men had to be coaxed to visit the tomb. Mary had already been there once, if not twice. The men were unwilling to wait around on a hunch. She waited, lax to leave if there was any possibility she might see his body again. The men lacked faith and doubted her claims. She was the definition of faith, though it was being sorely tested at that moment.

Close your eyes and imagine seeing Jesus through Mary's dark orbs. Do you have a clear picture of him standing there? Is he smiling or frowning? Are his eyes filled with grace or judgment? Are his hands outstretched or folded behind his back? Does he resemble a painting you once saw in a Bible bookstore, or a favorite teacher, or your father or husband as a young man of thirty-three?

Who is this Jesus? Would you know him if you saw him?

Mary Magdalene didn't.

...but she did not realize that it was Jesus. *John 20:14*

I'm shocked, aren't you? How could she *not* recognize a man she'd followed closely for years? Had he changed so completely?

Let's think through half a dozen possibilities of why Mary Magdalene didn't recognize Jesus.

1. *Too many tears.* Perhaps her endless crying clouded her vision and she "could not see him through her tears."[27]

2. *Too little light.* Since it was still quite early, maybe "she couldn't see him well in the early morning light."[28]

3. *Too little faith.* She wasn't yet convinced he was raised from the dead, and so "without the eyes of faith, Mary remains in her darkness."[29]

4. *Angelic overload.* Could be she was blinded by the lightning-white garments of the angels and was seeing spots.

238 UNVEILING MARY MAGDALENE

5. *Aerobic overload.* Sheer exhaustion from all that running back and forth might have hindered her judgment.

6. *Wardrobe changes.* The Lord's clothes were no doubt unfamiliar (his old ones were gambled away at the cross; his linen cloths were left behind at the tomb), or perhaps his attire included a hood that masked his features.

In my humble opinion, it was none of the above.

I think Jesus himself held back his identity, giving Mary Magdalene time to absorb the truth. Remember, when Jesus later appeared on the road to Emmaus with the two unnamed disciples, Luke included this brief but telling statement: "but they were kept from recognizing him."[30] *Kept* by whom? Jesus, of course. He slipped an unseen hand over the eyes of their hearts, temporarily filtering their vision. A few verses later we learned, "then their eyes were opened and they recognized him."[31] Now we know who opened them…the same One who closed them!

The very same One who kept Mary in the dark just a few heartbeats longer.

"Woman," he said… *John 20:15*

Honey, I love this! The first spoken word of the risen Christ was directed to one of us: "Woman." In a sense, it was meant for *all* of us. He sees us, sister. He knows we exist, that we are unique, that we are worthy, that we are *his*.

We've heard men use *woman* as a derogatory form of address. But here it's a term of "dignity and respect,"[32] the same word he used when speaking to his mother at the wedding feast in Cana. (Since he wasn't a teenager back then, we'll assume it was meant as a term of respect toward his mother as well!)

Though his appearance may not have been familiar, his compassion was instantly recognizable.

"…why are you crying?" *John 20:15*

There it is again, that question about the weeping, just as the angels had asked. *Poor, tender-hearted Mary.* Was it a sign of feminine weakness for her to cry? Not at all. The Lord delights in the tears of both men and women.

The bold apostle Paul wasn't embarrassed to confess that he cried: "For I wrote you out of great distress and anguish of heart and with many tears."[33] A thousand years earlier the mighty King David was not ashamed to moan: "all night long I flood my bed with weeping and drench my couch with tears."[34]

Tears aren't a sign of weakness. They signify a strength so mighty it can withstand sorrow and a love so powerful it stretches beyond the grave.

Jesus had demonstrated that very strength, that boundless love, earlier in his ministry when he came across Mary of Bethany heartbroken and sobbing over the death of her brother, Lazarus.

> When Jesus saw her weeping, and the Jews who had come along with her also weeping, he was deeply moved in spirit and troubled. *John 11:33*

Never doubt that tears speak louder than words! Seeking Lazarus, Jesus asked:

> "Where have you laid him?" *John 11:34*

My, my. Did you catch the parallel with Mary Magdalene's words at Jesus' grave, seeking the whereabouts of *his* body? Gives me shivers!

It's a sure bet that whenever Jesus was around tombs, the dead didn't stay dead very long! But before Lazarus's resurrection could take place, there were tears.

> Jesus wept. *John 11:35*

It's everybody's favorite two-word Scripture memory verse, but oh, the mercy and compassion packed in those words! "Jesus burst into tears. His grief was spontaneous."[35]

Bless you, Lord, for affirming Mary of Bethany's sorrow by joining her in it. And here, for acknowledging Mary of Magdala's weeping without making her feel foolish. For letting all of us know we can cry whenever the Spirit moves.

Gently, sympathetically, Jesus asked Mary Magdalene a simple question.

> "Who is it you are looking for?" *John 20:15*

Note the emphasis on *who.* Sadly, our Mary was still on a body hunt. "She had been looking for some*thing*, not some*one*,"[36] for a dead body, not a risen Christ.

Did the Lord admonish her for this? Make her feel less than faithful, less than worthy? Not our Jesus. The work of a Savior is not to belittle, shame, and ridicule. He comes and finds us where we are and calls us unto himself. "Though she had not found Christ, He had found her."[37]

Now that they were face-to-face, he asked her to put into words whom she was looking for. In doing so, she revealed her unspoken request: *what* she was looking for.

Jesus likes us to vocalize our needs. Once when he met a blind man, Jesus didn't simply zap away the man's disability. He asked him what needed zapping: "What do you want me to do for you?" The blind man said, "Rabbi, I want to see."[38]

Precisely what our girl Mary Magdalene needed—eyes to see who was standing right before her.

> Thinking he was the gardener… *John 20:15*

That tells me he was indeed human looking. Not larger than life, not shining like the angels, and *definitely not a dead man.* Did he appear different than his usual self—younger, older, paler, darker? Was he wearing gardening gear or toting some kind of first-century spade over his shoulder?

She *was* in a garden. Perhaps she simply *expected* a gardener. Sometimes it takes a moment for reality and expectation to sort themselves out. One misty September morn in the Scottish Highlands, my sister and I ventured out before breakfast, eager to stroll through the sprawling gardens surrounding our inn. Laboring silently among the tall sunflowers—his movements so economical we didn't see him until we nearly stepped on his Wellies—was the gardener, already at work in the cool of the day, wearing gray garb and a wreath of pipe smoke around his head. No wonder we never saw him—he was the same color as the mist!

Scared us silly, it did, lass.

But this supposed gardener didn't scare Mary Magdalene. She was too grief-stricken to be frightened. Not by angels and not by a man who looked like a groundskeeper. Besides, he might be able to help her. It was worth asking one more time.

...she said, "Sir,..." *John 20:15*

Just as he had been cordial in his address—"woman"—she, too, was polite. After all, this man was a stranger. Though she had turned toward him (to do otherwise would be highly rude), her chin may have been hanging down and her eyes still swimming with tears. It's possible she never looked at his face, never looked farther than his muddy feet.

The feet of a gardener.

> "...if you have carried him away, tell me where you have put
> him..." *John 20:15*

Mary's discouragement was fraying her thin thread of hope. Even with angels present, this had to be "the darkest passage in all Mary's life."[39] She didn't bother to identify herself nor explain which man she was talking about but simply "blurted out her worst fears."[40]

We get that. When we're burdened with grief, we often assume the whole world is up to speed on our suffering, knows what we're going through, won't ask stupid questions, won't place unnecessary demands on us, and above all will know what we need.

Mary no doubt assumed the gardener had been there all along, had heard her brief chat with the angelic men, and knew which body she was looking for.

> "...tell me where you have put him, and I will get him."
> *John 20:15*

Boldly she promises, "I will take him away" (KJV).

Wait. You mean she intended to carry this dead body all by herself?! She no doubt planned to find someone to help, but her willingness to take responsibility for him is so like our impulsive Mary Magdalene, who "always leads with her heart."[41]

Then again, as a woman of means, she might have meant she would arrange to have his body properly claimed and cared for. A sister with money often makes such offers without explanation—a slight nod at the waiter, and moments later the check for a table of friends lands discreetly beneath her plate.

At some point during her brief inquiry, Mary M. turned away from the gardener and looked at the empty tomb again, perhaps to hide another spate of tears.

Dry your eyes, sweet Mary!

That gardener is about to plant the seed of Truth in your heart, watered with love and nurtured with grace.

Perk up your ears, dear Mary!

The next word you hear will change your world, and ours, forever.

Jesus said to her, "Mary." *John 20:16*

Your name, Mary. He spoke your name!

In a single word, he revealed her identity.

And his own.

Mary! Of all the people in the world he might have revealed himself to in this sacred hour, he chose Mary Magdalene. A woman with a devilish past. A woman from a town with a tarnished reputation. A woman, period. *A woman!*

Perhaps Christ chose Mary because she who had once belonged to Satan now belonged to him. Victory upon victory! Jesus did not announce himself, nor issue a command, nor scold her for doubting. He spoke her name and with it her redemption. "Fear not, for I have redeemed you; I have summoned you by name; you are mine."[42]

No one ever spoke my name as my daddy did. If I answered the phone and heard him say that one word, I knew in an instant it was my father.

Now that he is gone, hearing him say my name is the single thing I miss the most. He always called me by my childhood name—"Ruthie"—a name long since lost to me, thanks to a radio career where my middle name, Elizabeth, seemed a better fit. When Daddy said my name, it carried forty-six years of memories, a lifetime in two syllables: "Ru-thie."

Is that how it was for our Mary, that morning outside the garden tomb? Was she longing to hear those two precious syllables, "Ma-ry"? True, the name was common to many women, but the voice—the tone, the warmth, the familiar cadence of it—was unique to only One.

She knew instantly who it was. The time had come, and "Jesus let himself be recognized."[43] He delivered her from the darkness of confusion to the bright light of comprehension with a single word that was music to her ears—her name. In that dark morning, "paradise itself had broken through."[44]

When she heard her name, Mary Magdalene's "tears of sorrow became tears of unspeakable joy,"[45] as she faced her future.

She turned toward him... *John 20:16*

Did she turn slowly, filled with awe and fear and apprehension, or spin about so fast the hood of her tunic fell around her neck, leaving her bareheaded and breathless? That second option gets my vote! The Greek verb for "turned"—*strapheisa*—means "she changed her course of action,"[46] not merely the direction she was facing.

She'd imagined him dead. There he stood, very much alive!

...and [she] cried out in Aramaic, "Rabboni!" (which means Teacher). *John 20:16*

Not lofty, la-di-da Greek. Down-to-earth Aramaic, the language of Jesus. And of Mary.

The word was personal, too. Not just anybody's Teacher. *Hers.* Never could it more appropriately be said, "He taught her everything she knew." Certainly everything that mattered.

Other scholars render *Rabboni* as a term of high respect—"My great Master"[47]—or a term of gentle endearment—"My dear Lord."[48] In either case, the personal tone comes through loud and clear.

My Teacher, my Master, my Lord.

Mine, said Mary Magdalene.

Yet, notice what she did *not* say. She did not cry out "Beloved!" or "Husband!" or his proper name, "Jesus!" She said, "Teacher!" In that one word the core of their relationship was captured for eternity. All other speculations may be quietly cast aside. He was, first and foremost, the one who taught her who he was and who she was in him.

No wonder Mary Magdalene's dawn tryst with her Savior among the garden shadows is considered "the greatest recognition scene in all literature."[49]

Not only did Mary see the risen Lord in all his splendor. She saw herself reflected in his eyes and heard his voice speak her name.

In discovering Jesus, her own identity in him was sealed for all time.

WHAT LESSONS CAN WE LEARN FROM MARY MAGDALENE AND HER DISCOVERY?

Go there.
In a culture that says "Don't go there," those of us who call ourselves followers of Christ really *must* go there—go to the cross, go to the grave, go to others and say, "Come and see for yourself." Let's not enter hesitantly like John or leave too soon, shaking our heads, like Peter. Mary Magdalene is our role model here: Show up. Come back. Ask questions. Look around. Persevere when others turn away. Make Christ the center of your life, and go where he goes, no matter how scary or uncertain the path. Even if you don't have all the facts, have all the faith, girl. Go there.

> I want to know Christ and the power of his resurrection and
> the fellowship of sharing in his sufferings, becoming like him
> in his death, and so, somehow, to attain to the resurrection
> from the dead. Not that I have already obtained all this, or
> have already been made perfect, but I press on to take hold
> of that for which Christ Jesus took hold of me.
> *Philippians 3:10-12*

Let's not overlook the obvious.
Like the apostle Paul—like you, like me—Mary Magdalene wasn't perfect. She who "witnessed the event of all the ages"[50] almost missed it! How many of us look beyond the Christ for something else, something more. Something complicated. Something we have to earn or learn. "We have some vague, yet stubborn idea of a Christ whom we must climb for, or dig for, or traverse sea and land for."[51] Mary was looking so hard at the empty tomb she didn't see

the open door to the truth. As patiently as Jesus waited for her to open her eyes, so is he waiting for us to do the same.

> See, I have placed before you an open door that no one
> can shut. I know that you have little strength, yet you
> have kept my word and have not denied my name.
> *Revelation 3:8*

"Woman, why are you *not* crying?"

How about it, sis? Does the thought of Jesus' hanging on a cruel cross and lying dead in a dark tomb move you to tears? Or is it nothing more than an intellectual exercise or a spiritual truth to tuck away in some dry-eyed corner of your soul? I realize not all of us are leakers, yet the Lord certainly honored those who mourned and wept as he did. Weeping is a healthy sign of brokenness, of sorrow, of longing, of repentance, and of joy. Don't be afraid to leak during worship, during your Bible studies, during prayer. Mary Magdalene was one of the wet ones…and look how she was rewarded!

> I tell you the truth, you will weep and mourn while the world
> rejoices. You will grieve, but your grief will turn to joy.
> *John 16:20*

Jesus knows your name.

More than merely your name, he knows *everything* about you. As fully as he knew Mary Magdalene, who was his constant companion for many seasons, that's how well he knows you. "But I've never seen him face to face," you say? You have only to turn, beloved, as Mary Magdalene turned. He is even now calling your name. Listen carefully. Do you hear all the promises of God that infuse that voice—all the love for you, the hope for you, the future he has planned for you? You can be sure, if he is calling your name, you belong to him forever. Put away doubt, and shout with Mary, "My great Master! My dear Lord!"

> "His sheep follow him because they know his voice." *John 10:4*

GOOD GIRL THOUGHTS WORTH CONSIDERING

1. Mary Magdalene and the other women at the tomb "hurried away" to tell the men back in Jerusalem what they'd discovered. Are you that eager to talk to others about Jesus? What empowered these women to do so? Why is it sometimes hard for us? Would it be easier with a group of sisters like this? How do you think they felt when the men didn't believe them? And why *didn't* the men believe what Mary and company had seen—because the messengers were women or because the men hadn't seen any angelic evidence for themselves? Should worrying about how our message will be received stop us from sharing the Good News?

2. What do you think Mary Magdalene hoped to accomplish by racing to the tomb with Peter and John? And why, if men didn't generally believe women, did they follow her in the first place? What does that tell us about Mary—and about Peter and John? With all we've learned about Mary Magdalene, why was she the one to return to the tomb, rather than Joanna, or Mary the mother of James, or Salome, or one of the other women? Does it seem to you that this is a *second* visit for Mary Magdalene that Easter morning? How is it like the first visit with the other women (described in Luke 24:1-8), and how is it dramatically different?

3. When Mary said, "They have taken the Lord," what "they" was she talking about, do you think? Who were the most likely suspects? Why would they have taken his body in the first place—and where? Were her fears grounded in truth or merely in desperation? Do we look for someone to blame when our faith is knocked for an unexpected loop? Might that be what happened to Mary? Do you feel as if your own faith has been sorely tested? How did you get answers to your questions? What might Mary have done to "see" more clearly and keep alive the Lord's promise that he would rise again?

4. It would have been much easier if the angels had stepped forward to confirm things while the men were still there. Why did they wait until Peter and John left to show up? Why do you think Mary was neither frightened nor awed by the angels this time? Since they did not bring her news but simply asked one question—a question Jesus repeats moments later—why do you think the angels were there?

5. Mary Magdalene certainly did lots of weeping! What were those tears all about? Had she lost something more than her Lord? Had she lost her faith in his resurrection? Her hope for the future? Her trust in his heavenly Father? What else might she have mourned? Why did both the angels and the Lord ask her why she was crying? Did they expect an answer, or do you think they were suggesting she had no more need for tears? What does crying do for us emotionally? Do the countless tears of Mary Magdalene make you think *more* favorably of her, seeing her as empathetic and compassionate, or *less* favorably, seeing her as overly emotional and weak?

6. Have you ever seen someone whom you knew yet did not recognize right away? How did you handle the situation? Asked his or her name outright? Looked the other way and kept walking? Started talking, hoping you'd somehow think of it? At the tomb do you think Jesus intentionally withheld his identity from Mary? If so, to what end? If not, then why do you think Mary Magdalene didn't recognize him? The two disciples on the road to Emmaus had the very same experience—confusion, then discovery. What significance do you see in this hidden, then revealed identity of the risen Christ?

7. How would *you* recognize the voice of Jesus? Have you ever had a sense of the Lord's speaking your name? If so, when, where, and why? Does the thought of hearing the voice of Jesus speaking to your heart delight you...or does it trivialize your relationship with a great and mighty God? Do Christians make too much of that experience...or too little?

8. Read again chapter 8 of *Unveiling Mary Magdalene.* Find all the ways in which Mary Delaney's experience paralleled Mary Magdalene's that morning long ago. And what are some of the obvious differences that make Mary Magdalene's morning at the tomb a one-of-a-kind story?

Chapter Fourteen

LETTER TO THE WORLD

HER DECLARATION

This is my letter to the World.
EMILY DICKINSON

Picture this: You've searched aisle after aisle at the grocery story, desperation growing because your four-year-old son has disappeared. Tears sting your eyes as you swing your cart around a wobbly display of paper towels. *Help, help!* The child was by your side less than two minutes ago, but now…

Suddenly there he is, standing among a stack of cereal boxes, sharing a toothy grin with Tony the Tiger. He turns and says the one word you've been straining your ears to hear: "Mom!"

Thank you, Lord!

What is the very first thing you would instinctively do? Ask this precious child why he ran off? Scold him for frightening you? Pick out his favorite cornflakes while you're there?

No way. You'd wrap your arms around that lost-and-found young man and hug him for dear life.

Do you suppose tender-hearted Mary Magdalene was any different?

The gospel of John doesn't describe Mary's immediate reaction when she saw the lost-and-found Christ. But, judging by what he said next, it sounds as if she behaved very much like our mom at the grocery store and threw her arms around his blessed body.

Jesus said, "Do not hold on to me…" *John 20:17*

Since the Greek verb means "to clutch or grip,"[1] it's easy to understand why hundreds of artists over the centuries have painted Mary Magdalene with her fingers clutching his garment or her arms encircling his knees. For my grammarian sisters who care about such things, this was written in the present imperative tense—"Stop touching me,"[2]—which tells us Mary didn't waste a second between exclaiming "Rabboni!" and reaching out to hold her teacher.

This impetuous, heart-on-her-sleeve display of affection endears Mary Magdalene to me all the more. Since how she touched him was not described, we don't know if she fell at his feet, clung to his knees, wrapped her arms around his waist, or hugged his shoulders, but whatever Mary Magdalene did, it was immediate, unplanned, and definitely physical.

Touching him must have been something she did often, spontaneously, without thinking. If she was indeed his mother's age or older, hugging him in a motherly fashion would have been natural and completely innocent.

Jesus touched people, didn't he? To heal, to comfort, to forgive. I've always imagined him as being the sort of man who gave really good hugs. Not one of those stiff-bodied, barely touching hugs, but a good full-court press, the kind that makes your spine tingle and crack while a warm glow of wellness radiates through your body.

Mary, who had known "love and mercy, healing and empowerment, through his voice and touch,"[3] did what came naturally to her: She called out to him. And she reached out to him.

Jesus' statement, "Do not hold on to me," is often known by its Latin translation: *"Noli me tangere."* Despite what the phrase looks like—"no looking at my tangerine"—*tangere* has the same Latin root as touchy words like *tangible* and *tangent.* I nearly choked on my coconut Jelly Belly when I discovered that back in the fourth century a scholar named Ambrose "interpreted the words *noli me tangere*…to mean that women were forbidden to teach in church."[4]

Hold it right there, fella.

Jesus said "no *touching*," not "no *teaching*"!

Yet Mary *did* touch him…and Jesus said stop. How hard it must have been for our Mary to hear that. She had always been able to minister to him, touch him, anoint his head, bathe his feet, but now…no more touching? Having lost him to death, then welcomed him to life, she was *not* about to let go. Jesus was fully aware of that, which is why "the check given to Mary is of the kindest character."[5]

You can let go, Mary. He will never leave you again.

Any vignette from my own life pales to nothing by comparison, but I remember my heartbroken response when, as a brand-new Christian, I learned that the godly couple who introduced me to Jesus planned to move two thousand miles away.

I was devastated and clung to their hands, if not their garments. "Don't leave me! I'll never make it spiritually without you!" They assured me I was in good hands (the Lord's) and pressed on, urging me to study the Bible on my own, seek out other believers, and expand my boundaries. It was months before I began to see some small benefit in their departure. Although I missed them greatly, I learned to stand on my own, leaning only on the Christ.

Mary Magdalene had a much bigger lesson to learn and only minutes to assimilate it. Not only did she need to release her grip on his clothing, she also needed to let go of her old definition of who Jesus was. Her friend and teacher had suddenly become a great deal more than a righteous man rooted to her time and place. He was now a risen Savior for all mankind, for all time.

If Mary thought he had "simply 'come back' from the dead, and that he was again the man she knew as 'Teacher' "[6]—like Lazarus who was raised from the dead and resumed his old life—boy, was *she* in for a surprise! Jesus had a very different agenda, and he needed Mary Magdalene to make that adjustment and fast.

Perhaps he longed for her to stop weeping and start walking her faith. To stop clinging and start singing his praises. To stop looking back to Friday's crucifixion and start looking forward to the coming of the Holy Spirit at Pentecost.

Our tearful Mary was given a difficult assignment: "transcend the old relationship with its limitations and discover him anew as the risen, free Christ."[7] She knew him as her deliverer, she knew him as her disciple maker, and she knew him as her dearly departed friend. But *this* was Someone else again. This Jesus defied description and did away with day-old definitions. He was "freshly hatched" and "soaked in glory,"[8] wholly new and utterly alive.

> I am the Living One; I was dead, and behold I am alive for
> ever and ever! *Revelation 1:18*

Order a Mocha Grande, baby! It's a brand-new day.

Like Mary Magdalene, many of us can point to a time when Christ presented himself to us alone, individually, heart to heart, and asked us to rethink our relationship with him. To let go of our concept of a "manageable" Christ, a Sunday-only Christ, and embrace the fullness of his risen, eternal self. The *Oxford Book of Prayer* beautifully states what might have been Mary Magdalene's thoughts: "I know that what has died is not thou, my Lord, but only my idea of thee."[9]

There was another reason Mary had to stop clinging to Jesus. He had places to go and things to do.

> "…for I have not yet returned to the Father." *John 20:17*

"Returned," as in "ascended" (RSV). After his resurrection, he was caught between two worlds. The Son of God was about to become the Son of Heaven again. Mary Magdalene was the first to see him in this sacred transitional state, the first to "spy the future of a glorified God."[10] The very garden air shimmered with the miraculous in this "place of *mysterion*."[11]

Just as God chose Mary of Bethlehem to bring the baby Jesus into the world, so God chose Mary of Magdala to bring news of the risen Christ to the world.

Does the Lord use women in a major way or *what?*

> "Go instead to my brothers and tell them…" *John 20:17*

Jesus gave her two direct commands—"go" and "tell." No wonder she had to let go of his garments! She, too, had places to go and things to do, and it didn't behoove her "to draw any nearer or to tarry any longer."[12] Time for a little show and tell.

The disciples may not have trusted Mary Magdalene as a witness, but Jesus did. God seldom selects the obvious person for ministry. Darlin', I'm a walkin', talkin' example of that! I've got "Least Likely to…" stamped all over my forehead. But God will send whomever he pleases wherever he chooses, and that's exactly what happened that morning in the garden.

It's clear that Jesus saw Mary as "a unique person in whom the life and power of God flowed with the same degree of intensity as it did in Peter, James, or John."[13] He trusted this woman to spread the news and get the story straight. Not just any woman—a former madwoman, a Former Bad Girl, a delivered demoniac!

The One who "healed her mind and knew it was a complete healing"[14] also knew her steadfast nature could be trusted. She'd been at the cross, at the burial, at the empty tomb. While others wandered off, she waited. When others strayed, she stayed. Loyalty was her middle name, and perseverance was her game.

That morning when she rose and dressed before dawn, gathering an armload of spices and a truckload of courage, Mary couldn't have imagined that before the sixth hour she would become "not only the first witness of the resurrection, but the first preacher of it."[15]

Go tell it on the mountain, Mary M.!

And here's what Jesus commanded her to tell the disciples:

> "I am returning to my Father and your Father, to my God and
> your God." *John 20:17*

That "I am returning" phrase reminds us she'd caught him in the very act, as it were. In the process of returning. The Greek word, *anabaino,* literally means "to go up, to ascend, to arise."[16] He wouldn't be returning to that old tomb. Jesus was heaven bound. And look at the personal pronouns he used—"my" and "your" Father and God.

His Father from before the dawn of time. Our Father by grace.

His God from forever ago. Our God from the day we hear his voice and acknowledge him as Lord.

For those women among us who chafe at the idea of a loving heavenly Father because our earthly dads were emotional write-offs, Jesus took care of that at the cross and "made a loving son and daughter relationship with the Father possible."[17]

At that precise moment, Mary probably wanted to do nothing more than celebrate their relationship and stay right where she was, in the presence of her Lord. But that was not to be. Jesus had a job for her to do. She who had turned toward him in mere acknowledgment, then turned away in disappointment, then turned toward him again with a shout of joy, now had to turn away once more and concentrate on communicating his message. Mary Magdalene needed—oh, girlfriend, would *this* be difficult!—to convince herself she loved "carrying Christ's message, better than enjoying Christ's fellowship."[18]

That's the reality check of loving God.

We wanna sit at his feet, bask in his presence, worship all day, but we've got work to do. His work. Kingdom work. The glorious news is, in serving him our fellowship is enhanced, not diminished.

Jesus tested her self-control with "Touch not," then tested her obedience with "Go tell."[19] She passed both tests with flying colors.

Like the woman at the well who left behind her water jar, Mary Magdalene abandoned her ointment jar and pointed her toes toward town, prepared to share her amazing story. Perhaps a lesson she'd once heard Jesus share danced through her thoughts as she turned away from her beloved teacher: "If anyone stands before other people and says he believes in me, then I will say that he belongs to me."[20]

Mary Magdalene went... *John 20:18*

We aren't told that she *ran* on her mission, though that woulda been her style. I picture her walking resolutely, occasionally slowing to glance over her shoulder at the spot where Jesus had stood. Did he watch her go or disappear in the twinkling of an eye? Did she square her shoulders and lift her chin, realizing the time had come for her to "rise up as an independent woman of faith, as a leader of the early Christian movement,"[21] or did she stumble along, mentally practicing what she would say when she got to Jerusalem?

Half a mile, a brisk ten-minute walk, and Mary was there.

Take a deep breath, everybody.

> Mary Magdalene went to the disciples... *John 20:18*

Not just to Joanna and Susanna and the other Marys. To the men as well.

Augustine declared, "The Holy Spirit made Magdalene the apostle of the apostles."[22] The *what?* You got it, babe. In Latin, that's *apostolorum apostola*—apostle of the apostles, "messenger" and "witness of truth."[23] An apostle in the broadest sense of the term: "one sent on a mission."[24]

Oh, yeah. She was all that.

Her witness was bold and without apology, the single biggest announcement in world history. As Paul said, "if Christ has not been raised, our preaching is useless and so is your faith."[25] Since Mary Magdalene was the one who witnessed and proclaimed that resurrection, she was the prime minister of information that Easter morning.

One commentator put it bluntly: "Without Magdalene, the Jesus movement would have died."[26] You and I know better. *Nothing* could have stopped Jesus. But Mary—passionate, nothing-held-back Mary Magdalene—*was* his chosen vessel. She's "an everywoman" who calls us "into the liberation she experienced in her radical savior. I want to know and be like this woman who gave her life to telling about the light of Jesus."[27]

Amen, and put my name down too!

What began as a "magnificent commission" led to a "triumphant message."[28]

> Mary Magdalene went to the disciples with the news...
> *John 20:18*

No question, "her news" (NEB) was the "most wondrous news in the world."[29] Though she's been described as "the dignified and solemn proclaimer of the mystery of resurrection,"[30] that's not the voice I hear shouting through the streets of Jerusalem that day.

Huh-uh.

The voice I hear was breathless from hurrying and strained with excitement.

Bold with confidence and infused with awe. The voice of a woman whose life had been transformed—twice—at his appearing.

Tell the world, woman!

"I have seen the Lord!" *John 20:18*

With her own eyes, she saw him.

With her own ears, she heard him.

With her own hands, she touched him.

This was no angelic message whispered down the lanes of Jerusalem. This was a testimony, a threefold validation. Not "I know about" or "I heard about" or "I read about."

"I have seen the Lord!"

And note, she does not say, "*We* have seen the Lord." It's personal. "*I* have."

Here's the key to Mary Magdalene's story: Mary shared the gospel with everyone and anyone who would listen. Not because it was her *job,* but because it was her *joy* to do so. She didn't wait for someone to give her a church to pastor, she didn't require a robe and stole, she didn't demand an ordination or title. She went and told people about her experience with the risen Christ: "I have seen him with my own eyes!"

This is *it,* sister mine. This is the lesson for all of us.

Go and tell.

Go and tell the guy who delivers your mail. Go and tell the hygienist who cleans your teeth. Go and tell the women in your Bunco group. Go and tell anyone who will stand still long enough to listen. Male, female, young, old, *tell them.*

What was it that propelled Mary forward, without hesitation, taking the huge risk of being seen as mad again? Boundless love. Endless gratitude. Matchless devotion. I remember the first time I heard the phrase "So-and-so is sold out to God." *That's it!* It describes the thing perfectly. Mary was bought and paid for, no longer her own person, released from the concern of "what should I do?"

When you are sold out to God, you cannot *not* go and tell.

Mary Magdalene was not the only woman the Lord sent out to proclaim his truth. John's gospel records the story of the woman at the well who shared the good news with the men of her town—"Come, see a man who told me everything I ever did. Could this be the Christ?"[31] Martha of Bethany also made a confession of faith that echoed Peter: "Yes, Lord,...I believe that you are the Christ, the Son of God, who was to come into the world."[32]

And now, here's our anything-but-mad Mary using the same words as the apostle Paul: "Have I not seen Jesus our Lord?"[33] Without question, the Lord does call women to be witnesses to what we have seen, experienced, and know to be true. It's time for us to follow Mary Magdalene's example and simply shout in the marketplace, "I have seen the Lord!"

Don't be hiding behind some "evangelism isn't my gift" excuse. You may not be called to travel from platform to platform sharing the gospel, but you are without any shadow of any doubt called to go and tell the people in your sphere of influence. The question isn't your gift or your calling. The question is, are you sold out? Do you love him with a boundless love welling in your soul? Do you look upon his face with endless gratitude shining in your eyes? Do you take risks and give generously of everything that matters to you because of your matchless devotion to him?

Is Jesus Lord of your life?

Mary Magdalene knew the answer to that one: "Yes!"

> And she told them that he had said these things to her.
> *John 20:18*

"These things" were his statements about returning to their heavenly Father, although I bet the disciples were still reeling from her opening line: "I have seen the Lord!" Whole songs have been written about that statement; entire sermons have been preached on it; many chapters in many books focus on the power of that single line and its life-altering truth.

Say it with me, sis: "I have seen the Lord!"

Doesn't it make shivers run along your arms? *Woo-hoo!* If Mary did nothing else in her life but say those few words, she would have done enough. And if we can proclaim the same truth in our own corners of the world, think of the impact we might have.

Ooh, baby! More shivers. Lots more.

The gospel of Mark gives us a few more details about Mary's audience that morning.

> She went and told those who had been with him and who
> were mourning and weeping. *Mark 16:10*

The men and the women as well then—all of whom were convinced the Savior was dead. And here came Mary with the best news in the world: "He is *not* dead, and I know so, because I've just seen him!"

Hallelujah!

Did they stop weeping? Nope. They wrote her off as a madwoman. Again.

> When they heard that Jesus was alive and that she had seen
> him, they did not believe it. *Mark 16:11*

What? I'm about ready to pull out my hair here!

Mary Magdalene not only saw the Lord, she spoke with him. She not only spoke with him, she touched him. He was most assuredly alive! But they didn't believe her.

When the women returned with their first message—the one about the empty tomb and the talking angels—I can see how that might have been a tad suspect. It was early; it was dark; they were frightened and joy filled, crying one minute and laughing the next. Easy to see why the disciples might have questioned that one.

No visible proof.

But not this second declaration from Mary Magdalene! She had visible proof, tangible truth, and a message for them straight from Jesus. They still missed the message. No, it was worse than that. They didn't *believe* it. They rejected the truth of the resurrection.

Celsus, one of Christianity's early detractors, wrote off Mary Magdalene's declaration as the "hallucination of a 'hysterical woman.'"[34] Origen, a patriarch in the early church, complained that Mary Magdalene was a "wholly unsuitable first witness."[35]

Look, gentlemen. Jesus chose a woman. Adjust.

Before the sun set Easter night, Jesus appeared to two disciples on the road to Emmaus[36] and to the Eleven and those with them in Jerusalem,[37] convincing them in person that he had indeed risen. A week later he offered a gentle but firm word of admonishment to Thomas: "Because you have seen me, you have believed; blessed are those who have not seen and yet have believed."[38]

The disciples were the first to hear the news and not believe, but they would not be the last. For two thousand years—one hundred generations—various Mary Magdalenes and Simon Peters all over the world have been crying out, "I have seen the Lord!" and people have been shaking their heads.

Madwoman. Madman.

We beg. We plead. We point to the Bible, the Word of God, and say, "Look, right here—the gospel of John, twentieth chapter, eighteenth verse. Mary saw him alive. He rose from the dead. It happened!"

"Oh, really?" the person we're talking to might say, flipping back several pages. "Then how come over in the twenty-eighth chapter of Matthew, the ninth verse, it says, 'They came to him, clasped his feet and worshiped him.' *They,* huh? Sounds like more than just Mary Magdalene to me. Explain *that* one."

Gulp.

The truth is, scholars can't agree on why the gospel accounts have slight variations. "The sequence of events cannot be worked out. Each account is a separate summary of early Christian testimony to the fact of Jesus' resurrection."[39] It would seem there were two or three different scenes that incredible morning or the same scene was described different ways.

My pastor, Bob Russell of Southeast Christian Church in Louisville, was once challenged by a college student: "How can you base your belief on the Gospels when the accounts of the resurrection contradict each other?" In good rabbinical fashion, Bob answered his question with a question: "If you had four witnesses in a courtroom and all four testimonies were verbatim, what would you conclude?" The student replied, "I'd figure they had collaborated and were probably lying."

Exactly.

Differing accounts simply mean four different writers are giving us their unique viewpoints of that momentous morning. The four gospel accounts don't include the same number of details, nor are they presented in the same order, but they all add up to the same message: Jesus Christ rose from the dead. As Bob put it, "Each writer tells the story from a different perspective. Far from undermining the credibility of Scripture, instead it enhances it."[40]

I can rest in this: In all four accounts Mary Magdalene was the first at the tomb, the stone was rolled away, the angels announced that Christ was risen, and the Lord appeared first to Mary Magdalene. That is astounding enough truth for anyone to comprehend! And that passage in Matthew, by the way, still sends the women on a mission: "Go and tell my brothers,"[41] so Mary having others with her doesn't change the message one iota.

My faith in Christ is not dependent on a neatly filled out page marked "Easter" in my Day Runner, with every fifteen minutes accounted for. I have no problem picturing a lot of running back and forth from the tomb that day. An early trip in the predawn darkness made by several women, including Mary Magdalene, who hurried back to describe the empty grave. A return trip by Mary M. with two male disciples, who walked away scratching their heads and therefore missed her thrilling solo sighting of the risen Christ. Mary Magdalene's announcement to the disciples, "I have seen the Lord!" Then yet another visit by Mary with a couple of her faith sisters (the passage in Matthew 28:9-10), women who *did* believe what she'd said and wanted to see for themselves, only to find themselves falling at the feet of the risen Christ.

Perhaps you've read other harmonies that ring more true to you. Or perhaps you've never given it a moment's thought and don't intend to now. No problem. It's not precisely *when* but exactly *what* happened on that earth-shaking day that matters most.

One wise soul commented, "Had they wanted to produce accounts more easily harmonized, they could have done so and made the present task much easier. But that would have diverted them from the direction in which the Spirit led them."[42] I always wanna go where the Spirit goes, and surely the apostle John felt the same way.

So what do you say to the skeptic who refuses to believe and blames differing gospel accounts as the reason?

You say what Mary Magdalene said. "I have seen the Lord!"

"I read about it in the Bible" is true and good. Yet, "I have seen him with the eyes of my heart" is often more convincing. And convicting.

How do I know that Jesus has risen? Because he has risen to the throne of my own heart. I have seen him work miracles in my life, one after another, big and small. He has changed my desires; he has remodeled my thinking; he has shown me how to love the unlovable, forgive the unforgivable (including myself), and move the unmovable barriers in my path.

The undeniable gospel is this: a transformed life.

Mary Magdalene was the perfect person to go and tell the disciple the news, because she knew what it was to be spiritually dead and in the clutches of the Adversary. And she knew—oh, how very well she knew!—what it was to be spiritually alive in Christ. "She is the messenger and she is the one who understands who this risen Jesus is."[43]

Precisely so: He is the One who has overcome the Prince of Darkness. First for her, and now for the entire world.

Mary the Demoniac became Mary the Declarer of Good News.

Like Rahab the prostitute from the pages of the Old Testament, who was still called Rahab the Harlot some fourteen hundred years after the fact, Mary Magdalene's identity will forever be linked to her demon-filled past.

A bad thing? No, a wondrous thing.

Those of us with a past we're not proud of—oh, my precious sister, are there any among us who don't cringe when we look back at some of the things we've said and done?—can rise to our feet with Mary Magdalene and say, "I am a woman, made in the image of God, claimed for a dark season by God's enemy, then recreated by God in the image of his Son Jesus, who is alive in me."

"I have seen the Lord!"

Christ's appearing first to Mary Magdalene was without question his finest assurance to women throughout the ages that he values us, that he died for us, that he rose for us. He could have appeared before his beloved disciple John, he could have sent his spirited disciple Peter to proclaim his resurrection to the world, but the undeniable fact is, Jesus chose Mary Magdalene.

He chose a woman. Yes, he did.

Here's one detail about which the gospels are in perfect harmony: Although others saw Jesus that Resurrection Sunday, only one saw him *first*.

> When Jesus rose early on the first day of the week, he appeared
> first to Mary Magdalene, out of whom he had driven seven
> demons. *Mark 16:9*

In a sentence, a single verse, we are shown once again the amazing range of Christ's compassion: He drove out the seven demons and filled her completely with the revelation of himself. As a perfect example of "the last shall be first," Mary's story "begins with the darkest of all human misery and ends with the most glorious day in the history of the world."[44]

What about the *next* day? What happened to Mary Magdalene after her big Easter morning scene?

We don't know.

Groan.

The Bible doesn't tell us, and all the conjectures about her postresurrection ministry come from noncanonical accounts, medieval literature, and hagiographical writings (*Say what?!* Those are "idealized biographies") from the eleventh century, some of which suggest that she ended up in southern France. That legend has since been "seriously questioned."[45] Indeed.

Mary Magdalene is not mentioned by name in the book of Acts but is almost certainly among those who waited in the Upper Room at Pentecost where they "all joined together constantly in prayer, along with the women and Mary the mother of Jesus, and with his brothers."[46] It's not a stretch to conclude that, as one of Jesus' most faithful followers, Mary Magdalene "was among the women in this group."[47]

She's also not mentioned in the rest of the New Testament, at least not by name, unless—and this is a long shot—Paul was referring to her when he wrote among his personal greetings in the book of Romans, "Greet Mary, who worked very hard for you."[48] If he meant Mary Magdalene, she would have been a very old woman indeed by this point. Seventy-something. And remember how common the name *Mary* was. I say we chalk this woman up as one of those seven Marys in the Bible, but not *our* Mary.

Nonetheless, look at all the *women* listed in this letter to the believers in Rome, and be encouraged!

> I commend to you our sister Phoebe, a servant of the church in Cenchrea. I ask you to receive her in the Lord in a way worthy of the saints and to give her any help she may need from you, for she has been a great help to many people, including me. *Romans 16:1-2*

She "became a patron of others [and] aided or defended them in their cause."[49] Go, Phoebe girl! And here's another spiritual sis:

> Greet Priscilla and Aquila, my fellow workers in Christ Jesus. They risked their lives for me. Not only I but all the churches of the Gentiles are grateful to them. *Romans 16:3-4*

Okay, Aquila is a fella—Priscilla's husband—and a good man at that, but she's listed first. Go, Pris! A few verses later, more women appear.

> Greet Tryphena and Tryphosa, those women who work hard in the Lord. Greet my dear friend Persis, another woman who has worked very hard in the Lord. *Romans 16:12*

Now, *there* are a couple of names you don't hear around the church nursery much! T. & T. were "two holy women...who ministered to the sick."[50] Hard-working women of all ages, no doubt. Recognized as *women,* named and honored with respect, gratitude, and admiration.

Actually the first-century church was replete with women; not a few but lots. In the following verses from Acts, check out all the ways that author Luke emphasized the fact that *women* were openly included in the new church. As usual, the italics are mine...

> Even on my servants, both men *and women,* I will pour out my Spirit in those days, and they will prophesy. *Acts 2:18*

> Nevertheless, more and more men *and women* believed in the Lord and were added to their number. *Acts 5:14*

> Many of the Jews believed, as did also *a number of prominent
> Greek women* and many Greek men. *Acts 17:12*

Love that "prominent women" tag! It's also been translated "important" (ICB), "honourable" (KJV), "women of standing" (NEB), and "women...of influence" (MSG). Mary Magdalene and the other sisters paved the way for these prominent women to openly, unashamedly proclaim the Christ as their Messiah.

Whether you see yourself as a "woman of influence" or not, God does.

If he can use Mary Magdalene—and he did—he can certainly use you!

But first you have to be set free from your past, released from your demons, filled with the Holy Spirit, and sent by the One who knows exactly where you need to go.

Are you ready? Are you willing? Because, honey, he is able!

Our role models are not women who've *made it*—not Martha Stewart, not Madonna. Our role models are women like Mary Magdalene who've been *made new*. That's what "the gospel does for woman—elevates her, heals her, saves her."[51] Mary M.'s joyful declaration of Christ's victory over death "shouts to women everywhere how an encounter with Christ changes a life forever."[52] And ever, girl. And ever.

Have you come to love Mary Magdalene, as I have? Not because she got it all right. On the contrary, because she followed and provided, then worried and wept, then clung to him, refusing to let her relationship with him grow and change, then responded to his calling and proclaimed his truth. Her walk was not unlike my own—three steps forward, two steps back. You, too?

Just as we're moving forward in a positive direction, so at last is Mary Magdalene's reputation. July 22, the Feast of Mary of Magdala, has become a day of celebration for Catholics across America who long to "erase the image of Mary Magdalene as a whore...and restore her to her place as a well-respected spiritual leader and member of Christ's inner circle."[53]

Hooray!

And a note of caution. As we've reshaped our image of Mary M. to bring it in alignment with the historical and biblical Mary, we must always remember she was simply a woman, like us, at a unique juncture in history. The

LETTER TO THE WORLD   265

temptation is to lift Mary Magdalene above all others. One writer effusively
described her as "The daughter of time / The woman of all ages / The mother
of all humans and all spirit."[54]

Sounds like worship to me. Idolatry, in fact.

We are not called by God to worship Mary Magdalene or any other mortal in Scripture. Like us, they were sinners in need of grace. Mary Magdalene the Perfect would not only stretch beyond biblical truth, she'd also be beyond our grasp. Give me a woman who knows she needs grace every day just to keep breathing, and I'll follow her example and seek the Christ.

It has been my goal in *Unveiling Mary Magdalene* to scrub her tainted image clean and give us a clear picture of the *real* Mary Magdalene—both before the demons were cast out and, more to the point, after they were gone. When all is read and done, the demons are barely a footnote on her résumé. She will ever be remembered as the one who declared, "I have seen the Lord!"

No fifteen minutes of fame for this girl. Her name, her story, her shame, her glory are all preserved for eternity in the Word of God.

We, who may never be famous, can simply rejoice that our names are written down where it matters most. As Paul phrased it, "Help these women who have contended at my side in the cause of the gospel…whose names are in the book of life."[55]

Until the day that heavenly book is opened, let's stand together with our ancient role model, Mary Magdalene, and our millions of sisters in faith through the ages "while we wait for the blessed hope—the glorious appearing of our great God and Savior, Jesus Christ."[56]

Amen, and come quickly!

WHAT LESSONS CAN WE LEARN FROM MARY MAGDALENE AND HER DECLARATION?

Be bold.
Mary Magdalene boldly reached out for what she needed most on that amazing morning—assurance—and touched her risen Lord. Though Jesus asked her to stop, he did not scold her for reaching out to him. That boldness

served her well when it came time for her to "go" and "tell." She did both with gusto! If you are by nature a bold woman, use that boldness to God's glory. We all know the difference between a pushy woman and a strong one. One is determined to get her way. The other is determined to do things God's way. Big difference, babe.

> Therefore, since we have such a hope, we are very bold.
> *2 Corinthians 3:12*

Go crazy.

Mary Magdalene never stopped being "mad," you know. After she was delivered from those demons, she gave her life away to Jesus. Ignoring social conventions, she had no male "sponsor," no home address, no family ties. She staked *everything* on him. Maybe you and I need to go a little crazy too. Do something—*one* thing—that defies common sense but makes utter biblical sense. Give something away that we still need but someone else needs more. Risk looking foolish by sharing the gospel with a stranger. Pray openly at a restaurant—eyes closed, out loud, the whole bit. Include the waitress. A little craziness for Christ is a good thing!

> If any one of you thinks he is wise by the standards of this age,
> he should become a "fool" so that he may become wise.
> *1 Corinthians 3:18*

Give honor where honor is due.

The women around Jesus—Mary M. most of all—deserve our highest praise. "All honor to them, to their courage, and to their love."[57] They set the standard for women in ministry today. Don't let the word *minister* scare you, beloved. It's not only a title; it's a verb. To minister means to care for, to aid, to serve. We can all do that for one another. We're also called to honor those who *do* minister in a more official capacity. As we would honor the Christ, so should we honor all who serve under his authority. It's not easy for a pushy girl like me to submit to authority (see "Be Bold" above!). But if their leadership agrees with God's Word, it's always right.

Now we ask you, brothers, to respect those who work hard
among you, who are over you in the Lord and who admonish
you. Hold them in the highest regard in love because of their
work. *1 Thessalonians 5:12-13*

A "Mary" heart doeth good like a medicine.

There's a verse in Romans that says straight out what we have to do to inherit
eternal life. See if this sounds familiar: "If you confess with your mouth,
'Jesus is Lord,' and believe in your heart that God raised him from the dead,
you will be saved."[58] Wow...that describes Mary Magdalene to a T! She said,
"I have seen the Lord!" and she believed in her heart—and with her eyes—
that he was raised from the dead. Ta-da! She proclaimed "the total change in
her life, which...resulted from her encounter with the Lord."[59] He changed
her life. He changed my life. Has he changed your life, sis? If you confess that
change with your mouth and believe it in your heart, what joy it will be to see
you in heaven!

> Take hold of the eternal life to which you were called when
> you made your good confession in the presence of many
> witnesses.... I charge you to keep this command without
> spot or blame until the appearing of our Lord Jesus Christ.
> *1 Timothy 6:12-14*

GOOD GIRL THOUGHTS WORTH CONSIDERING

1. Before she could "go and tell," Mary had to "let go." What are some of
   the things she had to let go of that day in the garden? Which of those
   things can you identify with? Has the Lord asked you to let go of
   anything tangible in your life? If we do let go, what can we hold on to
   instead? Are those things—close relationships, God's eternal Word, the
   support of friends, or whatever else you might choose to cling to—
   enough for you? What if God asked you to let go of everything and
   trust him completely? Could you do it? If not, what might be stopping
   you?

2. Have you had a spiritual mentor in your life? How did he or she help you? Did a time come when you had to strike out on your own? What did you learn in the process? Have you learned more in your spiritual life from men or from women? How did their styles of teaching or encouragement differ? Do both men and women bring something of value to mentoring? To ministry?

3. Jesus could have chosen to reveal himself to anyone that sacred morning, but he chose Mary Magdalene. Think of some reasons why she was the worst choice…and the best choice. Did she handle her important task well? Why didn't the disciples believe her? Was she not trustworthy, honest, or faithful? How might the disciples have felt toward Mary by day's end when many had seen Jesus for themselves? What does this teach us about focusing on our mission—to share the gospel—rather than on how others respond—or don't respond—to what we tell them?

4. How might Christ's ministry and message have changed if Mary of Magdala had been Marcus of Magdala instead? Does the fact that she's a woman enhance the gospel story or detract from it or not matter at all? Might a man just as easily have been there at the tomb that morning? At what points in her story does the fact that she's a "she" make a significant difference? Does it matter to *you* that Mary was a Mary and not a Marcus? Why or why not?

5. Have you ever made a Mary kind of declaration to a group of people: "I have seen the Lord!" or something similar? What was your experience? How were you received? And how was your message received? Can you separate the two? Did it make you want to be bolder on another occasion or vow never to make a fool of yourself like that again? How do we look at people who proclaim their faith visibly, noisily, publicly? Does God ask us to do that? If so, for what purpose?

6. Were you aware before studying Mary's story how the gospel accounts of the resurrection seem to differ? Does that challenge your faith at all? How do you reconcile those apparent story variations in your own mind? How do you explain them to others? Is God able to handle our

doubts and concerns? How can we stand on his Word and know that it is trustworthy and true?

7.   Mary Magdalene quietly disappeared from Scripture after her big morning in the garden. Why might that be the case? How did the listing of other women from Acts and Romans encourage you? Can you imagine your own name alongside Phoebe's and Priscilla's? How will you be remembered among your sisters in Christ when you are gone? What legacy of faith will you leave behind?

8.   Now that we've studied Mary Magdalene from every angle, what lesson has she taught you above all others? Are you prepared to "go" and "tell," as Mary did? Have you been wondering what happened when our contemporary Mary Margaret Delaney returned to the church that Easter morning with the gardener's reminder to "tell the others" still fresh in her mind? Suppose we find out...

WHEN WE SPEAK WORDS

We know not what we do
When we speak words.
PERCY BYSSHE SHELLEY

"*Psst!* Mary!"

Mary Margaret Delaney heard the whispered entreaty behind her and turned around long enough to acknowledge Suzy with a solemn wink. *Soon!*

Undaunted, her friend leaned forward, propping her chin on Mary's shoulder. "So. Are you going to say something or not?"

"Yes," Mary Delaney whispered back. When the time was right. *Show me when, Lord.*

The mood was subdued, appropriately funereal. Even the lilies looked somber, their white blossoms drooping like elderly women with bowed heads. An undercurrent of noise filled the crowded sanctuary as the small choir took their seats and another VIP rose to honor the memory of a young pastor slain in his prime. Mary listened carefully to their words while she weighed her own.

A city official spoke in favor of justice and retribution.

Mary Margaret prayed on behalf of mercy and grace.

A police detective declared victory: an apprehended assassin.

Mary Margaret knew of a greater victory: an empty tomb.

When the string of civil servants finished their pronouncements, Pete approached the pulpit with weary steps, the strain of the long weekend etched on his features. "Before we conclude our ceremony in memory of Jake Stauros, would anyone else care to add their comments?"

Mary Margaret was on her feet before he finished, moving down the aisle as though propelled by an unseen power. She stopped short of the pulpit, choosing instead to stand in front of it, remaining close to her audience, just as Jake had often done.

Drawing in a deep breath, Mary exhaled slowly, allowing her taut nerves to relax as countless eyebrows rose with anticipation and the constant murmuring ceased.

Mary met their curious gazes with a steady one and made a simple declaration.

"He is not dead."

A gasp moved through the crowd. Their faces revealed their thoughts. *Was she a madwoman…again? Still?*

Mary spoke again. "Jesus Christ conquered death on Easter morning—*this* morning. He is not dead." Her voice grew stronger with each word. "Jake staked his future on that cross. He's alive in Christ."

Mary stepped closer, her heart pounding against her ribs. "But *I* was dead. Dead to the things of God." She swallowed, determined to continue. "You all knew that. You saw me. You judged me and found me wanting."

She looked up at the wooden cross above the door, grateful for its silent assurance. "But Jake saw something different. He saw who I *could* be, not who I was. He saw past the demons, past the darkness, past the death wish that was my life."

Tears began flowing down her cheeks unchecked, running into the upturned corners of her mouth. "I saw the Christ alive in Jake." She smiled at the Sisters, whose radiant faces infused the air around them. "And I saw the Christ alive in you."

Mary's joy, impossible to contain, spilled out in laughter that sounded like music. "And now I see the Christ alive in me. He is not dead. He is risen. He is risen indeed!"

Mary Margaret Delaney's Irish Soda Bread

4 cups all-purpose flour

1½ teaspoons salt

1 teaspoon baking soda

1 tablespoon baking powder

2 tablespoons sugar

¼ cup butter, softened

2 cups buttermilk

1 egg

Preheat oven to 375 degrees.

Mix flour, salt, baking soda, baking powder, and sugar in a large bowl. Add softened butter and mix with your fingers.

In a small bowl, beat egg and buttermilk together. Pour the egg and milk mixture over the dry ingredients, and mix well until dough forms.

Knead dough on a lightly floured surface only until it is smooth, about a dozen times. Divide dough evenly, and form into two round loaves. Place on greased baking sheet. Use a sharp knife to cut a cross into the top of each loaf.

Bake at 375 degrees for about 40 minutes. When done, the loaves should sound hollow when thumped.

Remove loaves from the oven and brush with a bit of melted butter. Cool for a few minutes on a wire rack. Serve bread warm.

Study Guide

The questions at the end of chapters 9 through 14 were included for your personal study and reflection and/or for small-group discussion. In many cases there are no right or wrong answers; such questions are designed simply to stimulate your thinking and to encourage you to examine your heart on certain issues. Other questions point directly back to Scripture, which is where the following verses may come in handy.

These are by no means the only solutions one might find in the Bible...no way! I merely want to offer a good starting point in order to keep things "on track" biblically. Have fun checking out all the possibilities that time permits. May the Lord bless you abundantly, sister mine, as you open his Word!

Chapter 9: Her Legend

1. Romans 8:33; 1 Corinthians 12:4-6; Acts 5:14
2. Proverbs 10:23; Galatians 6:10; Titus 3:1-2
3. 1 Thessalonians 5:15; 1 Peter 2:12; 2 Corinthians 4:2
4. Proverbs 6:25-26; Proverbs 6:32; Romans 3:9-11
5. Job 12:12; Hebrews 5:14; Proverbs 16:31
6. Matthew 7:1-2; Romans 14:10; Philippians 2:3
7. 1 Peter 5:8; Romans 16:17-18; 1 Corinthians 4:5

Chapter 10: Her Demons

1. Mark 1:27; Matthew 6:13; Luke 6:17-19
2. Matthew 12:28; John 10:27-29; 1 John 4:10; 1 John 5:18-20
3. Psalm 9:18; Psalm 22:24; Psalm 43:5
4. Romans 13:12; 2 Corinthians 10:4-5; Ephesians 6:11-18
5. Ephesians 1:18-21; Jude 24-25; Colossians 1:13-17

6. Matthew 9:27-31; Matthew 9:32-33; Luke 17:12-19; Colossians 3:17
7. Acts 1:8; Matthew 10:18-20; 1 Peter 2:21

CHAPTER 11: HER DEDICATION

1. Romans 12:16; Romans 14:13; 2 Timothy 2:22-26
2. Ephesians 5:31-32; Philippians 3:13-14; Jeremiah 29:11
3. Proverbs 11:16; 1 Corinthians 11:11-12; 1 Timothy 2:9-15
4. John 4:25-29; Luke 7:37,47-50; John 8:10-11
5. Deuteronomy 4:2; Psalm 119:89; Isaiah 55:10-11; Jeremiah 23:28
6. Ephesians 5:3; James 1:13; Hebrews 7:25-26
7. Matthew 10:37-39; John 12:26; James 4:10

CHAPTER 12: HER DESPAIR

1. John 12:44-46; Mark 4:10-13; Luke 18:31-34
2. Mark 8:34-35; Mark 15:21; Matthew 11:29-30
3. 1 Chronicles 28:9; Philippians 2:5-8; Matthew 26:56
4. Matthew 21:11; Luke 19:41-44; Matthew 23:37
5. Lamentations 5:15-16; Psalm 23:4; 2 Corinthians 1:3-5
6. Genesis 1:2; Matthew 6:23; Isaiah 45:7; John 12:35
7. Psalm 14:2; Deuteronomy 4:29; John 14:19

CHAPTER 13: HER DISCOVERY

1. Acts 2:32; 1 John 1:5; Ephesians 6:19-20; 1 Corinthians 2:12-13
2. 2 Corinthians 5:11; 1 Peter 3:13; Psalm 25:4-5
3. 2 Corinthians 4:8; Romans 8:25; Hebrews 6:11; Romans 5:3-5
4. Hebrews 1:14; Exodus 23:20; Psalm 103:20
5. Acts 20:19; Psalm 56:8; Psalm 126:5
6. Matthew 11:25; Luke 8:17; 1 Peter 1:20
7. Deuteronomy 5:24; Isaiah 6:8; Acts 22:6-10

CHAPTER 14: HER DECLARATION

1. Genesis 12:1; Psalm 9:10; Psalm 56:3-4
2. Ephesians 4:11-13; Job 32:7-8; Hebrews 10:25
3. Romans 1:16; 1 Corinthians 9:16; 1 Thessalonians 2:3-4
4. Matthew 12:50; John 4:25-27; Acts 16:14-15
5. 2 Corinthians 4:5; John 3:11; John 4:39
6. Psalm 93:5; James 1:5-6; 1 Peter 1:23-25
7. 2 Corinthians 3:3; Deuteronomy 11:18-21; Hebrews 12:1-2

NOTES

Prologue: Wings of Madness

1. Morton Bryan Wharton, *Famous Women of the New Testament* (Chicago: W. P. Blessing, 1890), 247.

2. Mary Ellen Mize, *Profiles of Biblical Women* (Cadiz, Ky.: Barkley Printing, 1984), 95.

3. Sue Richards and Larry Richards, *Every Woman in the Bible* (Nashville: Nelson, 1999), 184.

Chapter Nine: Her Infinite Variety

1. Mark 1:7.

2. Donald Guthrie et al., ed., *The New Bible Commentary: Revised* (Grand Rapids: Eerdmans, 1970), 901.

3. Matthew Henry, *Matthew Henry's Commentary on the Whole Bible,* vol. 5 (1706; reprint, Peabody, Mass.: Hendrickson, 1991), 530.

4. Henry, *Matthew Henry's Commentary,* vol. 5, 530.

5. Mary R. Thompson, *Mary of Magdala: Apostle and Leader* (New York: Paulist, 1995), 47.

6. Matthew 21:31, MSG.

7. Renita J. Weems, *Just a Sister Away* (San Diego: LuraMedia, 1988), 88.

8. Thompson, *Mary of Magdala,* 121.

9. Merriam-Webster's Collegiate Dictionary, 10th ed., s.v. "magdalen."

10. Esther de Boer, *Mary Magdalene: Beyond the Myth* (Harrisburg, Pa.: Trinity Press International, 1997), 2.

11. F. F. Bruce, *The Gospel of John* (Grand Rapids: Eerdmans, 1983), 384.

12. "Mary Magdalene: The Hidden Apostle," *Biography,* prod. Bram Roos, A&E Television Networks, 2000, videocassette.

13. Matthew 27:61.

14. John 11:1.

15. Neal W. May, *Israel: A Biblical Tour of the Holy Land* (Tulsa, Okla.: Albury, 2000), 63.

16. John 11:2.

17. Susan Haskins, *Mary Magdalen: Myth and Metaphor* (New York: Harcourt Brace & Co., 1993), 24.

18. Matthew 26:13.

19. Henry Thorne Sell, *Studies of Famous Bible Women* (New York: Revell, 1925), 129.

20. Luke 7:11.

21. Raymond E. Brown, *The Gospel and Epistles of John* (Collegeville, Minn.: Liturgical Press, 1988), 66.

22. Morton Bryan Wharton, *Famous Women of the New Testament* (Chicago: W. P. Blessing, 1890), 251.

23. Luke 7:50.

24. Elisabeth Moltmann-Wendel, *The Women Around Jesus* (New York: Crossroad Publishing, 1980), 64.

25. William Hendricksen, *New Testament Commentary: The Gospel of John* (Grand Rapids: Baker, 1961), 432.

26. Virginia Stem Owens, *Daughters of Eve* (Colorado Springs, Colo.: NavPress, 1995), 231.

27. Moltmann-Wendel, *The Women Around Jesus,* 65.

28. Woodeene Koenig-Bricker, *365 Saints* (San Francisco: HarperSanFrancisco, 1995), July 22.

29. Kenneth C. Davis, *Don't Know Much About the Bible* (New York: Morrow, 1998), 385.

30. *Mary Magdalen: An Intimate Portrait,* prod. and dir. Charles C. Stuart, V.I.E.W. Videos, Inc., 1996, videocassette.

31. Thompson, *Mary of Magdala,* 4.

32. de Boer, *Mary Magdalene,* 8-9.

33. Wharton, *Famous Women of the New Testament,* 247.

34. Diane Apostolos-Cappadona, "Saint and Sinner: Mary Magdalene in Art History," *U.S. Catholic* 65, no. 4 (April 2000): 17.

35. Haskins, *Mary Magdalen,* 63.

36. *JESUS,* prod. John Heyman, Inspirational Films, 1980, videocassette.

37. Herbert Lockyer, *All the Women of the Bible* (Grand Rapids: Zondervan, 1967), 100.

38. Rose Salberg Kam, *Their Stories, Our Stories* (New York: Continuum, 1995), 234.

39. Kay D. Rizzo, *Face to Face with Forgiveness* (Nampa, Idaho: Pacific Press, 1997), 10.

40. Luke 10:18.

41. 2 Corinthians 11:3.

42. Romans 3:23.

43. Frances Vander Velde, *Women of the Bible* (Grand Rapids: Kregel, 1985), 215.

44. Edith Deen, *All the Women of the Bible* (New York: Harper & Row, 1955), 203.

45. Leviticus 19:32.

46. 1 Peter 3:3-4.

47. Moltmann-Wendel, *The Women Around Jesus,* 69.

48. Henry, *Matthew Henry's Commentary,* vol. 5, 671.

49. Joy Jacobs, *They Were Women Like Me* (Camp Hill, Pa.: Christian Publications, 1993), 144.

50. May, *Israel: A Biblical Tour,* 244.

51. Richard Atwood, *Mary Magdalene in the New Testament Gospels and Early Tradition* (Bern, Germany: Peter Lang, 1993), 23.

52. Frederick Drimmer, *Daughters of Eve* (Norwalk, Conn.: C. R. Gibson, 1975), 28.

53. Atwood, *Mary Magdalene in the New Testament Gospels,* 25.

54. George Arthur Buttrick, *The Interpreter's Dictionary of the Bible,* vol. 3 (New York: Abingdon, 1962), 221.

55. Carla Ricci, *Mary Magdalene and Many Others* (Minneapolis: Fortress, 1994), 130.

56. William P. Barker, *Women and the Liberator* (Old Tappan, N.J.: Revell, 1972), 124.

57. Lockyer, *All the Women of the Bible,* 100.

58. Atwood, *Mary Magdalene in the New Testament Gospels,* 26.

59. John 1:46.

Chapter Ten: Moonstruck Madness

1. William P. Barker, *Women and the Liberator* (Old Tappan, N.J.: Revell, 1972), 124.

2. Richard Atwood, *Mary Magdalene in the New Testament Gospels and Early Tradition* (Bern, Germany: Peter Lang, 1993), 32.

3. Mark I. Bubeck, *The Adversary* (Chicago: Moody, 1975), 144-6.

4. Mary Ellen Ashcroft, *The Magdalene Gospel* (New York: Doubleday, 1995), 55.

5. Albert Barnes, *Barnes' Notes on the New Testament: Luke and John* (1884-85; reprint, Grand Rapids: Baker, 1998), 55.

6. Warren W. Wiersbe, *The Strategy of Satan* (Wheaton, Ill.: Tyndale, 1979), 148.

7. Robert Lightner, *Angels, Satan, and Demons* (Nashville: Word, 1998), 130.

8. Gien Karssen, *Her Name Is Woman, Book Two* (Colorado Springs, Colo.: NavPress, 1977), 203.

9. Alexander Moody Stuart, *The Three Marys* (1862; reprint, Edinburgh, Scotland: The Banner of Truth Trust, 1984), 31.

10. Margaret E. Sangster, *The Women of the Bible* (New York: Christian Herald, 1911), 278.

11. Carla Ricci, *Mary Magdalene and Many Others* (Minneapolis: Fortress, 1994), 131.

12. Donald Guthrie et al., ed., *The New Bible Commentary: Revised* (Grand Rapids: Eerdmans, 1970), 901.

13. Sylvia Charles, *Women in the Word* (South Plainfield, N.J.: Bridge Publishing, 1984), 173.

14. Katherine Ludwig Jansen, *The Making of the Magdalen* (Princeton, N.J.: Princeton University Press, 2000), 33.

15. Morton Bryan Wharton, *Famous Women of the New Testament* (Chicago: W. P. Blessing, 1890), 247-8.

16. Lightner, *Angels, Satan, and Demons,* 133.

17. Stuart, *The Three Marys,* 30.

18. Lightner, *Angels, Satan, and Demons,* 134.

19. Bob Buess, *Setting the Captives Free* (Van, Tex.: Bob Buess, 1975), 2-3.

20. 1 John 1:10.

21. 1 John 4:4.

22. Stuart, *The Three Marys,* 46.

23. Stuart, *The Three Marys,* 26.

24. 2 Corinthians 4:6.

25. Rose Salberg Kam, *Their Stories, Our Stories* (New York: Continuum, 1995), 233.

26. Elisabeth Moltmann-Wendel, *The Women Around Jesus* (New York: Crossroad Publishing, 1980), 65.

27. Albert Barnes, *Barnes' Notes on the New Testament: Matthew and Mark* (1884–85; reprint, Grand Rapids: Baker, 1998), 41.

28. Lightner, *Angels, Satan, and Demons,* 131.

29. Stuart, *The Three Marys,* 29.

30. Sangster, *The Women of the Bible,* 278.

31. Harold J. Ockenga, *Have You Met These Women?* (Grand Rapids: Zondervan, 1965), 125.

32. William Menzies Alexander, *Demonic Possession in the New Testament* (Edinburgh, Scotland: T. & T. Clark, 1902), 4.

33. Alexander, *Demonic Possession in the New Testament,* 91.

34. Alexander, *Demonic Possession in the New Testament,* 137.

35. Ashcroft, *The Magdalene Gospel,* 84.

36. Luke 4:32.

37. Alexander, *Demonic Possession in the New Testament,* 69.

38. Guthrie et al, *The New Bible Commentary: Revised,* 896.

39. Stuart, *The Three Marys,* 50.

40. Guthrie et al, *The New Bible Commentary: Revised,* 896.

41. Stuart, *The Three Marys,* 63.

42. Alexander, *Demonic Possession in the New Testament,* 63-4.

43. Wharton, *Famous Women of the New Testament,* 247.

44. Psalm 3:8.

45. W. E. Vine, *Vine's Expository Dictionary of Old and New Testament Words,* vol. 4 (Old Tappan, N.J.: Revell, 1981), 62.

46. John 1:1.

47. Hebrews 1:3, NASB.

48. Wiersbe, *The Strategy of Satan,* 135-6.

49. Robert Don Hughes, *Satan's Whispers* (Nashville: Broadman Press, 1992), 174.

50. Lightner, *Angels, Satan, and Demons,* 139.

51. Exodus 7:11.

52. Guthrie et al, *The New Bible Commentary: Revised,* 826.

53. George Arthur Buttrick, *The Interpreter's Dictionary of the Bible,* vol. 1 (New York: Abingdon, 1962), 811.

54. Alexander, *Demonic Possession in the New Testament,* 78.

55. Alexander, *Demonic Possession in the New Testament,* 78.

56. Frank E. Gaebelein, ed., *The Expositor's Bible Commentary,* vol. 8 (Grand Rapids: Zondervan, 1992), 217.

57. Romans 14:11.

58. Guthrie et al, *The New Bible Commentary: Revised,* 862.

59. *Merriam-Webster's Collegiate Dictionary,* 10th ed., s.v. "legion."

60. Herbert G. May and Bruce M. Metzger, eds., *The New Oxford Annotated Bible, Revised Standard Version* (New York: Oxford University Press, 1962), note, 1255-6.

61. Guthrie et al, *The New Bible Commentary: Revised,* 862.

62. Ricci, *Mary Magdalene and Many Others,* 133.

63. Frances Vander Velde, *Women of the Bible* (Grand Rapids: Kregel, 1985), 215.

64. Julie-Allyson Ieron, *Names of Women of the Bible* (Chicago: Moody, 1998), 161.

65. John 15:3-4.

66. Wharton, *Famous Women of the New Testament,* 257.

67. Elizabeth George, *Women Who Loved God* (Eugene, Oreg.: Harvest House, 1999), 10,18.

Chapter Eleven: Through Thick and Thin

1. Morton Bryan Wharton, *Famous Women of the New Testament* (Chicago: W. P. Blessing, 1890), 257.

2. Mary R. Thompson, *Mary of Magdala: Apostle and Leader* (New York: Paulist, 1995), 50.

3. Dorothy Kelley Patterson, ed., *The Woman's Study Bible, the New King James Version* (Nashville: Nelson, 1995), 1707.

4. Julie-Allyson Ieron, *Names of Women of the Bible* (Chicago: Moody, 1998), 166.

5. Esther de Boer, *Mary Magdalene: Beyond the Myth* (Harrisburg, Pa.: Trinity Press International, 1997), 42.

6. Mary Ellen Ashcroft, *The Magdalene Gospel* (New York: Doubleday, 1995), x.

7. Sue Richards and Larry Richards, *Every Woman in the Bible* (Nashville: Nelson, 1999), 185.

8. Leonard J. Swidler, *Biblical Affirmations of Woman* (Philadelphia: Westminster John Knox, 1979), 164-5.

9. Luke 15:2.

10. Luke 15:3-9.

11. Luke 15:10.

12. Ross Saunders, *Outrageous Women, Outrageous God* (Alexandria, New South Wales, Australia: E. J. Dwyer, 1996), 8.

13. Saunders, *Outrageous Women, Outrageous God,* 18.

14. Henry Thorne Sell, *Studies of Famous Bible Women* (New York: Revell, 1925), 127.

15. *Mary Magdalen: An Intimate Portrait,* prod. and dir. Charles C. Stuart, V.I.E.W. Videos, Inc., 1996, videocassette.

16. Richard Atwood, *Mary Magdalene in the New Testament Gospels and Early Tradition* (Bern, Germany: Peter Lang, 1993), 17.

17. Herbert Lockyer, *All the Women of the Bible* (Grand Rapids: Zondervan, 1967), 101.

18. Thompson, *Mary of Magdala,* 48.

19. Rose Salberg Kam, *Their Stories, Our Stories* (New York: Continuum, 1995), 233.

20. 2 Timothy 2:2, NLT.

21. Janice Nunnally-Cox, *Foremothers* (New York: Seabury Press, 1981), 100.

22. Swidler, *Biblical Affirmations of Woman,* 163.

23. Swidler, *Biblical Affirmations of Woman,* 163.

24. Swidler, *Biblical Affirmations of Woman,* 342.

25. Swidler, *Biblical Affirmations of Woman,* 348.

26. Alexander Moody Stuart, *The Three Marys* (1862; reprint, Edinburgh, Scotland: The Banner of Truth Trust, 1984), 18.

27. Susan Haskins, *Mary Magdalen: Myth and Metaphor* (New York: Harcourt Brace & Co., 1993), 13.

28. Luke 9:13.

29. John 2:12.

30. Sell, *Studies of Famous Bible Women,* 130.

31. Matthew Henry, *Matthew Henry's Commentary on the Whole Bible,* vol. 5 (1706; reprint, Peabody, Mass.: Hendrickson, 1991), 530.

32. Stuart, *The Three Marys,* 64.

33. Renita J. Weems, *Just a Sister Away* (San Diego: LuraMedia, 1988), 86.

34. Albert Barnes, *Barnes' Notes on the New Testament: Luke and John* (1884–85; reprint, Grand Rapids: Baker, 1998), 55-6.

35. Carla Ricci, *Mary Magdalene and Many Others* (Minneapolis: Fortress, 1994), 53.

36. Atwood, *Mary Magdalene in the New Testament Gospels,* 17.

37. Saunders, *Outrageous Women, Outrageous God,* 61.

38. Atwood, *Mary Magdalene in the New Testament Gospels,* 19.

39. Margaret Starbird, *The Goddess in the Gospels* (Santa Fe, N.M.: Bear & Company Publishing, 1998), 22.

40. Haskins, *Mary Magdalen: Myth and Metaphor,* 33.

41. Elaine Pagels, *The Gnostic Gospels* (New York: Random House, 1979; reprint, New York: Vintage Books, 1989), xv.

42. Susanne Heine, *Women and Early Christianity: A Reappraisal* (Minneapolis: Augsburg, 1988), 55.

43. Pagels, *The Gnostic Gospels*, xv.

44. *Merriam-Webster's Collegiate Dictionary*, 10th ed., s.v. "lacuna."

45. de Boer, *Mary Magdalene: Beyond the Myth*, 71.

46. "Mary Magdalene: The Hidden Apostle," *Biography*, prod. Bram Roos, A&E Television Networks, 2000.

47. "Mary Magdalene: The Hidden Apostle."

48. Sandra M. Rushing, *The Magdalene Legacy* (Westport, Conn.: Bergin & Garvey, 1994), 78.

49. Denise Lardner Carmody, *Biblical Woman* (New York: Crossroad, 1988), 118.

50. Psalm 139:2-3.

51. Nunnally-Cox, *Foremothers*, 115.

52. Hebrews 13:8.

53. Isaiah 53:2.

54. Sarah Towne Martyn, *Women of the Bible* (New York: American Tract Society, 1868), 275.

55. Leigh Norval, *Women of the Bible* (Nashville: M. E. Church, South, Sunday School Department, 1889), 246.

56. de Boer, *Mary Magdalene: Beyond the Myth*, 39.

57. Luke 18:28.

58. John 6:65.

59. John 8:12.

60. John 14:6.

61. John 4:25-26.

62. William Barclay, *The Gospel of John*, vol. 2 (Philadelphia: Westminster, 1975), 68.

63. Luke 22:53.

64. Stuart, *The Three Marys*, 78.

65. John 20:24-25.

66. Luke 22:24.

67. Luke 22:34.

68. Margaret E. Sangster, *The Women of the Bible* (New York: Christian Herald, 1911), 279.

69. Matthew 27:19.

70. Luke 22:51.

71. Thompson, *Mary of Magdala,* 36.

Chapter Twelve: Path of Sorrow

1. Matthew 16:22.

2. Matthew 16:23.

3. Matthew 17:23.

4. Matthew 27:32.

5. *Merriam-Webster's Collegiate Dictionary,* 10th ed., s.v. "maudlin."

6. Albert Barnes, *Barnes' Notes on the New Testament: Luke and John* (1884–85; reprint, Grand Rapids: Baker, 1998), 155.

7. Donald Guthrie et al., ed., *The New Bible Commentary: Revised* (Grand Rapids: Eerdmans, 1970), 923.

8. Neal W. May, *Israel: A Biblical Tour of the Holy Land* (Tulsa, Okla.: Albury, 2000), 171.

9. Mary Ellen Ashcroft, *The Magdalene Gospel* (New York: Doubleday, 1995), 123.

10. Mark 15:40.

11. Ashcroft, *The Magdalene Gospel,* 124.

12. Susanne Heine, *Women and Early Christianity: A Reappraisal* (Minneapolis: Augsburg, 1988), 77.

13. Matthew 27:5.

14. Luke 23:46.

15. John 19:30.

16. Morton Bryan Wharton, *Famous Women of the New Testament* (Chicago: W. P. Blessing, 1890), 262.

17. Albert Barnes, *Barnes' Notes on the New Testament: Matthew and Mark* (1884–85; reprint, Grand Rapids: Baker, 1998), 315.

18. Isaiah 53:9.

19. Barnes, *Barnes' Notes on the New Testament: Matthew and Mark,* 315.

20. John 3:1.

21. John 7:50.

22. John 3:2.

23. Penelope Ody, *The Complete Medicinal Herbal* (New York: DK Publishing, 1993), 50.

24. Guthrie et al, *The New Bible Commentary: Revised,* 965.

25. F. F. Bruce, *The Gospel of John* (Grand Rapids: Eerdmans, 1983), 379.

26. William Hendricksen, *New Testament Commentary: The Gospel of John* (Grand Rapids: Baker, 1961), 442.

27. Rose Salberg Kam, *Their Stories, Our Stories* (New York: Continuum, 1995), 236.

28. May, *Israel: A Biblical Tour,* 171.

29. John 15:1.

30. May, *Israel: A Biblical Tour,* 183.

31. Dorothy Kelley Patterson, ed., *The Woman's Study Bible, the New King James Version* (Nashville: Nelson, 1995), 1797.

32. Guthrie et al, *The New Bible Commentary: Revised,* 965.

33. Deuteronomy 21:22-23.

34. Isaiah 53:10, NASB.

35. Frank E. Gaebelein, ed., *The Expositor's Bible Commentary,* vol. 8 (Grand Rapids: Zondervan, 1992), 584.

36. Guthrie et al, *The New Bible Commentary: Revised,* 924.

37. William E. Phipps, *Assertive Biblical Women* (Westport, Conn.: Greenwood Press, 1992), 115.

38. Heine, *Women and Early Christianity,* 77.

39. Virginia Stem Owens, *Daughters of Eve* (Colorado Springs, Colo.: NavPress, 1995), 233.

40. Harold J. Ockenga, *Have You Met These Women?* (Grand Rapids: Zondervan, 1965), 128.

41. Leviticus 23:32, NASB.

42. Matthew Henry, *Matthew Henry's Commentary on the Whole Bible,* vol. 5 (1706; reprint, Peabody, Mass.: Hendrickson, 1991), 671.

43. Psalm 30:5, KJV.

44. John 20:1.

45. Barnes, *Barnes' Notes on the New Testament: Matthew and Mark,* 317.

46. Leon Morris, *The Gospel According to John* (Grand Rapids: Eerdmans, 1971), 832.

47. Revelation 22:16.

48. Song of Songs 8:6.

49. Gaebelein, *The Expositor's Bible Commentary,* vol. 8, 584.

50. Alexander Moody Stuart, *The Three Marys* (1862; reprint, Edinburgh, Scotland: The Banner of Truth Trust, 1984), 82.

51. Guthrie et al, *The New Bible Commentary: Revised*, 885.

52. Matthew 28:2.

53. Barnes, *Barnes' Notes on the New Testament: Matthew and Mark*, 318.

54. Barnes, *Barnes' Notes on the New Testament: Matthew and Mark*, 318.

55. Sister Margaret Magdalen, *Transformed by Love: The Way of Mary Magdalen* (Mineola, N.Y.: Resurrection Press, 1989), 76.

56. Henry, *Matthew Henry's Commentary*, vol. 5, 671.

Chapter Thirteen: The Trysted Hour

1. Esther de Boer, *Mary Magdalene: Beyond the Myth* (Harrisburg, Pa.: Trinity Press International, 1997), 45.

2. Ross Saunders, *Outrageous Women, Outrageous God* (Alexandria, New South Wales, Australia: E. J. Dwyer, 1996), 64.

3. Matthew Henry, *Matthew Henry's Commentary on the Whole Bible*, vol. 5 (1706; reprint, Peabody, Mass.: Hendrickson, 1991), 672.

4. Elizabeth M. Tetlow, *Women and Ministry in the New Testament* (New York: Paulist Press, 1980), 114.

5. F. F. Bruce, *The Gospel of John* (Grand Rapids: Eerdmans, 1983), 390.

6. Bruce, *The Gospel of John*, 383.

7. Frank E. Gaebelein, ed., *The Expositor's Bible Commentary*, vol. 9 (Grand Rapids: Zondervan, 1992), 188.

8. Mark 9:24, NLT.

9. Susan Haskins, *Mary Magdalen: Myth and Metaphor* (New York: Harcourt Brace & Co., 1993), 9.

10. Gaebelein, *The Expositor's Bible Commentary*, vol. 9, 189.

11. Mary R. Thompson, *Mary of Magdala: Apostle and Leader* (New York: Paulist, 1995), 68.

12. Gaebelein, *The Expositor's Bible Commentary*, vol. 9, 190.

13. Henry, *Matthew Henry's Commentary*, vol. 5, 675.

14. Joyce Hollyday, *Clothed with the Sun* (Louisville, Ky.: Westminster John Knox, 1994), 234.

15. Dorothy A. Lee, "Partnership in Easter Faith: The Role of Mary Magdalene and Thomas in John 20," *Journal for the Study of the New Testament* (Sheffield, England: Sheffield Academic Press, 1995), 41.

16. Alexander Moody Stuart, *The Three Marys* (1862; reprint, Edinburgh, Scotland: The Banner of Truth Trust, 1984), 66.

17. Janice Nunnally-Cox, *Foremothers* (New York: Seabury Press, 1981), 115.

18. Eugenia Price, *God Speaks to Women Today* (Grand Rapids: Zondervan, 1964), 168.

19. Julia Staton, *What the Bible Says About Women* (Joplin, Mo.: College Press, 1980), 108.

20. Donald Guthrie et al., ed., *The New Bible Commentary: Revised* (Grand Rapids: Eerdmans, 1970), 965.

21. William Hendricksen, *New Testament Commentary: The Gospel of John* (Grand Rapids: Baker, 1961), 453.

22. Leon Morris, *The Gospel According to John* (Grand Rapids: Eerdmans, 1971), 837.

23. Paul D. Duke, *Irony in the Fourth Gospel* (Atlanta: John Knox, 1985), 104.

24. John 20:2.

25. Sister Margaret Magdalen, *Transformed by Love: The Way of Mary Magdalen* (Mineola, N.Y.: Resurrection Press, 1989), 53-4.

26. Duke, *Irony in the Fourth Gospel,* 105.

27. William Barclay, *The Gospel of John,* vol. 2 (Philadelphia: Westminster, 1975), 269.

28. Carolyn Nystrom, ed., *The Bible for Today's Christian Woman* (Nashville: Nelson, 1998), note, 1242.

29. Francis J. Moloney, *Woman: First Among the Faithful* (London: Darton, Longman and Todd, 1985), 81.

30. Luke 24:16.

31. Luke 24:31.

32. Thompson, *Mary of Magdala,* 74.

33. 2 Corinthians 2:4.

34. Psalm 6:6.

35. Gaebelein, *The Expositor's Bible Commentary,* vol. 9., 119.

36. Hendricksen, *The Gospel of John,* 454.

37. Edith Deen, *All the Women of the Bible* (New York: Harper & Row, 1955), 201.

38. Mark 10:51.

39. Stuart, *The Three Marys,* 83.

40. Guthrie et al, *The New Bible Commentary: Revised,* 965.

41. Michael Card, *The Parable of Joy: Reflections on the Wisdom of the Book of John* (Nashville: Nelson, 1995), 239.

42. Isaiah 43:1.

43. Carla Ricci, *Mary Magdalene and Many Others* (Minneapolis: Fortress, 1994), 143.

44. Ann Spangler and Jean E. Syswerda, *Women of the Bible* (Grand Rapids: Zondervan, 1999), 397.

45. Hollyday, *Clothed with the Sun,* 234.

46. Thompson, *Mary of Magdala,* 75.

47. W. E. Vine, *Vine's Expository Dictionary of Old and New Testament Words,* vol. 3 (Old Tappan, N.J.: Revell, 1981), 243.

48. Gaebelein, *The Expositor's Bible Commentary,* vol. 9, 191.

49. Barclay, *The Gospel of John,* 268.

50. Carolyn Nabors Baker, *Caught in a Higher Love* (Nashville: Broadman & Holman, 1998), 148.

51. Stuart, *The Three Marys,* 98.

Chapter Fourteen: Letter to the World

1. Frank E. Gaebelein, ed., *The Expositor's Bible Commentary,* vol. 9 (Grand Rapids: Zondervan, 1992), 192.

2. William Barclay, *The Gospel of John,* vol. 2 (Philadelphia: Westminster, 1975), 271.

3. Joyce Hollyday, *Clothed with the Sun* (Louisville, Ky.: Westminster John Knox, 1994), 233.

4. Katherine Ludwig Jansen, *The Making of the Magdalen* (Princeton, N.J.: Princeton University Press, 2000), 54.

5. Alexander Moody Stuart, *The Three Marys* (1862; reprint, Edinburgh, Scotland: The Banner of Truth Trust, 1984), 125.

6. Richard Atwood, *Mary Magdalene in the New Testament Gospels and Early Tradition* (Bern, Germany: Peter Lang, 1993), 133.

7. Sister Margaret Magdalen, *Transformed by Love: The Way of Mary Magdalen* (Mineola, N.Y.: Resurrection Press, 1989), 71.

8. Mary Ellen Ashcroft, *Spirited Women* (Minneapolis: Augsburg Fortress, 2000), 11.

9. Magdalen, *Transformed by Love,* 62.

10. Sandra M. Rushing, *The Magdalene Legacy* (Westport, Conn.: Bergin & Garvey, 1994), 64.

11. Rushing, *The Magdalene Legacy,* 65.

12. Stuart, *The Three Marys,* 134.

13. Susan Haskins, *Mary Magdalen: Myth and Metaphor* (New York: Harcourt Brace & Co., 1993), 399.

14. Eugenia Price, *God Speaks to Women Today* (Grand Rapids: Zondervan, 1964), 170.

15. Morton Bryan Wharton, *Famous Women of the New Testament* (Chicago: W. P. Blessing, 1890), 265.

16. W. E. Vine, *Vine's Expository Dictionary of Old and New Testament Words,* vol. 1 (Old Tappan, N.J.: Revell, 1981), 74.

17. Michael Card, *The Parable of Joy: Reflections on the Wisdom of the Book of John* (Nashville: Nelson, 1995), 240.

18. Alexander Moody Stuart, *The Three Marys,* 134.

19. Stuart, *The Three Marys,* 134.

20. Matthew 10:32, ICB.

21. Rushing, *The Magdalene Legacy,* 59.

22. Elisabeth Moltmann-Wendel, *The Women Around Jesus* (New York: Crossroad Publishing, 1980), 64.

23. Jansen, *The Making of the Magdalen,* 65.

24. *Merriam-Webster's Collegiate Dictionary,* 10th ed., s.v. "apostle."

25. 1 Corinthians 15:14.

26. *Mary Magdalen: An Intimate Portrait,* prod. and dir. Charles C. Stuart, V.I.E.W. Videos, Inc., 1996, videocassette.

27. Ashcroft, *Spirited Women,* 10.

28. Edith Deen, *All the Women of the Bible* (New York: Harper & Row, 1955), 204.

29. Frederick Drimmer, *Daughters of Eve* (Norwalk, Conn.: C. R. Gibson, 1975), 29.

30. Mary R. Thompson, *Mary of Magdala: Apostle and Leader* (New York: Paulist, 1995), 78.

31. John 4:29.

32. John 11:27.

33. 1 Corinthians 9:1.

34. F. F. Bruce, *The Gospel of John* (Grand Rapids: Eerdmans, 1983), 384.

35. Ashcroft, *Spirited Women,* 12.

36. Luke 24:13-35.

37. Luke 24:36-49.

38. John 20:29.

39. Herbert G. May and Bruce M. Metzger, eds., *The New Oxford Annotated Bible, Revised Standard Version* (New York: Oxford University Press, 1962), 1212.

40. Bob Russell, sermon at Southeast Christian Church, Louisville, Kentucky, 17 December 2000. Used by permission.

41. Matthew 28:10.

42. Robert L. Thomas and Stanley N. Gundry, *A Harmony of the Gospels* (New York: HarperCollins, 1978), 308.

43. Thompson, *Mary of Magdala*, 44.

44. Frances Vander Velde, *Women of the Bible* (Grand Rapids: Kregel, 1985), 213.

45. Atwood, *Mary Magdalene in the New Testament Gospels*, 147-8.

46. Acts 1:14.

47. Jansen, *The Making of the Magdalen*, 23.

48. Romans 16:6.

49. Albert Barnes, *Barnes' Notes on the New Testament: Romans* (1884–85; reprint, Grand Rapids: Baker, 1998), 327.

50. Barnes, *Barnes' Notes on the New Testament: Romans*, 329.

51. Wharton, *Famous Women of the New Testament*, 267.

52. Dorothy Kelley Patterson, ed., *The Woman's Study Bible, the New King James Version* (Nashville: Nelson, 1995), 1797.

53. Kimberly Winston, "Magdalene's Disciples Grow Across Nation," http://www.dallasnew.com/religion/9717rel12magdalene.htm, 17 July 1999.

54. Flo Aeveia Magdalena, *I Remember Union: The Story of Mary Magdalena* (Putney, Vt.: All Worlds Publishing, 1999), 470.

55. Philippians 4:3.

56. Titus 2:13.

57. William Hendricksen, *New Testament Commentary: The Gospel of John* (Grand Rapids: Baker, 1961), 432.

58. Romans 10:9.

59. Thompson, *Mary of Magdala*, 78.

A Final Word from the Author

I'm truly honored to hear from my readers, and I enjoy keeping in touch twice a year through my free printed newsletter. For the latest issue, please write directly to me:

Liz Curtis Higgs
P.O. Box 43577
Louisville, KY 40253-0577

Or visit my Web site:
www.LizCurtisHiggs.com

Bless you for your encouragement and support. May you, too, have a "Mary" heart!

Liz

Contemporary fiction.
Timeless truths.
Changed lives.